GREAT DECISIONS 2015

About the cover

People attend a rally to support the annexation of Ukraine's Crimea to Russia in Red Square in central Moscow, Mar. 18, 2014. The flags display portraits of Russia's President Vladimir Putin and read "We are together!"

Photo Credit:
MAXIM SHEMETOV/
Reuters/Corbis

© COPYRIGHT 2015 BY FOREIGN POLICY ASSOCIATION, INC., 470 PARK AVENUE SOUTH, NEW YORK, NEW YORK 10016.

All rights reserved.

No part of this book may be reproduced in any form, or by any means, without permission in writing from the publisher.

PRINTED IN THE UNITED STATES OF AMERICA BY DARTMOUTH PRINTING COMPANY, HANOVER, NH.

LIBRARY OF CONGRESS CONTROL NUMBER: 2014957266

ISBN: 978-0-87124-247-1

Researched as of No[...]
The authors are responsi[...]
and for the view[...]

FPA itself takes no position on issues of U.S. foreign policy.

Underwriting those who set forth together.

From brokers in the commercial insurance industry to the risk managers of global organizations, Starr Companies is the global insurance organization whose purpose is bigger than insurance. We service clients that have a vision of a greater tomorrow. By joining our expertise with yours, we can chart the best possible path to success together. In short, we believe in collaboration. Whether it's reducing risk exposure or expanding into emerging markets, Starr signs our name in ink right below yours to accomplish the amazing. To see how a partnership with our team can take you further and help you soar to new heights, visit us at www.starrcompanies.com

STARR
COMPANIES
GLOBAL INSURANCE & INVESTMENTS

ACCIDENT & HEALTH · AVIATION & AEROSPACE · CASUALTY · CONSTRUCTION · CRISIS MANAGEMENT · ENERGY · ENVIRONMENTAL
FINANCIAL LINES · MARINE · PROFESSIONAL LIABILITY · PROPERTY · PUBLIC ENTITY · SPECIALTY PRODUCTS · TRAVEL ASSISTANCE

Starr Companies: Underwriting the future.

As incubators of new technologies of information transfer and communication, institutions of higher learning have accelerated integration of the world economy. Indeed, universities are key players in the phenomenon known as globalization, characterized by unprecedented movement of people, goods, capital and, of course, ideas.

Ironically, the prodigious pace of globalization has called into question whether universities themselves have adapted to this bold new world. Are universities preparing graduates for the challenges they will encounter over the course of their lives? Opportunities to plunge into international life abound at some institutions of higher learning while others have yet to make a credible global offering available to their students.

With the blurring of international and domestic issues, we can foresee that so-called "intermestic" developments will loom large in the future. Arguably, we are already facing challenges today, ranging from climate change to nuclear proliferation, that are among the most ominous in all of human history. Fully engaging higher education communities will be critical to addressing these challenges. In this regard, at the direction of Secretary-General Ban Ki-Moon, the United Nations has rolled out its Academic Impact program:

"i) To bring into association with the United Nations, and with each other, institutions of higher learning throughout the world.

ii) To provide a mechanism for such institutions to commit themselves to the fundamental precepts driving the United Nations mandate, in particular the realization of the universally determined Millennium Development Goals.

iii) To serve as a viable point of contact for ideas and proposals relevant to the United Nations mandate.

iv) To promote the direct engagement of institutions of higher education in programs, projects and initiatives relevant to this mandate."

In addition to helping achieve the Millennium Development Goals, institutions of higher learning can contribute to the renewal of the international system, with emphasis on preventing violence, through education, mediation and early warning. These "pillars of prevention," as set out by Dr. David A. Hamburg, need to be institutionalized if the international community is to resolve conflicts constructively and peacefully.

While we must be prepared, as it has been said, for challenges we cannot yet foresee, with knowledge not yet developed, using tools not yet invented, Abraham Lincoln had it right when he observed that the best way to predict the future is to create it.

At the Foreign Policy Association, we see education as the bridge to a better future for humankind. We welcome partnerships with universities in the United States and around the world to help prepare future generations to be responsible citizens in their communities and in the world.

Noel V. Lateef
President and CEO
Foreign Policy Association

(Adapted from remarks delivered at the FPA-Bosphorus University Conference on Higher Education and Globalization, marking the 150th anniversary of Bosphorus University, the oldest American-founded institution of higher learning outside the United States.)

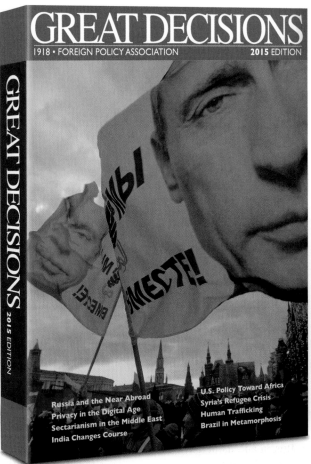

Russia and the Near Abroad
by Oxana Shevel

A man poses with a Russian flag in front of a Black Sea Fleet ship in Sevastopol, Ukraine, on Mar. 16, 2014. (HANNIBAL HANSCHKE/DPA/CORBIS)

Years after the end of the Cold War, the question of whether Russia is a stabilizing or destabilizing power, globally and in the post-Soviet region, has yet to be answered. Relations between Russia and its neighbors—as well as among Russia, the U.S. and other Western powers—have featured instances of both cooperation and conflict. On one hand, Russia allowed the Soviet Union to disintegrate largely peacefully and cooperated with the West on a range of issues, including German reunification, nuclear containment of Iran and North Korea, counterterrorism operations in Afghanistan, and chemical weapons removal in Syria.

On the other hand, the West and Russia have butted heads over the Yugoslav war (1991–99) and Kosovo's independence, the North Atlantic Treaty Organization's (NATO) eastward expansion, and the Russian-Georgian war (2008). Between Russia and its neighbors, points of contention have included the treatment of Russians and Russian-speakers in the former Soviet republics, as well as the newly independent states' geopolitical orientation between Russia and the West.

Over the past year, these tensions reached crisis propor-

tion. Russia's response to street protests known as the Euromaidan, or "Euro Square," and the overthrow of Ukrainian president Viktor Yanukovych, as well as its annexation of Ukraine's Crimean peninsula in March 2014, plunged Russia's relations with the West to a new low.

How and why did it come to this? Are Russia's actions in Ukraine a prelude to further aggressive acts in the areas of its former dominance? What can be done to contain Russia, and is it possible to restore cooperative relations between Russia and Ukraine, and Russia and the West, and if so, how? To answer these questions we need to look into the causes of the current crisis and drivers of Russian foreign policy in its neighborhood and in relations with the West. ■

OXANA SHEVEL *is an associate professor in the Department of Political Science at Tufts University and an Associate at the Davis Center for Russian and Eurasian Studies and the Ukrainian Research Institute at Harvard University. She is the author of* Migration, Refugee Policy, and State Building in Postcommunist Europe *(Cambridge 2011). The book received the 2012 American Association of Ukrainian Studies (AAUS) book prize. Shevel holds a PhD in Government from Harvard University, am M.Phil in International Relations from the University of Cambridge in England.*

Foreign policy in the 1990s

Soviet Union President Mikhail Gorbachev signs a treaty prohibiting the Communist Party on the territory on Aug. 23, 1991. (GEORGES DE KEERLE/SYGMA/CORBIS)

Foreign policy of the post-Soviet Russia has its origins in the late Soviet period. In 1985, Mikhail Gorbachev took leadership of the Communist Party of the Soviet Union and launched a new approach in relations with the West. Gorbachev advocated the philosophy of "new thinking," which postulated that the Union of Soviet Socialist Republics (USSR) and the West could coexist and pursue common interests. Nuclear disarmament, the withdrawal of Soviet troops from Afghanistan, the reunification of Germany, and the fall of Communism in the Eastern European Soviet satellite states in 1989–1990 were all made possible by Gorbachev's "new thinking." But the seeds of later tensions between Russia and the West were sown as well. When Gorbachev agreed to the reunification of Germany, he was given informal promises that NATO would not expand to the east. Such promises were never formalized, and Gorbachev's USSR received substantial financial aid for not opposing reunification. Nevertheless, in later years, when NATO expanded east of united Germany to former Soviet block countries, and by 2004, to three of the former Soviet republics (Estonia, Latvia and Lithuania), NATO expansion was bitterly resented

in Russia. Russian leaders and political commentators claimed the West cheated Russia by breaking its earlier promise. Putin called NATO expansion "a direct threat to the security of our country."

The dissolution of the Soviet Union at the end of December 1991 ushered the first phase of Russian foreign policy in the post-Soviet period. Russia's new foreign policy was initially shaped by pro-Western liberals, who believed that Russia's interests were best served by pursuing closer ties and integration into a Euro-Atlantic world. These new Russian leaders saw Russia as an organic part of Western civilization; in the words of Russian liberal foreign minister Andrei Kozyrev, they wanted it to become a "normal" Western country. The expectation was that the West would help Russia transition to a market economy and democratic system, integrate it into transatlantic economic and security institutions and overall treat it as an equal. This pro-Western approach was helped by Russian President Boris Yeltsin's and U.S. President Bill Clinton's friendship.

As early as 1993 the liberal idea of cooperation and common interests with the West faced challenges from powerful forces within Russia. Following strong showing in the 1993 legislative

elections by Communists and nationalists opposed to Yeltsin's domestic and foreign policy course, the discourse critical of Russia's bowing to Western interests grew in prominence and popularity. By 1996 Kozyrev was out of the job, and Russia's cooperation with the West was marred by, on one hand, Western criticism of Russia's war in Chechnya and, on the other, Russian criticism of NATO action against Bosnian Serbs and plans for expansion of the Alliance.

The clash that led to the silencing of liberal voices in Russia's foreign policy by the middle of the 1990s has historical parallels. As far back as the pre-Soviet era, the Russian intellectual tradition has been split between the "Westernizers" and "Slavophiles." Westernizers saw Russia as a part of Western civilization and advocated forming Russia in the West's image; Slavophiles regarded Russia as a unique and exceptional civilization—one that was not only morally superior to the West, but whose national interests were by definition anti-Western. In the post-Soviet period, the "Westernizers" (at times called Atlantists) favored Russian integration into Western political and economic institutions, as well as a democratization and marketization agenda. They stood in opposition to the "Slavophiles" (often referred to as Eurasianists), who were suspicious of the West and saw Russia as a center of Eurasian civilization, which included the post-Soviet region but excluded the West. Neither the Westernizers nor the Atlantists had stood at the helm of Russian state policies unchallenged for long, so the backlash against unabashedly pro-Western policies of the late Gorbachev and early Yeltsin era can be seen as a repeat of this historical pattern.

However, there have been more immediate reasons as to why the pro-Western period following dissolution of the USSR proved to be so short-lived. This period in the early 1990s coincided with economic collapse that resulted in a sharp drop in living standards and imposed tremendous material hardship on

Russian citizens. In this context, the rhetoric of Yeltsin's opponents—who argued that the West was actively weakening, or at least not sufficiently aiding, Russia by imposing free-market capitalism and fostering the rise of oligarchs—fell on receptive ears.

Yet another factor contributing to the abandonment of an explicitly pro-Western Russian foreign policy were the ethno-cultural consequences of the disintegration of the USSR. The USSR's collapse left Russia with borders that mirrored its reach in the 17th century. Overnight, some 25 million ethnic Russians and 33 million Russian-speakers found themselves cut off from the new Russian state. Russians in the "near abroad"—the term coined in Russia in the early 1990s to refer to the former Soviet states, which reflected the perception that they are not "really" foreign—became a national minority and no longer members of the leading nationality as they had been in the Soviet era. In some cases ethnic Russians even faced discrimination in citizenship and employment matters. As a result, millions of former Soviet citizens, most of them ethnic Russians, moved to Russia from the former Soviet republics in the early- and mid-1990s. Migration came with its own set of socio-economic burdens, as the government had pledged to assist migrants and adopted special legislation to this effect. Mass migration of Russian-speakers from neighboring states also fostered resentment against the governments' of the newly independent states Russians were fleeing and against the West.

This "ethnic unmixing" was prompted by a number of factors: citizenship denial in Latvia and Estonia; language policies in most state that elevated the status of titular languages, often at the expense of Russian; economic hardship; and armed conflicts that flared in some of the USSR successor states, such as Azerbaijan, Georgia, Moldova and Tajikistan. Many in Russia felt that the West, while criticizing Russia for rights abuses in Chechnya, turned a blind eye to the infringement of the rights of ethnic Russians in the post-Soviet states, particularly in Western-aligned Estonia and Latvia. For similar reasons, the West and Russia also butted heads with regards to Russian support for separatists in breakaway regions, such as Transdniestria in Moldova and Abkhazia and South Ossetia in Georgia. While Russia presented its support of separatists in these regions as a defense of the rights of Russian-speaking minorities against rising nationalism, Western governments saw as Russia's meddling in its newly independent neighbors' affairs and as attempts to keep them from leaving Russia's orbit by creating simmering pockets of domestic instability that challenged their territorial integrity.

The attempt to turn Russia into a "normal" Western state did not succeed, and many in Russia began to doubt that the transformation was in their interests. Western support was called into question as well. The West supported Yeltsin's policies of questionable democratic merit, which instigated the country's economic collapse and culminated in the rise of wealthy oligarchs. Western governments backed Yeltsin in his struggle with a Communist and nationalist-dominated parliament, and they took his side when Yeltsin ordered troops to shell the legislature in October 1993 during constitutional crisis. In the 1996 presidential elections, when an unpopular Yeltsin was challenged by the hardline leader of an unreformed Russian Communist party, Western governments stood by Yeltsin the "democrat," who narrowly won by means questionable from the point of view of democratic process. Among such means was the infamous "loans-for-shares" scheme, wherein the state allowed a select group of Russian businessmen to take control of a dozen key state owned enterprises, including major parts of the energy, telecommunications, and metallurgical sectors, in return for receiving some $800 million in loans for the federal budget. The justification of the loans-for-shares was that it would create a permanent capitalist class with a stake in the Russian market. Instead, loans-for-shares gave rise to the so-called oligarchs, who, with their great wealth, became an independent source of political power and were able to wield vast influence over the state during Yeltsin's second term.

Given the botched process and pitiful results of transferring Western economic models and democracy during the Yeltsin years, the second half of the 1990s led many to believe that Russia needed to pursue its own interests. With a powerful Communist and nationalist presence in the legislature, as well as the growing perception that the West is not taking Russian concerns into account, there was growing consensus that following the West's lead was no longer an ideal path. ∎

An elderly homeless woman covers her dog with her coat in a shantytown near the Kremlin.
(PETER TURNLEY/CORBIS)

Foreign policy under Putin

President-elect Vladimir Putin watches tactical exercises of Russia's Northern Fleet on in the Barents Sea on April 6, 2000. (-/EPA/CORBIS)

Vladimir Putin rose to political prominence by developing a reputation for defending Russian interests, asserting its rightful place as a global superpower, and demonstrating a willingness to restore its damaged pride. These themes would come to form Russian foreign policies and its relations with the West after Putin became president in 2000, but they also underlined Putin's meteoric rise from a virtual unknown in August 1999, when an ailing Yeltsin appointed him prime minister. As the new prime minister, Putin vowed to restore control of the breakaway Chechen republic. (The republic had been a site of lawlessness and gross human rights abuses in 1996–1999, after Russia lost de facto control of the republic following the 1994–1996 war.) Putin's assertive stance against the Chechen separatists and his tough language—including his infamous promise to kill Chechen terrorists "in the outhouses"—catapulted him to popularity. His approval rating jumped from 31% in August 1999 to 79% in December 1999.

The need for a strong state and the subordination of private interests were important elements of Putin's ideology before he assumed presidency. In his 1997 dissertation and in a subsequent article published in 1999, he wrote about the need for Russia's mineral resources and key strategic enterprises managing them (the "national champions") to be operated with state interests in mind, rather than private interests. As president, Putin put this vision into practice.

The most iconic case is that of Yukos, then Russia's largest oil and gas company, whose owner and Russia's richest man, Mikhail Khodorkovsky, was arrested, imprisoned, and lost his assets. Khodorkovsky's plight sent a clear signal to the oligarchs that Putin would not allow them to maintain independence. With his KGB background, Putin could rely on the support of the siloviki, or elites from the security and military sector. Critics argued that the Yeltsin-era reality of oligarchs wielding power over the state had been replaced by a new, and equally undemocratic reality, where siloviki control state

polices and amass personal wealth.

Putin's rise to power also coincided with the growth in oil prices, giving him the fortune to preside over the first major economic recovery after the disastrous 1990s. Economic recovery boosted his popularity at home and allowed him to lessen Russia's dependency on Western loans and other forms of economic aid, which in turn put it in a stronger position to pursue more assertive foreign policies.

With the Russian government more willing and better able to stray from the West's path, Western actions, such as the U.S. circumventing the UN Security Council to deploy NATO in airstrikes against Serbia in March 1999 and the incorporation of Poland, Hungary and the Czech Republic into NATO the same year, also contributed to the redefinition of Russian foreign policy goals and strategies vis-à-vis the West and its neighbors. During his first year in office, Putin signed new editions of Russia's major security documents into law—the National Security Concept (January 2000), the Military Doctrine (April 2000) and the Foreign Policy Concept (June 2000). If the 1997 National Security Concept of the Yeltsin era saw internal problems, not international developments, as the greatest threat to Russian national security and regarded the post-Cold War international system as cooperative rather than competitive, the 2000 security documents saw the current trends in international politics as threatening to Russia. The documents considered Western security policy to be a threat to Russia and prioritized counter-balancing such threats with political, military and economic cooperation with members of the Commonwealth of Independent States (CIS).

By the early 2000s several factors came together, contributing to and enabling a more assertive Russian foreign policy and a rift in Russia's relations with the West: the drastic political and economic fallout of the 1990s led to a definitive shift away from earlier Western-oriented policies, Putin's personal beliefs in the strong state and great

Russia, the period of economic growth under Putin, the West's unilateral actions in Kosovo, and NATO's expansion. None of these factors, however, ruled out the possibility of cooperation between Russia and the West on issues of mutual interest—indeed since Putin took helm of Russian politics, Russia cooperated with the West on nuclear nonproliferation, energy and the war on terror. Under Putin, Russian and U.S. leaders signed and ratified the New Strategic Arms Reduction Treaty (START) and Russia joined the World Trade Organization (WTO).

One popular explanation for Putin's activity in Ukraine is NATO expansion. A number of experts have asserted that in 2014 the West essentially provoked Russia to take action in Ukraine in order to prevent NATO reaching there after the overthrow of former Ukrainian president Viktor Yanukovych. Others have pointed out that while Russia has consistently opposed NATO expansion since the mid-1990s, its relations with the West have evolved and Ukraine's NATO membership was not forthcoming. The intention to enlarge NATO was made public already in 1994, and in 1999 the Czech Republic, Hungary and Poland joined. In 2004 they were followed by seven more post-Communist countries: Bulgaria, Romania, Slovakia, Slovenia, Estonia,

Latvia and Lithuania. The current crisis in Ukraine took place years after the last round of NATO expansion. Furthermore, no moves on the part of Ukraine or NATO have taken place since 2008, when the alliance declared that Ukraine and Georgia will be able to join one day but took no further steps to admission. For NATO, enlargement to the east became essentially a non-issue after Russia's incursion into Georgia in August 2008 in response to Georgia's attempt to retake control of the breakaway region of South Ossetia. Before Russia's invasion of Crimea, NATO membership was mostly a non-issue in Ukraine. Russian aggression made support for NATO in Ukraine stronger than it has ever been, with a November 2014 poll showing 51% of Ukrainians would vote for NATO membership in a referendum.

Another causal factor behind the current crisis over Ukraine is Putin's fear of popular mobilization against his regime. The political system created in Russia under Putin is centered on a strong presidency that cannot be challenged by the either opposition in the legislature, by regional elites or independent economic interests. Political elites loyal to the president, not voters, control the political process in the country. This political order is claimed to be the model best able to stimulate economic development, identify and address key social needs of

the society, and ensure social stability. The Putin system was also presented as the return to law and order. Thus, independent societal mobilization in Russia's backyard on a scale that would have the potential to unseat governing elites were seen as threatening because: 1.) they would encroach on Russia's sphere of influence through the installation of pro-Western governments in former Soviet states; 2.) popular revolutions offered a model of political change and the destruction of authoritarian regimes through "people's power."

Of all the post-Soviet states, the removal of Ukraine from Russia's sphere of influence by way of a popular revolution was, at least from the Russian perspective, the worst of the bad outcomes. Ukraine occupies a special place in Russia's historical narrative and national identity. One historical mythology that originated in the tsarist period and perpetuated by the Soviets identified Ukraine and Russia (together with Belarus) as three "branches" of the same family tree. Kyiv, the center of the medieval kingdom of the Kyivan Rus', was "the mother of Russian cities" and the cradle of Russian identity and culture. A separate Ukraine with a right to statehood, as well as the notion that Ukraine as a state could pursue "anti-Russian" policies was anathema in Russia, both

LUCIDITY INFORMATION DESIGN, LLC

to the elites and to the public. One 2006 poll found that 58% of Russians said that there were no national differences between Russia and Ukraine; another in 2005 identified that 78% of Russians had a positive attitude toward the unification of Russia and Ukraine; yet another poll in 2007 showed 48% of Russians would vote for unification in a hypothetical referendum. Indeed, in April 2008, Putin told President George W. Bush that "Ukraine isn't even a state" and that "there are only Russians" living in the south of Ukraine. What Russia saw in 2013–14 was the West attempting to drive Ukraine away from Russia, and ultimately into NATO, by supporting the Euromaidan uprising. To Russia, the West orchestrated the overthrow of an autocratic president by means of popular protests, brought a pro-Western government in office, and in so doing, was laying the groundwork for Ukraine's NATO membership and a Ukrainian identity that was distinct, if not outright hostile, to the narrative of eastern Slavic unity.

U.S.-Russia relations

The roots of the current crisis in Russia-Ukraine and Russia-West relations goes back to 2004, when a popular uprising that became known as the "orange revolution" prevented Yanukovych from becoming Ukraine's third president after flawed presidential elections. Russia perceived the orange revolution as a Western-financed ploy aimed at installing pro-Western government in Ukraine under the leadership of Yanukovych's opponent, Viktor Yushchenko. Russia's elites wanted to prevent Ukraine from moving westward, as well as a repeat of an electoral revolution at home. By 2004, Putin had already strengthened his presidential authority by taming business tycoons, taking over or closing all independent national television channels, and creating a pro-presidential party that dominated both houses of parliament. Following events in Ukraine in 2004, Putin delivered another blow to independent political activity and civil society by creating pro-Kremlin youth groups, passing an electoral law that abolished single-member constituencies and increased

the electoral threshold for the party list vote, making it harder for smaller parties and independent candidates to win seats, as well as tightening state control over non-governmental organizations (NGOs), especially ones that received funding from Western donors.

Russia's fears that Ukraine's orange revolution would lead to either a diffusion of electoral revolution to Russia or Ukraine's decisive turn to the West did not materialize. Yushchenko's tenure in Ukraine was marred by constant infighting between the former members of the "orange" team, in particular between Yushchenko and Yulia Tymoshenko, a key supporter turned bitter rival. Domestic gridlock damaged prospects for Ukraine's integration into Western institutions, as well as domestic reforms. The disarray and disappointment that followed the orange revolution allowed Yanukovych to win presidential elections in 2010. Yanukovych relied on the support of his core electorate in the south and east, which were alienated by many of Yushchenko-era cultural policies. He narrowly defeated Tymoshenko in the second round (49% to 45%) after Yushchenko, eliminated in the first round, called on his supporters to abstain from supporting either candidate.

Yanukovych's electoral victory in 2010 was fairly clean, but regional vote polarization in Ukraine meant he entered office with the support of one half of the country and opposition from another. Yanukovych began pursuing foreign

Supporters for opposition candidate Viktor Yushchenko demonstrate on Nov. 30, 2004, in Independence Square. (IGOR KOSTIN/CORBIS)

and cultural policies that further alienated the pro-Western electorate in central and western Ukraine. He rammed through the 25-year extension of the Russian Black Sea Fleet lease of naval bases in Sevastopol in Crimea, endorsed Russia-supported characterization of the 1932–33 killer famine in Ukraine as a "common tragedy" of all Soviet people (not "genocide of the Ukrainian people"), and dropped the language of Euro-Atlantic integration from the law on the foundations of Ukrainian domestic and foreign policy.

During his first year in office, Yanukovych not only dismantled the few accomplishments of the orange period, namely a free press and stronger parliament—he also undertook a number of changes to secure and widen his power, as well as to clamp down on the opposition. He had Tymoshenko arrested and imprisoned on abuse of office charges that independent observers uniformly saw as politically motivated. He changed rules governing coalition formation in the legislature to create a pro-presidential majority and pushed the Constitutional Court to revert a 2004 constitutional reform that had weakened presidential powers and strengthened the legislature. Yanukovych elevated elites from his home region of Donets'k to key positions in government and the judiciary, and the growing power of the so-called "family"—elites close to Yanukovych and his sons—as well as massive corruption were contributing to the growing dissatisfaction with Yanukovych rule in Ukraine.

The immediate precursor to the current crisis was Yanukovych's decision in November 2013 not to sign the association and free trade agreement with the European Union. The preparatory process had been going on for several years, and in September 2013 Ukraine still intended to sign it. But the decision was not simple—the EU put pressure on Yanukovych to live up to democratic standards, commit to reforms and release Tymoshenko from jail. Russia, for its part, blocked exports from key Ukrainian industries in the months preceding the planned signing date to show that it can make Ukraine, which relied on Russia for a quarter of its exports, pay if it turned West. Russia argued that the Ukraine-EU agreement would have hurt its economy, a debatable claim. It ultimately prefers to bring Ukraine into the Russia-led customs union with Belarus and Kazakhstan—a plan that proved to be successful in the case of Armenia, which had also been in similar negotiations with the EU but agreed to join the Russian customs union instead. Russia welcomed Yanukovych's decision not to sign the agreement with the EU.

After the Ukrainian government adopted a decree halting the effort to sign the agreement one week before an EU summit on Nov. 21 in Vilnis (where Yanukovych made an unexpected demand for an astounding 175 billion dollars through 2017 from the EU in compensation for the costs of adopting European standards), popular protests erupted in Ukraine. The protests, sparked by Yanukovych's decision not to sign the agreement with the EU, became known as Euromaidan, or "Euro Square." They culminated with Yanukovych's escape from the country on Feb. 22, 2014.

Russian state media portrayed Euromaidan as a Western-financed ploy to unseat Yanukovych and tear Ukraine away from Russia. A number of Western leaders, including U.S. Assistant Secretary of State Victoria Nuland, visited the main protest sight in a show of support, and U.S. and European governments spent billions on the development of democratic institutions in Ukraine and other post-Soviet states since independence. Euromaidan, however, was hardly a Western pet project but a protest movement with complex causes, and the goals of the movement also evolved over time as the protests progressed. As surveys have shown, what started as a protest for the agreement with the EU became a protest against police brutality after violent dispersal of demonstrators by the end of November. When police violence was unpunished and escalated, demand for government resignation grew. Only at the tail end of the protests did the removal of Yanukovych and a return to the 2004 constitution take center stage.

Eventual success of the protests to

A teenager waves a Ukrainian national flag over a crowd of pro-European Union activists on Dec. 8, 2013, in Kyiv's Independence Square. (SERGEI GRITS/AP/CORBIS)

drive out Yanukovych was a humiliating defeat for Putin's strategy on Ukraine. Putin firmly backed Yanukovych throughout the protests as he came under increased pressure from the West. After a Dec. 17 meeting with Yanukovych, Putin announced that Russia would buy $15 billion in Ukrainian debt by investing in Ukrainian bonds and reduce the price of Russian gas delivered to Ukraine. Russian leadership also urged Yanukovych to take an aggressive stance against the protesters, but the escalation of repression and violence eventually backfired. On Jan. 16, Yanukovych supporters in the parliament voted by a show of hands a law that criminalized much of the protest activity and NGO work. This fateful vote energized but also radicalized the protests, and the first three protesters were killed in clashes with police on Jan. 22. A month later, on Feb.18–20 dozens of people were shot dead by police on the streets of Kyiv during the violence following parliament's decision not to consider returning to the 2004 constitution limiting presidential powers. The worst street clashes between police and protesters ensued and were followed by the police assault on the main protest site, as well as a subsequent shooting of the protesters in broad daylight on the morning of Feb. 20. As violence escalated in Kyiv, protesters in western and central Ukraine occupied government buildings.

On the morning of Feb. 21, in a last ditch effort to reach a compromise and prevent state collapse and civil war, for-

eign ministers from France, Germany and Poland, as well as a Russian special envoy, brokered an agreement between Yanukovych and the leaders of the three largest parties present on the Euromaidan. The deal—which would have restored the 2004 constitution in Ukraine, created a coalition government, but left Yanukovych in office until the end of 2014—was announced as protesters were holding public funerals for those killed in previous days. The three protest leaders were booed as they announced the deal. The deal was seen as too little too late, and the continuation of Yanukovych's rule unacceptable. Protesters called on Yanukovych to resign, and a commander of one of the self-defense units protesters formed promised to drive him out if he does not resign by the following morning.

But the protesters did not drive Yanukovych out. As the stillborn deal was announced at the site of protests, Yanukovych's party began to crumble in parliament. On Feb. 21 dozens of lawmakers defected from his party, and the parliament voted to dismiss Yanukovych's interior minister, overturn the law under which Tymoshenko was convicted and jailed, and restore the 2004 constitution. By the end of the day, police withdrew from the streets and public buildings, and Yanukovych fled from his suburban estate by helicopter, first to the east, then to Crimea, and finally to Russia. Evidence subsequently uncovered at his estate suggested that he was pre-

Protestors clash with police on Jan. 22, 2014, in central Kyiv during Ukraine's escalating political crisis. (EFREM LUKATSKY/AP/CORBIS)

paring for his departure ahead of time.

The following day, Feb. 22, the parliament met and voted by a constitutional majority of 328 votes to remove Yanukovych from office and to hold early presidential elections on May 25. Russia called developments in Ukraine a "constitutional coup" and slammed the opposition and European leaders for the failure to uphold the Feb. 21 agreement. The constitutional aspects of Yanukovych's removal are complex, but independent experts described it as an extra-constitutional development, as Ukraine's constitution—similar to the constitutions of most western states—did not prescribe a course of action for the president fleeing the country. Russia's insistence that the Feb. 21 agreement was the best solution to the crisis was also not its original position, as the Russian representative was the only one of the negotiation participants to not sign the agreement in endorsement, possibly seeing it as not sufficiently reflecting Russia's preferred outcome.

Was the crisis inevitable?

Was Euromaidan a triumph of people's power over a corrupt authoritarian leader, or was it a Western-supported coup that brought a "fascist junta" to power in Ukraine? Because Russia has adopted a vastly different interpretation of the Euromaidan than the West and Ukraine, it is difficult to speak of an "objective reality" that can be understood by all sides. This gulf in perceptions has contributed

to the current crisis, including Russia's decision to swiftly annex Crimea after Euromaidan's victory. It also makes the crisis difficult to end.

Euromaidan's success triggered Putin's annexation of Crimea, the rationale for which was multifaceted. The annexation was purportedly to save Crimea's ethnic Russians and Russian-speaking "compatriots" from the "fascists" who took power in Kyiv, but it also aimed to prevent the Russian Black Sea Fleet from being evicted from its base in Sevastopol and prevent Ukraine from joining NATO. Crimea's majority ethnic Russian population and the fact that it was a part of Russia from the time Catherine II took it from the Ottoman Empire until the peninsula was transferred from the Russian republic to the Ukrainian republic within the USSR in 1954 were offered as additional justifications for Russia's actions. If Russia's objectives were to ensure non-discrimination of Russian-speakers in Crimea and Ukraine, to prevent Ukrainian membership to NATO and the country's decisive tilt westward, and to keep its naval base in Crimea, it is not evident that annexation—which turned Russia into an international pariah and saddled it with sanctions as its economy was already lagging—was the best course of action for Russia to achieve these goals. Russia could have chosen to exercise any of the many levers it had over Ukraine—levers that did not dis-

appear with the victory of Euromaidan and that were strong enough to enable Russia to advance these objectives.

Russia has enormous economic leverage over Ukraine. It is the destination for about a quarter of Ukrainian exports, and Ukraine is also heavily dependent on Russian gas. European markets could not fully replace Russian markets, and Ukrainian exports, especially its industrial output, will remain more attractive to Russian markets than to the West for a long time. Russia could have exploited extensive trade and economic links to undermine, on a case-by-case basis, moves by the new Ukrainian government that Russia considered undesirable. Ukraine's new president, Petro Poroshenko, who took office after the May 2014 elections, is someone with whom Russia could have easily found common ground. Poroshenko is not a radical anti-Russian revolutionary but a long-term member of the Ukrainian political establishment and an economic tycoon with business interests in Russia. He is an interlocutor not much different from previous Ukrainian presidents, with whom Russia was always able to conduct business.

Domestic divisions in Ukraine that have time and again produced a substantial Russia-friendly, if not outright pro-Russian, lobby in the Ukrainian parliament did not disappear after the victory of Euromaidan. According to a February 2014 Gallup poll, 45% nationwide supported the Euromaidan protests while 51% did not. The same poll found that 41% favored economic integration with the EU, and 35% with the Customs Union of Russia, Belarus and Kazakhstan. Had Putin not invaded Ukraine, such popular preferences could have been leveraged to establish a strong pro-Russian lobby in parliament through which Russia could have continued to influence Ukrainian politics.

Ironically, it was Putin's actions that upended these long-standing domestic divisions in Ukraine and made it much less pro-Russian than before the annexation. By annexing Crimea and supporting the insurgency in the Donbas region, which have reliably voted for pro-Russian parties and politicians, Russia effectively removed several million pro-Russian voters (approximately 10% of the electorate) from election rolls in Ukraine. (Residents of Crimea and of the insurgent-controlled parts of the Donbas—some 4.6 million registered voters—are now unable to take part in Ukrainian elections.) Unlike in previous elections where the margin of victory between "pro-Russian" and "pro-Western" parties or presidential contenders has always been narrow, 2014 marked the first time the electoral field shifted decisively away from pro-Russian forces. Poroshenko won by a wide margin in the first round in May 2014 presidential elections; in the October 2014 legislative elections, pro-European parties gained a constitutional majority for the first time in Ukrainian history. Only one party that can be considered pro-Russian made it into the parliament with 9.4% of the vote. As a result, the overall size of the pro-Russian lobby in parliament is unlikely to exceed a quarter of its composition.

The perceptions of Russian-speaking voters have also changed. In the southern and eastern regions of Ukraine—which Putin has referred to as Novorossia ("New Russia")—Russian-speakers are no longer reliably pro-Russian or even Russia-friendly. One illustrative example is the victory of Dmytro Yarosh, the leader of the radical nationalist Right Sector, in a single member district race in the Russian-speaking Dnipropetrovs'k region, which Russia counts as belonging to Novorossia. In October 2014 legislative elections, the pro-Western parties in the southeast won more votes than pro-Russian parties in most southern and eastern districts. (In previous elections, virtually all districts in the southeast voted for pro-Russian parties.)

Ukraine's NATO membership and the eviction of the Russian navy from Crimea were far from imminent. Indeed, as far as NATO membership is concerned, Russia's annexation of Crimea and incursion in the Donbas may have made it more, rather than less, likely. Ukrainian NATO membership did not have significant support domestically or within NATO itself. Even pro-western Ukrainian politicians had not advocated NATO membership for Ukraine, but

now the tides are changing. After the October 2014 legislative elections, five pro-Western parties agreed to form a coalition and set NATO membership as a goal. Tymoshenko's party, for example, has called for a referendum on NATO membership and started collecting signatures for it. The Ukrainian public also began to view membership more favorably, with 50% supporting membership in the alliance. Rising popular support for NATO membership in Ukraine is invariably a result of Russian aggression.

Likewise, the Russian Black Sea Fleet previously faced no danger of losing its bases in Crimea under a post-Yanukovych government. Yanukovych signed an agreement in February 2010 with Putin to extend the lease of the naval bases by the Russian Black Sea fleet in Crimea until 2042. (The earlier lease term was due to expire in 2017). The lease extension was negotiated in secret and rammed through the Ukrainian parliament by pro-Yanukovych majority despite protest from the opposition. While it is possible that the new Ukrainian government would have wanted to revisit the agreement at some point, Russia was well positioned to secure favorable terms for any new deal, provided its control over Ukrainian energy and the pro-Russian population in Crimea. No Ukrainian leader spoke of

revoking the lease after Euromaidan.

Further, the strength of radical nationalism and threat to Russian-speakers in the post-Euromaidan Ukraine was exaggerated by Russian leadership and state media. Radical nationalists and far right groups were present at the Euromaidan protests, and probably played a significant role in the violence from the protesters side, but the far right and extreme nationalists do not enjoy much support in Ukraine, as polling data and electoral results show. Under Yanukovych, Svoboda was the only far right nationalist party to gain legislative representation in 2012 parliamentary election. (It received 10% of the vote.) In May 2014 presidential elections, leaders of Svoboda and the Right Sector, the two main nationalist groups, together received less than 2% of the vote. The post-Yanukovych government included a few individuals with connections to the radical nationalist parties, although the most prominent appointment—that of the head of the national defense and security council, Andriy Parubiy, who was also the commander of self-defense units of the Euromaidan—had a connection that was a decade old. The radical nationalists have been nowhere close to dominating political life in post-Yanukovych Ukraine and have little chance to do so, as both right-wing parties failed

ETHNIC MAJORITIES IN UKRAINE
by Administrative Division

MAJORITY RUSSIAN

50% TO <90% UKRAINIAN

90% TO 100% UKRAINIAN

In March 2014, the Russian Federation annexed Crimea, an action not recognized by the international community.

SOURCE: 2001 UKRAINIAN CENSUS   LUCIDITY INFORMATION DESIGN, LLC to clear the 5% threshold for representation in the October 2014 elections.

Finally, claims of assaults on the rights of ethnic Russians and Russian-speakers in Ukraine and in Crimea specifically were exaggerated. Since 1989 Ukrainian has been the only state language in Ukraine; in Crimea, which enjoyed autonomous status within Ukraine, there were three official languages: Ukrainian, Russian and Crimean Tatar. In the years since independence Ukraine's government moved to reverse the Russification policies of the last decades of the Soviet era, particularly in government and education, but Russian remained widely used and dominant in the media, business and popular culture. The absolute majority of Ukrainians are bilingual and few were inconvenienced by Ukrainian as the only state language policy in daily lives. According to March 2014 Gallup poll, only 12% felt that Russian-speakers are under pressure because of their language. Among ethnic Russians this share stood at 29%; however, 66% of ethnic Russians (and 85% overall) did not consider Russian-speakers in danger of discrimination.

A key piece of evidence Russian leaders evoked when justifying the need to "defend compatriots" from the "fascist junta" in Kyiv was Ukrainian parliament's recent decision to repeal a 2012 law that gave Russian the status of a regional language in areas where over 10% of the population were Russian-speakers. The provocative nature of the vote was quickly recognized, and the parliament speaker and acting president at the time refused to sign it. As a result, the 2012 law remained in force. But even if the 2012 law was repealed—a law which at the time of its adoption was bitterly contested domestically and criticized by the Venice Commission of the Council of Europe for undermining the position of Ukrainian—the situation of Russian-speakers was unlikely to worsen. The 2012 law was more symbolic than consequential in practice; before and after promulgation of the law, the language policies and the situation of Russian-speakers in Ukraine were not distinct in any discernible way. Ukraine ratified the European Charter for Regional and Minority languages in 2005. Russian had been designated as one a regional language by then, and the courts routinely upheld decisions of local authorities to use Russian as regional language based on the charter's provisions. To advance language rights of Russian-speakers in Ukraine, Russia could have worked with and pressured Ukraine through European institutions to uphold the rights of Russian-speakers even in the absence of the 2012 language law.

So why, instead of exercising one or more of the many levers it had over Ukraine to influence the policies of the new Ukrainian government, did Putin opt for open conflict, upending the post-World War II security system and making Ukraine more anti-Russian than it has ever been? One compelling explanation is that Putin acted because the success of the Euromaidan uprising—and the possible success of Ukraine as a democracy in its aftermath—posed a great threat to the political system Putin has created. Putin may be pursuing a twin goal: first, preventing Ukraine from turning West and leaving the Russian sphere of influence by creating simmering conflict within its borders and a territorial dispute; and second, destabilizing post-Yanukovych Ukraine to discredit the people-led model of political and economic change in the country that is Russia's closest neighbor.

Policy options

As the crisis over Ukraine plunges U.S.-Russia relations to their lowest point since the end of the Cold War, the West continue to puzzle over how to reverse Russia's aggressive behavior in Ukraine, deter any similar future actions by Russia against other states in its neighborhood, and normalize relations with the Kremlin so that cooperation can continue in areas of mutual interests. Failing to accomplish these goals could lead to an even greater crisis in Ukraine and the spread of the crisis to other states. The possibility of Russia pushing further into Ukraine cannot be excluded. The areas Russian-backed insurgents control in the Donbas region are smaller than the territory of Novorossia envisaged by Putin. Since Crimea is dependent on mainland Ukraine for most of its supplies of fresh water and electricity and that the insurgent-controlled areas of the Donbas are home to Ukraine's rundown heavy industry and mines that need subsidies to stay operational, Russia may at some point look to carve a land corridor to Crimea. Russia may even push further along southern Ukraine into Moldova's breakaway region of Transdniestria, which has been under a pro-Russian unrecognized government since 1992.

If tensions created by the current crisis in Ukraine are not diffused, the possibility that Russia will violate the territorial integrity of other post-Soviet states under the pretext of protecting Russian-speakers is not out of the realm of possibilities, albeit more remote. The Baltic states—particularly Latvia and Estonia, which have large Russian minorities and tense relations with Russia over issues such as citizenship, language rights, and commemorative politics—could be future targets. However, because Latvia and Estonia are members of NATO, Russia is unlikely to risk open military action. Russia nevertheless could destabilize these states by acting aggressive but short of an outright invasion. Provocative moves, like Russia's kidnapping of an Estonian security officer from Estonian territory two days after President Obama visited the country, could become more frequent.

Kazakhstan is another state where a large and territorially concentrated Russian minority along the Kazakh-Russian border in the north of the country could become the locus of destabilization or conflict. Kazakhstan has been a reliable ally of Russia since the fall of the Soviet Union, and its president, Nursultan Nazarbayev, has been an active proponent of Russia-led Eurasian integration projects, such as a common economic space, the customs union, and the Eurasian economic community. But Kazakhstan is not a democracy, and Nazarbaiev, who is 74 years old, does not have a designated successor. Hence, any transition from Nazarbaiev to the next leader will be unpredictable, and mass mobilization and another "colored revolution" cannot be ruled out. Some have interpreted Putin's recent statement that Nazarbaiev has "done a unique thing" because he "created a state in a territory that had never had a state before" as an ominous warning that if Kazakhstan were to depart Russia's orbit, its borders may be challenged.

So what options do the U.S. government and its Western allies have when dealing with Putin? It will not be easy to diffuse the current crisis in relations with Russia, prevent new ones from emerging and continue cooperation on areas of mutual interests for several reasons. For one, the West and Russia have different views of what lead to the current crisis in Ukraine. These varied interpretations of reality are profound; in fact, after several conversations with Putin over Crimean crisis in March 2014 German Chancellor Angela Merkel reportedly told President Obama that Putin is "in another world." Following the October 2014 meeting in Milan between Putin and European leaders, Putin's spokesman said that the West shows "complete unwillingness to understand the real situation in the southeast of Ukraine." An inability to agree on the nature of the problem makes it so much harder to solve it.

One mechanism the West does have at its disposal are sanctions. Western sanctions, which both targeted individuals and companies in Russia, have already had a considerable impact on the Russian economy, resulting in a weakened ruble, growth in consumer prices and substantial burden on the state budget. Targeted energy companies have asked the government for funds to offset the losses caused by sanctions. Rosneft, Russia's largest state owned oil company, for example, asked for more than $49 billion to help withstand Western sanctions. That sum amounts to over half the cash stored in Russia's National Welfare Fund, a sovereign wealth fund created as a backstop to Russia's pension system.

Still, sanctions are unlikely to change Russia's course, especially in the short term. Russian leaders have said they have no intention of returning Crimea to Ukraine under pressure of sanctions. Despite mounting evidence, Russia continues to deny that its troops are aiding insurgents in the Donbas. That covert support for the insurgents is unlikely to be

Russian President Vladimir Putin watches military exercises with Defense Minister Sergei Shoigu. (GETTY IMAGES)

cut, given that the Ukrainian army came close to defeating the insurgency in August and that local support for the insurgency, while substantial, is not enough. The West faces a choice between two problematic options: to continue with sanctions that are unlikely to yield results in the short term (and possibly long term as well—Putin is widely popular in Russia and his term in office can go until 2024), or to relax or annul the sanctions, effectively signing off on Russia's annexation of Crimea, its violation of the international law, and its sponsorship of insurgency in eastern Ukraine.

Since NATO countries ruled out military action against Russia over Ukraine, the West has few options. Two sets of additional specific actions may prove effective—even if not immediately—in influencing Russia's behavior and the course of events in its neighborhood going forward. These would be helping democracy succeed in Ukraine, and recognizing and responding to legitimate Russian concerns.

Helping democracy succeed in post-Yanukovych Ukraine would offer long-term benefits, not only to Ukrainians but also to Russia and other countries in the post-Soviet space. It would show that regime change driven by popular mobilization could serve public interests and welfare as well or better than the model of managed democracy, which limits pluralism and public participation. The success of democracy in Ukraine should not be confused with success of pro-Western foreign policy

or political dominance of pro-Western elites, however. The West should scrutinize its pro-Western allies and call them on violations of democratic standards, just as it has been doing with regard to the pro-Russian actors. This will both aid democratic prospects in Ukraine, and may earn some good will with Russia, which has maintained that the U.S. has supported pro-Western forces in Ukraine without question.

More specifically, such a policy would involve recognizing the danger the far right can pose for democracy in Ukraine, even if it is not strong electorally. Rights groups have documented worrisome practices already, such as extrajudicial detention and ill treatment of suspected separatism supporters by the volunteer militias with links to the far right. Questionable lustration policies, physical assaults on political figures from the old regime, and legislation that limits basic constitutional rights in areas where a state of emergency or anti-terrorist operation is in force (including the right not to be detained without a court order) are clearly undemocratic and should be recognized as such, even if they are initiated by Ukrainian political forces friendly to the West.

Finally, addressing Russia's legitimate concerns when it comes to developing closer partnerships between states in Russia's near abroad and the West could serve to improve U.S.-Russian relations. Here, the West needs to walk a fine line between recognizing Russia's concerns about what happens in its neighborhood and working in good faith to address them without letting Russia veto integration of its neighbors in Western institutions if they so choose. The one year delay in the implementation of free trade part of the EU association agreement with Ukraine to allow time for consultations on the impact of this agreement on Russian economy and its trade with Ukraine is one example of a compromise solution. This considers the consequences such an agreement could have on Russia's economy. Distinguishing between "wants" and "needs" on a case-by-case basis, while not easy, is necessary on the part of both the West and Russia to prevent the crisis from deepening and spreading. ∎

discussion questions

1. The brief period that followed the fall of the Soviet Union was characterized by Russia's attempts to adopt pro-Western principles. Explain why Russia initially sought foreign policies with the West. How did Russia try integrating itself into the Western world? Identify the goals it hoped to achieve by doing so. In addition, name some of the challenges that it faced.

2. The rise of Vladimir Putin to power resulted in Russia's pursuit of assertive foreign policies, and relations between Russia and the West have become strained. What are some of the causes of this rift and crisis in Ukraine? How does Putin's leadership style differ from that of Yeltsin's? How has his leadership style changed throughout his time in politics?

3. How big of a role does ideology play in Putin's treatment of Ukraine? Are Putin's actions motivated by ideology or purely out of political and economic interests?

4. .The crisis in Ukraine can be traced back to the 2004 orange revolution. This prevented Viktor Yanukovych from becoming the third Ukrainian president, due to flawed presidential elections. How did Russia respond to the orange revolution? Why did Viktor Yanukovych decide not to sign the association and free trade agreement with the European Union, and what role did Russia play in this particular event? In light of the Ukrainian demonstrations and protests that ensued, how have Russian-Ukrainian and Russian-Western relations been affected by Euromaidan?

5. How did Russia's removal of several million pro-Russian voters (through its annexation of Crimea) from Ukrainian election polls affect Ukraine's 2014 presidential and legislative elections? How will the changes in Ukraine's Russian-speaker demographics affect its foreign policy?

6. In response to the crisis, Western sanctions have been imposed on Russian individuals and companies. How effective is this method in the long- and short-run? In addition, NATO countries have since ruled out using military action against Russia over Ukraine. In your opinion, what other options does the West have in dealing with the crisis?

suggested readings

Freire, Maria Raquel and Roger E. Kanet. **Russia and Its Near Neighbors.** Houndmills, Basingstoke, Hampshire: Palgrave Macmillan, 2012. 320 pp. The book analyzes Russia's return to power in the international arena and its future foreign policies toward former Soviet nations.

Gvozdev, Nikolas and Christopher March. **Russian Foreign Policy: Interests, Vectors, and Sectors.** Los Angeles: CQ Press, 2014. 436 pp. An up to date volume that provides a comprehensive overview of actors shaping Russia's foreign policy, and an account of these policies in different regions of the world.

Legvold, Robert. "Russian Foreign Policy During Periods of Great State Transformation," in Robert Legvold, ed. **Russian Foreign Policy in the Twenty-First Century and the Shadow of the Past**. New York: Columbia University Press, 2007. pp.77-143. This chapter offers a broad historical sweep of the periods of great transformation in Russian history and Russia's foreign policy during these turbulent times.

Mearsheimer, John. "Why the Ukraine Crisis Is the West's Fault." **Foreign Affairs**. September/October 2014. McFaul, Michael and Stephen Sestanovich, "Faulty Powers: Who Started the Ukraine Crisis." **Foreign Affairs.** November/December 2014. (online). These articles offer alternative explanations of Russia's actions vis-à-vis Ukraine.

Remnick, David. **Lenin's Tomb: The Last Days of the Soviet Empire.** New York: Random House, 1993. 626pp. Remnick, who at the time covered the events for the *Washington Post*, details the last days of the USSR through a series of short first-hand accounts.

Remnick, David. **Resurrection: The Struggle for a New Russia.** New York: Vintage Books, 1998. 432pp. Remnick follows up on *Lenin's Tomb* in this account of rebuilding the Russian state in the aftermath of the USSR.

Service, Robert. **A History of Modern Russia: From Nicholas II to Vladimir Putin (Revised Edition).** Cambridge: Harvard University Press, 2005. 659pp. A detailed account of modern Russian history from around 1900-2000.

Stent, Angela. **The Limits of Partnership: U.S.-Russian Relations in the Twenty-First Century.** Princeton: Princeton University Press, 2014. 384pp. This volume by Clinton's and Bush's advisor on Russia offers an account of U.S.-Russian relations since 1990, and overview of the obstacles that have prevented a closer relationship.

Tolz, Vera. **Russia: Inventing the Nation**. Arnold/Hodder Headline Group, 2001. 320pp. A comprehensive analysis of different Russian national identity conceptions, their historical evolution, and ways in which they influence Russian policy making towards its neighbors.

✔ **DON'T FORGET TO VOTE!**
WWW.FPA.ORG/BALLOT

KEY TO ABBREVIATIONS AND ACRONYMS FOR EACH ARTICLE NOW AVAILABLE ONLINE!

TO LEARN MORE ABOUT THIS TOPIC AND TO ACCESS WEB LINKS TO RESOURCES GO TO www.greatdecisions.org

Privacy in the Digital Age
by Nuala O'Connor and Alethea Lange

National Security Agency surveillance revelations continue to surface following the disclosure of classified documents to The Guardian *and* Washington Post *by Edward Snowden.* (ALEX MILAN TRACY/NURPHOTO/NURPHOTO/CORBIS)

There is no universal legal or practical definition of privacy in the digital age. In fact, there was not a particularly instructive definition before the digital age. The framers of the U.S. Constitution do not explicitly use the word "privacy" anywhere in the document. Instead, the Constitution focused on the idea of protecting your right to control your property and papers, as any information about you would likely have been sufficiently covered under that principle in a world lacking mechanical reproduction or electronic proliferation.

But preventing government authorities from rifling through your file cabinets has become an outdated concept of privacy. Although the term does appear in international human-rights treaties, those treaties were drafted in the era of telegrams and party telephone lines—a time when today's ubiquity of tracking, recording and otherwise invasive technology was unimaginable. The question of how to define privacy in the digital age is fundamental to all policy, legal and cultural discussions about managing the explosive growth of data we are facing, and there are many different ways to approach the question. As we think about what is next, another re-imagining of what privacy means may be on the horizon.

While there are important insights in previous interpretations of the law and privacy-protecting innovations, there is no teleology of technology, and the future is uncertain. At its core, privacy is about giving those who utilize technology the right to control their information and positioning individuals such that they command their digital destiny. What precisely this entails can be unclear, though it is generally broken down into two pieces: privacy from the government and managing relationships with private companies. This article will approach the question broadly and discuss what privacy means with respect to the entire "digital self."

NUALA O'CONNOR *is the president & CEO of the Center for Democracy and Technology. She is an internationally recognized expert in Internet and technology policy, particularly in the areas of privacy and information governance. Nuala has experience in both the public and private sectors. Prior to joining CDT, she worked at Amazon.com and General Electric (GE). She was also the first statutorily appointed chief privacy officer in federal service when she was named as the first chief privacy officer at the Department of Homeland Security.*
ALETHEA LANGE *is a policy analyst on CDT's Consumer Privacy Project. Her work focuses on empowering users to control their digital presence, and includes topics such as developing fairness in algorithms, protecting digital assets, and the intersection of civil rights and big data. Prior to joining CDT, Alethea was an independent writer and researcher on emerging issues in technology policy.*

2

Digital privacy landscape

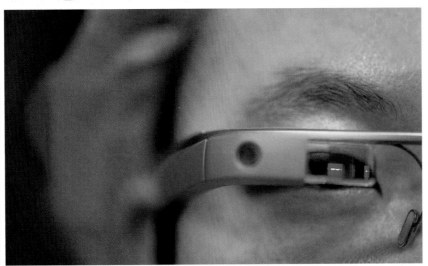

Dr. Patrick Hu, anesthesiologist, glances around UC Irvine's Medical Center hands free with Google Glass. Vital patient data from the operating room and more can be shared via Google Glass. (CINDY YAMANAKA/ZUMA PRESS/CORBIS)

The challenge of securing private information is not new to the digital age. For hundreds of years, people have sought to obscure and protect the contents of their private messages and documents. Surveillance of an individual's communications and personal information can have consequences for daily life.

Most protections for communication technologies are vulnerable. In the physical world, tamper-evident packaging and wax seals on letters may provide some security, but both can be meddled with, given enough time and motivation. In the digital world, security and surveillance measures are not always evident to an unsuspecting consumer. Methods for decoding information can fall anywhere between the simple and the artfully complex. Entire government agencies have been created for this purpose, from the Army Signal Corps of the post-World War I era to the National Security Agency (NSA). The history of communications technologies is also a story about wiretapping and taking advantage of telecommunications—from the telegraph to mobile phones—vulnerable to surveillance.

In recent years, two major incidents have forced the American public to confront their opinions on privacy. Following the attacks on Sept. 11, 2001,

the U.S. government implemented extreme surveillance systems in response to continued national security threats and to fill the intelligence gaps that make the attacks possible. The public, it seemed, wanted their government to do whatever it took to prevent an event like this from happening again. As the scope of these surveillance programs were revealed over the years, Americans were stunned to learn the extent of government surveillance revealed in documents leaked by former defense contractor Edward Snowden and others.

The Snowden documents, which came to light in 2013, showed, among many other things, that the NSA was collecting Verizon customers' phone records by the millions, deliberately undermining the encryption of emails and other private data, and gathering billions of cell-phone location records and millions of text messages from around the world on a daily basis. GCHQ, the NSA's British counterpart, was doing more, including directly tapping into some of the undersea cables that form the "backbone" of the Internet, thereby collecting almost unimaginable volumes of data, and—perhaps most disquieting to the average user—intercepting millions of images from Yahoo users' video chats. GCHQ shared much of this data with the NSA.

In the aftermath of these revelations, a Quinnipiac University poll found that a huge shift in public opinion on the balance of privacy and national security had taken place. In January 2010 the majority of those surveyed believed government anti-terrorism efforts did not go far enough; by July 2013 most reported that the government's activities infringed upon civil liberties.

Outside of government surveillance, the question of what privacy means today is mired in a debate about who is empowering whom when individuals utilize online platforms at little to no cost, often in exchange for allowing companies to collect data about them. The companies that provide the tools for us to create our digital selves—and interact with digital others—are undoubtedly critical in defining how Internet and mobile technology is experienced. However, those tools can come at the expense of privacy or self-determination. Still, the technologies that threaten our privacy offer a unique insight into our identity: The tailored ads and suggested content that guide us around the web, and the propensity toward digital echo chambers has transformed each individual's computer into a unique world that acts as a mirror as well as a window.

For an individual, digital privacy is about the ability to shape one's own online identity and decide when, how and where to share parts of that identity with people, companies or other selected entities. The freedom to create an identity online is the essence of conceptual privacy; in practice, it lies in the ability to develop and curate a digital portrait that reflects personal preferences.

Control over information is not always easily applied to a complicated technical and legal landscape. Different designs to address the practical implementation of privacy have developed in different fields; civil rights activists, industry, and government each have their own considerations and goals when defining privacy. While much international legal work focuses on defining and defending privacy as a fundamental right, U.S. Supreme Court cases have cobbled together versions of this right by applying a number of laws that may not mention privacy explicitly, such as the Fourth Amendment, to new technologies. But making and interpreting laws is a slow and cumbersome process. As this process lumbers along, companies and individuals continue to exist in a world of undefined or fluid digital boundaries where individuals must act with a degree of vigilance regarding commercial and government intrusions, and demand more control over their personal information. In response to this pressure, a market for privacy-protecting technologies has emerged, providing a practical solution to complex and ongoing political or legal wrangles.

The lack of a clear definition of digital privacy presents an opportunity to contemplate the underlying purpose of the question. There are two main avenues to consider this question: through experience with private companies and through the effect of government interferences—such as surveillance—on personal freedom. Privacy in government and commercial environments has different cultural and legal implications, but the technologies involved in either are often related. To understand different applications of privacy, it is helpful to look at the legal perspective, practical considerations and the technical capabilities that underlie the question. It is also necessary to explore past and present perceptions of the fundamental right to privacy.

In 1890, Supreme Court Justice Louis Brandeis addressed the concept of privacy in the context of a press whose infatuation with salacious stories was being fed by increasingly available means of mechanical reproduction, such as portable cameras and cheap means of printing. Prior to his Supreme Court appointment, Brandeis, along with Boston attorney Samuel D. Warren, published "The Right to Privacy" (1890) in the *Harvard Law Review*. They argued that the law must be responsive to the dynamic nature of technology and, hence, privacy. Both considered privacy to be a right that extends beyond traditional notions of property, and even beyond the "products and processes of the mind"

Advertisement for Kodak cameras from The Illustrated London News *in 1893 including Kodak's famous slogan "You press the button, we do the rest."* (GETTY IMAGES)

(e.g., art and trade secrets). They advance the value of privacy per se by arguing for a "right to be let alone."

In response to the journalism of that day, Brandeis and Warren wrote, "Gossip is no longer the resource of the idle and of the vicious, but has become a trade, which is pursued with industry as well as effrontery." The two men envisioned the "right to be let alone" as a way individuals could control the information that was captured and disseminated about them, even when they were in public spaces. Brandeis and Warren's reliance on the idea of preserving a right to privacy in the wake of technological and cultural changes was prescient and personal—Brandeis was a celebrity and often-photographed man of his time.

Brandeis and Warren's argument provides important insights into several aspects of the current privacy debate. The decrease in cost to collect and store data has permanently changed government surveillance, commercial data collection and the amount of information we store about ourselves with the aid of third-party services. We live now in a world with practically limitless data storage that costs next to nothing and is

becoming cheaper by the day, and the tools to analyze these vast amounts of data are becoming exponentially more sophisticated. The conversation around privacy has correspondingly shifted to questioning the implications for identity and security that "big data" brings with it, and the boundaries have not been conclusively defined.

Much like the innovation of portable cameras in Brandeis' time, the innovations supported by big data are starting to present challenges to privacy. The dust has yet to settle, but companies, advocates, courts, policymakers and researchers alike are considering whether to apply existing definitions of privacy in this new landscape or to introduce a completely new outlook.

Recent jurisprudence

Both within the U.S. and internationally, courts have done significant work in establishing boundaries that provide practical definitions of privacy. In doing so, they have had to make fundamental decisions about how and whether to apply old laws to new digital privacy challenges, and consider how to create new standards without losing baseline protections. Today's courts have had to navigate tensions between law enforcement and fundamental freedom that are often depicted as having greater and greater urgency.

The U.S. Supreme Court's seminal privacy cases tend to revolve around technology used by law enforcement—and so are argued under the Fourth Amendment—but the resulting decisions have also been applied to larger cultural and public policy conversations on privacy expectations. Technology's role in everyday life can be reflected in the opinions issued in these cases. Often, the deciding factor is about the way the technology works. These cases demonstrate fundamental values that underlie broader definitions of privacy.

Supreme Court rulings that hinge on technical details, such as *Kyllo v. United States* (2001) and *Riley v. California* (2014), provide some insights into the Court's understanding of a digital identity. In *Kyllo*, the fact that the technology—namely thermal imaging devices—was not widely available to the public was essential. In *Kyllo*, police used a thermal imaging device to observe heat patterns in Danny Kyllo's Oregon home. They observed a high amount of heat on the roof and used the information to obtain a search warrant for the property. Kyllo was subsequently charged with growing marijuana. The majority opinion of the Court argued that because the technology used was not widely available to the public, a warrant was required to search the home. The justices defined the reasonable expectation of privacy in practical terms: If it is uncommon for the heat signature of an individual's house to be scanned from a public street, then a warrant is required. This argument may not

stand against the increasing availability of surveillance technologies—thermal scanners are now available online for a few hundred dollars.

In *Riley*, the Court found that a warrant is required to search a mobile phone, even during an arrest. (Warrants generally are not required to search items on a person during an arrest.) Writing for a unanimous Court, Chief Justice John Roberts argued, "modern cell phones are not just another technological convenience. With all they contain and all they may reveal, they hold for many Americans the privacies of life. The fact that technology now allows an individual to carry such information in his hand does not make the information any

less worthy of the protection for which the Founders fought." That our phones come within the sphere of our personal privacy because the information contained within them can be so personal and comprehensive is an important cultural concept. The Court's decision to protect this iteration of the digital self has far-reaching consequences. This ruling allows for nuanced definitions of the distinctions between physical and digital property as well as the right to trust that the technology that empowers us to create and sustain a digital presence.

In addition to interpreting cultural expectations of privacy, court cases can establish norms based on rulings or to make strong arguments that a piece of

What Technologies are Involved?

*H*ardware is any physical component of a computer that performs in the digital environment: computers, cameras, servers, hard drives, as well as devices like cell phones and tablets. Anything that can be physically touched is likely hardware. Although the object may be physically in the hands of its owner, there is always the threat of unauthorized access through theft or insecure networks, among other potential gateways. Hardware also includes surveillance technology like Closed Circuit Television (CCTV) cameras and automatic license plate readers.

Software operates in two ways. System software is the set of rules that govern the way computer hardware functions such as an operating system. Application software is the set of rules that are manipulated by users to accomplish specific tasks, such as the creation of documents.

Mobile technology includes everything about a smartphone other than the device itself. The transmitting capability of a phone includes unique identifiers that pose challenges to privacy because they are not easily changed and are communicated with nearly every type of transmission. In recent years surveillance and commercial tracking technologies has developed that capitalizes on the fact that a phone is always looking for a signal when it is on. Technologies called "IMSI catchers" can be used to trick devices into sending identifying information by mimicking a cell tower, and is often used by law enforcement to track suspects. In the commercial space, retail analytics companies capture the passive communications of individuals' phones as they travel around a store or shopping center. Additionally, metadata—or data that defines or provides information about other data—is not protected by law in the same manner as the content being created or accessed. Metadata analysis poses significant threats to individual privacy.

The *cloud* is an evocative way to describe data storage via

file sharing that is outside of personal computer (PC) hardware, typically on the server of a private company. Data stored on the cloud is more vulnerable to unauthorized access than data stored on only on hardware because the cloud is an inter-networked mechanism that is typically accessed by users through mechanisms involving passwords, which can be lost, guessed or socially engineered by unauthorized parties to gain access. Cloud computing's security flaws are taken advantage of by the intelligence community. Cloud technology aggregates many users' data in one physical location and under the purview of one authority, which is one-stop shop, so to speak, for government surveillers.

The *Internet of Things* refers to computing and networking capability in everyday appliances and machines, such as a coffee machine that connects to the Internet so you can program it via a smartphone. There are significant interoperability problems in this space as there are many proprietary platforms competing for dominance that do not work well together. Additionally, this expansion of the network raises questions about what kind of data our appliances will be collecting, who will have access, and how it will be used. There are significant issues in terms of security and obsolescence; if your coffee maker is susceptible to malware but the company has gone out of business, you may never be able to update the software. It also increases the potential for invasion of the digital self— imagine if your refrigerator could track your calorie count.

Wearables are technology attached to the human body and includes anything from a watch with a built-in calculator to a networked Apple watch. Most recently, wearable technologies directly measure body data like heart rates and blood pressure to provide basic health data, and may function as a medical device by monitoring a patient's glucose levels and providing feedback to a diabetes application on a smartphone. This data is mostly unregulated and can be leveraged for good and bad purposes.

technology has fundamentally altered the playing field. For example, despite the presence of video cameras in many public places, those cameras do not usually include microphones. This is because *Katz v. United States* (1967) established a reasonable expectation of privacy in our conversations.

In her concurring opinion in the *United States v. Jones* (2012) case, Justice Sonia Sotomayor delivered a powerful narrative of the relationship between an individual, his/her digital trail, law enforcement and third parties. In the case, the police attached a GPS tracking device to Antoine Jones' vehicle and tracked him continuously for 28 days before arresting him on drug charges. The Court found his Fourth Amendment rights were violated but issued separate opinions. In her opinion, Sotomayor argued: "GPS monitoring—by making available at a relatively low cost such a substantial quantum of intimate information about any person whom the Government, in its unfettered discretion, chooses to track—may 'alter the relationship between citizen and government in a way that is inimical to democratic society.'" She continued, "More fundamentally, it may be necessary to reconsider the premise that an individual has no reasonable expectation of privacy in information voluntarily disclosed to third parties. This approach is ill suited to the digital age." Sotomayor situated information generated by or about an individual within his control, at least in principle if not in reality.

International trends

Similar legal and philosophical struggles can be seen at the international level, where human rights courts and United Nations (UN) institutions are confronting explicit questions about what the right to be free from arbitrary or unnecessary interferences with our "privacy" or "private life" means in the digital age. Although these bodies have addressed those questions primarily in the context of secret surveillance, the UN High Commissioner for Human Rights has highlighted general and "serious" concerns about "the extent to which consumers are truly aware of

what data they are sharing, how and with whom, and to what use [the data] will be put." The same report entered into the fray surrounding the question of whether individuals have less of an expectation of privacy in data about their communications (such as the sender, recipient, date, and time) than in the content of those communications. The report concluded that both types of data should be protected according to the same standards.

Meanwhile, highly influential judgments of the European Court of Human Rights (ECHR) suggest that we do not need new legal standards to protect privacy; we just need to be sure careful to apply the old ones as rigorously to email and Internet usage as we have historically done to letters and telephone calls. Governments around the world, however, continue to push back against this idea, citing new threats to public safety in legislation that expands surveillance powers, as the UK did when passing new surveillance and data retention legislation earlier this year.

Surveillance technologies will continue to advance at a rapid pace, and law enforcement will continue to push the boundaries of reasonable use. The interpretation of these tools and strategies by courts, legislators and international bodies provides a useful window into cultural understanding of both technical capability and the value of a digital life.

While scholars consider how to create a nuanced legal framework that defines modern privacy, the tech industry and its subscribers have been building a vibrant marketplace of privacy-enhancing innovation. Today's vast array of digital technologies is reflective of the many ways individuals interact with devices on a daily basis, from social media and baby monitors to fitness tracking and medical devices. All these technologies either produce or facilitate the generation of tremendous amounts of information about individuals. The revelation that the NSA exploits commercial technologies and the companies that make them have focused attention on privacy and with it the ability to control one's digital presence. Consumers are now more aware of the pervasiveness of tracking technology and the proliferating collection of big data.

Companies are now developing tools that allow users to prevent tracking, limit companies' ability to access or share user data, or use anonymity features in their products as a selling point, even if they do not always deliver. For example, many Internet browsers include an option to browse "privately" in their features. The widespread availability of this setting indicates that users are demanding some built-in privacy protecting modes of operation in everyday tools. These features are useful for preventing information about your

(NATE BEELER COURTESY OF CAGLE CARTOONS)

browsing habits from being stored on your device, but they do not keep activity private from servers or third-party tracking software embedded in some sites. Private browsing is based on a functional definition of privacy wherein users seek to protect themselves from someone in physically proximity or someone who has access to their devices. That is only one aspect of what it means to be private.

Other privacy-protecting products may disrupt tracking technology in order to limit or prevent targeted advertising and marketing. Two popular examples are Disconnect.me and Ghostery. These help users block tracking and advertising software by identifying tracking technologies and blocking them from reaching your browser. This technology contributes another layer of privacy protection by identifying third-parties (entities with whom the user does not have a relationship) that may be a threat to privacy.

Not all products claiming to protect privacy are created equal; there are several that over-promise anonymity or security features to users, an even worse offense than transparently exposing users' data. Snapchat and Whisper, among others, have had major hiccups after publicly advertising robust privacy and/or anonymity in their products while doing the opposite "under the hood." Snapchat allows users to send photos that disappear after a set amount of time; Whisper promises to allow users to anonymously express themselves online. Neither application did what it claimed, leaving sensitive photos undeleted on phone (Snapchat) and allowing sophisticated identified surveillance (Whisper). Despite the fact that the technology in these examples is flawed, their popularity indicates that the marketplace for privacy tools is strong. They also exhibit a unique mode of privacy protection: rendering a history of individual behavior inaccessible or untraceable.

In addition to building tools that support user privacy, companies have begun seeking ways to protect themselves from unwanted participation in unauthorized surveillance and hacking. Apple and Google have recently made substantial changes to the privacy protections in

their respective mobile operating systems, iOS and Android. The data stored on Android and iOS devices is encrypted and enabled by default. Encryption of data stored on the device means that when the device is lost or stolen, the increasingly intimate data stored on the device will be gibberish to anyone but the device owner, who has the encryption key. This has the promise of reducing some of the negative consequences associated with the loss of unencrypted devices; a user will be less susceptible to identity theft and other forms of crime.

Privacy policies

The lack of comprehensive baseline privacy legislation in the U.S. is at the heart of many U.S. privacy-related policy challenges. Instead of implementing a national standard for privacy, the U.S. has taken a sector-by-sector approach to the issue: access to electronic communications are regulated through Electronic Communications Privacy Act (ECPA), health records by the Health Insurance Portability and Accountability Act (HIPAA), credit reports by the Fair Credit Reporting Act (FCRA), student records by the Family Educational Rights and Privacy Act (FERPA), collection of children's personal information online by the Children's Online Privacy Protection Act (COPPA), and so on. Some laws are outdated and in need of a revamp; others offer sufficient privacy protections but are inconsistently applied.

Industries not falling within a particular privacy law may be left largely unregulated. In such circumstances, lawyers, judges and regulatory authorities attempt to reign in industry or government using state privacy law, state tort law, federal unfair competition laws or the Constitution. For example, while the Bill of Rights does not explicitly include a fundamental right to privacy, the Supreme Court has extended the doctrine to provide for individual privacy rights in certain circumstances.

At the crux of these debates is a desire to rebalance the power between states, companies and individuals. U.S. companies, as well as state and federal government, have historically embraced the "wild west" approach to

individual data collection, use, retention and sharing. Individuals have relatively little knowledge of or control over how their data is collected. Because there is no national legal standard articulating citizens' privacy rights, more often than not law is created after a company or the government is found to have disrupted citizens' reasonable expectation of privacy. Some industries have made efforts to self regulate—designing "best practices" and codes intended to enhance consumer privacy and avoid government regulation. There are stronger policy reasons for designing federal legislation to address individual privacy. For one, it would give businesses the incentive (and legal duty) to offer robust privacy protections for users from the start, as opposed to integrating protections after the fact. Baseline privacy law will speed the adoption of reasonable privacy practices across the marketplace, provide a level playing field, and ensure that bad actors are deterred.

While most collection and use of personal information by companies is unregulated in the U.S., many other nations have passed statutory protections to safeguard consumer data. In 1995, the EU passed the Data Protection Directive, requiring member states to adopt detailed privacy legislation requiring, among other things, transparency and proportionality in data processing operations, reasonable consumer access to information stored about them, and prohibitions on transferring to data to other countries with "inadequate" legal protections. Over time, dozens of other nations around the world have adopted similar laws based on the European model.

The varying laws including prohibitions on transfer to other jurisdictions have become more challenging and complicated over time. In the late 1990s, the U.S. and Europe entered into a "Safe Harbor" agreement to allow transfer of European's personal data to the U.S.— which hosted much of the world's cloud computing infrastructure—to companies who promised to abide by privacy-preserving practices. However, European policymakers have become increasingly skeptical about American data practices and surveillance capabilities. European policymakers are considering an update to the Data Protection Directive that would include more uniform rules and great enforcement powers for regulators. It may also rescind the Safe Harbor agreement, or require companies to get European permission to comply with extraterritorial governmental requests—forcing companies to choose which nation's laws to violate in considering a request for personal information.

Government surveillance

Both government and the private sector have vital role in fixing these emerging access issues. As so many important parts of our lives become digital, we need legal protections to replace practical ones that have faded away. Just as the Supreme Court stepped in when tapped phone lines and thermo-imaging let police look and listen past the security that the simple use of walls had offered for thousands of years, lawmakers must now step in to keep us safe from overly invasive surveillance practices.

The most pressing action for Congress in this regard is the USA FREEDOM Act. Over the last decade, technology has given the NSA the ability to employ a "collect it all" approach to surveillance, and gone into the realm of bulk data. The documents leaked by Snowden showed that the NSA has the ability to vacuum up all Americans' phone records through a single order from the secret FISA Court.

Limiting surveillance through legislation is difficult in a post-9/11 world, but the USA FREEDOM Act is the reform that proves "safe and free" is not just a political cliché. The bill's ban on bulk collection is supported by civil society groups, America's biggest tech companies, and politicians ranging from Bernie Sanders to Ted Cruz. It even has the backing of the intelligence community—Director of National Intelligence James Clapper stated the bill would not hinder security needs. It remains unclear if the USA FREEDOM Act will get a vote before the end of 2014. Even if USA FREEDOM passes Congress as written, it would be one step towards reform and not a complete solution—the bill, for example, provides almost no protection for non-U.S. persons.

Civil liberties activists hold a rally against surveillance of U.S. citizens in anticipation of President Obama's announcement regarding reforms of the NSA at the Justice Department in Washington, DC, on Jan. 17, 2014. (NICHOLAS KAMM/AFP/GETTY IMAGES)

Congress should also draft new laws to preserve the privacy of digital content stored in the cloud, such as email. Currently, police access is governed by the ECPA, a law created in the 1980s when cloud computing was science fiction. A loophole in the law allows police to access emails more than six months old without a warrant, and over 270 House members are cosponsoring the Email Privacy Act to address the problem. However, despite having such broad support, the bill has not even received a vote in its committee, leaving the public wondering how much longer their archived emails will be subject to warrantless government snooping.

While there are many areas where government should be building up privacy protections against overbroad surveillance, there is actually a risk that when Congress does act, it will be to tear existing protections down. Recently, FBI Director James Comey condemned Apple and Google's decision to encrypt phones by default, a protective measure that will keep smartphone users safe from cybercriminals. While Comey has argued this will make prosecutions impossible (a claim that has been strongly refuted), critics of encryption have failed to recognize that for normal smartphone users, encryption is one of the strongest tools the public has to prevent crime in the digital world.

International and economic trends

In Europe, two important and influential regional courts continue to take a strong stance in favor of the right to privacy. In balancing competing rights and values, these courts have arguably come to give privacy a paramount role.

The Court of Justice of the European Union (CJEU), whose interpretations of EU law are binding upon all 28 EU Member States, has issued what is known as the "Right to Be Forgotten" decision. Here, the court found that EU law requires search-engine operators to delete links from lists of search results concerning an individual where those links lead to information that is "inadequate, irrelevant or no longer relevant, or excessive in relation to the purposes" of the search—even if the information is true. The court also found that an individual's right to privacy and right to "personal data" protection outweigh the public's interest in being able to obtain information. The court did make an exception for information that the public has a "preponderant" interest in viewing, such as information concerning public figures. Many U.S.-based activists are concerned about how the judgment privileges privacy rights. Some believe that the "right to be forgotten" will have an impact on free expression, which the CJEU's judgment barely mentions.

Although the "right to be forgotten" decision has been more widely reported, the CJEU issued an important judgment a few months prior in a case known as Digital Rights Ireland in which the court struck down a number of critical laws governing companies' retention of user data. The laws, adopted in the aftermath of terrorist attacks in London and Madrid, required companies to retain certain user data in order to facilitate criminal investigations. The court made some significant and persuasive remarks what our metadata can reveal. Government surveillance regimes increasingly distinguish between communications metadata and content, and afford lesser protections to the former, so the remarks were particularly salient.

Over the past several decades, the European Court of Human Rights (ECHR) has also repeatedly grappled with questions concerning the extent to which the right to privacy extends to emerging technologies, as well as the fundamental-rights safeguards that must accompany secret government surveillance programs. In 2014, the ECHR plucked a case against Russia from relative obscurity and elevated it to the highest possible level of attention—consideration by the Grand Chamber. *Zakharov v. Russia* (2006) involves Russia's alleged surveillance of a journalist and the country's requirement that mobile-phone operators allow the installation of surveillance equipment in their facilities so that law enforcement can monitor phone calls. The court's judgment in the case could help companies around the world to argue that as a matter of human rights, governments cannot compel communications service providers to violate privacy rights.

Privacy and the U.S. economy

Technology policy can have a broad impact on the economy and innovation. The public is outraged about the Snowden revelations for many reasons, yet one of the most important harms of overbroad NSA surveillance has received little attention: the impact of surveillance on the U.S. economy.

NSA surveillance has a devastating impact on the American tech industry. Studies by the Information Technology and Innovation Foundation and Forrester Research estimate NSA surveillance will cost the U.S. tech industry between $22 billion and $180 billion over the next three years, a loss of up to 25% of total industry revenue. The U.S.' long-held strong competitive advantage in the tech sector is slipping due to the global perception that American products are insecure due to loose rules on surveillance.

Government surveillance also risks severe harm to innovation and the structure of the Internet. NSA surveillance has jumpstarted efforts abroad to require data to be stored in particular countries, which could splinter a once-global Internet into regional networks. These efforts could have negative repercussions for the competitiveness of the American tech industry, the free flow of information, and the Internet's ability to promote international entrepreneurship and innovation; any new American start-up would need the capacity to develop costly infrastructure in foreign counties.

These concerns are a major reason why the tech industry and both conservative and liberal advocacy groups are supporting the USA FREEDOM Act. Multiple independent reports have concluded that the program has not been critical to discovering or disrupting a terrorist plot, and the Attorney General and Director of National Intelligence have stated it would not inhibit essential operations. ■

A privacy framework

Over his life's work, Brandeis recognized that the rights to privacy and free speech travel together but are sometimes in tension. Yet he believed that together they were necessary components of the intellectual, moral, and spiritual development of individuals, "men and women who shall be free, self-respecting members of a democracy—and who shall be worthy of respect." In his dissent in *Whitney v. California* (1927)—which helped to lay the foundations of modern First Amendment doctrine—Brandeis stated that America's founders believed that "it is hazardous to discourage thought, hope and imagination," and that "the final end of the State was to make men free to develop their faculties." He saw that the freedom to develop one's faculties without fear is connected to one's ability to formulate opinions and participate in the in democratic self-governance. Today, people are enabled more than ever before to engage in the public discussion that Brandeis calls "a political duty." But fully embracing this potential requires we preserve the freedom of thought, the capacity for imagination and self-determination, and the ability to control our digital selves.

In today's world, the freedom to cultivate one's digital self and participate in digital life is an intellectual prerequisite to safeguarding individual privacy. At the same time, government and companies play an integral role in constructing or providing the platforms from which to construct a citizens' digital self. Moving toward an the specific legal fixes described and toward an understanding of how the individual user interacts with both companies and the government, and how these interactions shape the individual's digital self.

The digital self

The digital self is the sum total of a person's interactions with technology—their creative expressions, communications, curiosity as captured by a digital trail. Technology allows us to interact with the world in nuanced and creative ways, and has become strongly linked to our physical and emotional identity. It provides the mechanism for artistic production, as well as the ability to access content from around the world and to correspond with its producers. Individuals interact with technology in unique patters, and our online behaviors, communications, and creations represent an authentic and curated impression of who we are. There is a temptation to dismiss digital interactions as emotionally void or disingenuous, but this fails to appreciate the sincerity with which the majority of people engage in the process of creating and communicating online.

Not all technologies are equally malleable, however. Researcher and advocate danah boyd describes the empowering nature of the early iterations of social media. Consider the contrast between MySpace, where users could design their own pages using HTML, creating rich and diverse expressions of themselves while also learning about the technology, to something like Facebook where the visual layouts is a standard features, as is the algorithm that determines and populates the content you see.

In daily life, technology serves as a tool to help us express ourselves, communicate, or manage our content. Typically, we only contemplate the privacy and security implications of these tools as needed, either in response to world events or to personal embarrassments or violations. But the work of advocates like those at CDT is to stay constantly wary of the threat to an individual's digital self and thoughtful about how to protect that self through enhanced self-determination. Our phones and computers transport and hold a bevy of information about us. Collectively, these data and metadata that compose our digital identities can weave a detailed narrative about our actions, thoughts, and personal lives (though not necessarily an accurate one). With only information about where we were and to whom we spoke, government officials may make ill-informed conclusions about our intentions.

For an individual who does not know that he or she is part of a database monitored for terrorist activity, something as simple as a call to someone in the Middle East or an errant Internet search could draw a false portrait. Data that others produce about you can have an equally ill effect. For instance, Facebook allows users to tag other users in photos; additionally, its built-in facial

recognition tool is now very advanced and regularly assigns names and profiles to photos. As a user you at least have the option to remove the tag, but whether you have a profile or not, Facebook can plainly identify your face and connect it to the profiles of your acquaintances. So, whether or not you have deliberately handed over your personal information, friends, companies, and strangers are still able to supply it without your explicit consent.

Policy options

Given the myriad unique ways individuals define themselves and their identities, defining the digital self becomes exponentially complicated in the context of national security and network surveillance. Often, the structure of these programs is contradictory. They remove control of data from the individual and absorb the digital impressions of our selves into a system founded on scrutiny. But in these structures we can find the building blocks of a common framework for understanding and governing the digital self. Ultimately, we should seek a foundation on which we can build, as individuals and societies, freedom to express the digital self, explore the digital community, engage in the digital society, and actively participate in digital democracy.

Some policy efforts would specifically contribute to or deter privacy goals in the digital age. These largely fall into one of two categories: those focused on commercial data collection or use and those focused on government surveillance. Each of these policies has unique political context and policy objectives.

ECPA: One of the most overdue reforms in Washington is basic privacy for our emails. When you put Halloween pictures of your niece in a Gmail folder marked "Family" or archive an electronic medical bill, you expect that private information to be secure from snooping, just like a paper copy in your desk drawer. When the ECPA, the law governing email privacy, was enacted in 1986, an inbox could only hold a dozen emails, and letters over a month old were considered "abandoned." Today's inboxes can hold years, or even decades, worth of messages, all of which could be subject to warrantless surveillance. Our email privacy laws from the pre-dial-up age need to be desperately reconsidered.

It is no surprise this problem has many lawmakers calling for change, on both sides of the aisle. With Congress so often in stalemate, and bipartisan consensus so rare, it's hard to understand why a commonsense and widely agreed upon reform such as this is being held up.

USA FREEDOM ACT: Congress

Former National Economic Council Director Gene Sperling speaks at a White House event highlighting information economy and privacy Feb. 23, 2012 in Washington, DC. (WIN MCNAMEE/GETTY IMAGES)

is considering legislation that would reform some of the NSA's overbroad surveillance practices. The USA FREEDOM Act would rein in the NSA's bulk collection of domestic phone call and email records and create new safeguards to limit large-scale surveillance of Americans. It also gives private parties greater ability to report on surveillance orders received and establishes a panel of external experts tasked with protecting privacy and civil liberties at the Foreign Intelligence Surveillance Court (FISC). A related, but weaker, version of the bill passed the House, and a stronger version awaits a vote in the Senate. While the bill may not cross the finish line before the new session of Congress begins in Jan. 2015, Congress will have ample opportunity to advance this and other critical NSA surveillance reform legislation.

CRYPTOGRAPHY: Technology companies are providing increasingly secure commercial products, such as popular smartphones and email services, with strong encryption. Encrypting smartphones and other tech products will help protect against malicious hacking, identity theft, phone theft and other crimes. The move to more secure communications has prompted the FBI to push for legislation that would require tech companies to build "backdoor" access in order to facilitate surveillance. However, a government requirement that companies to build a "backdoor" would put consumers at grave risk and impose heavy costs on U.S. businesses. If the U.S. government can exploit a security vulnerability to access a consumer's device, so will malicious hackers, identity thieves and foreign governments. This will reduce the security of not just individual consumers around the world, but also the many businesses that use American commercial tech products day-to-day. Congress and the Executive Branch should decline to take up any technical mandate that undermines encryption.

CYBER SECURITY: Another missed opportunity in Washington is cybersecurity. With major data breaches happening regularly and threats from foreign governments on the rise, establishing new protections should be straightforward. Unfortunately, Congress' efforts have failed to provide security or offer a path forward. The main Senate bill on cybersecurity—the Cybersecurity Information Sharing Act—ignores the scandal surrounding NSA surveillance, and requires private communications given to the government for cybersecurity purposes immediately and automatically go to agencies like the NSA. It also would create no affirmative obligation on companies to strip out users' sensitive information unrelated to cyber threats. Giving the NSA more power to collect our communications is an unwise policy and untenable politically. If Congress intends to take cybersecurity threats seriously, it needs to offer a better solution.

Protecting privacy is not the only way that NSA revelations should inform our cybersecurity policy. Over the last year a great deal of cyber operations conducted by our own government have been exposed, including breaking into Google and Yahoo servers and storing "zero day" security vulnerabilities. These practices place American Internet users at risk—if our government can exploit vulnerabilities, so can cyber criminals and foreign adversaries. The President's Review Group on Intelligence and Communications Technologies has recommended a range of significant reforms to offensive cyber operations that put Americans at risk, but these have been completely ignored in Congress.

BASELINE PRIVACY LEGISLATION: The current system of piecemeal privacy regulation often results in the Federal Trade Commission (FTC) regulating consumer privacy through Section 5 of the FTC Act, which includes a provision against "unfair or deceptive authority." Even with limited resources, the FTC has done an admirable job of bringing important privacy concerns to the public; however, this type of regulation creates administrative burdens on agencies, may hamper technological and marketing innovations by creating an uncertain regulatory playing field for businesses, and offers limited protections to consumers as a whole. Comprehensive baseline privacy

legislation would build consumer trust, support technological innovation, and represent the best interests of the government, industries and the public.

President Obama proposed a Consumer Privacy Bill of Rights in 2012 and called on Congress to write these recommendations into law. His recommendations, loosely based on the Fair Information Practice Principles (FIPPs), focused on fundamental measures such as individual control over personal data, transparent and understandable privacy and security practices, and secure and responsible handling of personal data. He argued that privacy is fundamental to our democracy and economy: "Citizens who feel protected from misuse of their personal information feel free to engage in commerce, to participate in the political process, or to seek needed health care."

A federal law codifying a privacy bill of rights is unlikely in the current Congressional climate. However, the president's recommendations provide a useful framework of protections for privacy advocates and the technology industry to grapple with in legislative and self-regulatory initiatives.

THE PRIVACY ACT OF 1974: Because the American government is a prolific data repository for information about citizens, robust privacy safeguards are a necessity. One of these safeguards is the Privacy Act of 1974, which prohibits federal agencies from sharing information about individuals without their written consent. The Privacy Act currently does not apply to non-citizens. Recent leaks illustrating the reach of government surveillance and the lack of legal privacy protection for foreigners have placed enormous pressure on the government to provide more transparency, access and control for the subjects of this collection. Amending the Privacy Act of 1974 to include protections for non-citizens is one avenue to achieve these goals.

These protections should include, but are not limited to, equal access to agency records and judicial redress if an agency violates an individual's rights under the Act. In June, the Obama administration committed to

An employee fixes part of a web server inside the Facebook Inc. Prineville Data Center in Prineville, Oregon, U.S., on April 28, 2014. (MEG ROUSSOS/BLOOMBERG VIA GETTY IMAGES)

passing legislation that would extend the Privacy Act to EU member state citizens. Such legislation would allow EU citizens to access and correct errors in their collected information, as well as seek judicial redress for willful disclosures of personally identifiable information (PII) without their consent. Congress, however, has yet to introduce such legislation.

DATA BREACH LEGISLATION:
Nearly every U.S. state has a data breach law that incorporates breach notification provisions, providing both strong protection for consumers in those states and a headache for industries trying to comply with a patchwork of regulations. Congress is considering multiple bills that would create a federal standard for data breach notification but how this federal standard would work is unclear. Creating federal data breach legislation that goes beyond breach notification and reasonable security, which are already required under existing law, would provide useful safeguards. These safeguards should encourage companies to establish internal privacy practices that seamlessly protect data throughout its lifecycle. Ideally, any data breach notification mandate would require companies to develop front-end data security procedures, regularly monitor data storage, and limit data collection and retention to that which is needed to conduct a valid business purpose.

This law should offer protections at least as robust as the most stringent state laws. At minimum, a federal data breach notification law should require: 1.) appropriately scoped preemption to limit preemption of state to only those provisions that increase protections for consumers; 2.) a "notify unless" trigger that would require consumer notification by default unless a company makes an affirmative determination that there exists no serious risk that data will be misused; and 3.) outside scrutiny that would require companies to report all breaches to an outside regulatory authority regardless of whether the breach was determined to pose no risk.

No formal process for review or approval of a company's determination would necessarily be required. Simply knowing that a brief explanation would need to be filed with the regulatory body, and that the regulatory body may respond if it noticed a pattern, will push companies to be vigilant in their efforts to secure consumers' data. This would also equip the regulatory authority with information from which it can flag dangerous patterns or other concerns.

LOCATION PRIVACY ACT:
Location data is one of the most revealing pieces of information that can be collected about a person. In aggregate, location can paint a detailed picture of one's day-to-day life, including private practices such as attending Alcohol-ics Anonymous meetings, doctor visits or weekly trips to practice a faith. The proliferation of mobile devices with GPS technology has made location data enticing for advertisers and marketers. The abundance of mobile applications that passively collect location data has made it extremely easy for companies to obtain and sell to advertisers. Despite its sensitivity, there are few regulations governing what kinds of notice must be given to consumers or how location data can be used.

Sen. Al Franken has introduced a bill called the Location Privacy Protection Act that aims to provide some regulation for location data. Franken specifically points to the threat posed by stalking apps that use GPS data to enable abusers to locate or follow victims. This legislation would also apply to both commercial and government entities, but includes exceptions for emergency situations and lawful searches with warrants. Although the bill had several co-sponsors, it was not considered in the 113th Congress.

This type of narrowly focused legislation might be a fruitful strategy for avoiding partisan gridlock and putting useful privacy legislation on the books. Rather than attempting to address the whole of data collection, increasing oversight of particularly vulnerable data streams offers incremental benefits and protections to users.

Looking forward
Privacy protections are integral to an individual's ability to cultivate their digital self. Technology is not intrinsically valuable; its value lies within the adoption and application of it by users. The government is responsible for setting reasonable limits on data collection and use in order to empower all users equally such that they can control this application, as well as their digital experience and destiny. This includes not undermining that principle by conducting opaque surveillance with the same systems and tools. In the meantime, the marketplace for privacy and anti-surveillance technologies will continue to thrive and individuals will continue to iterate on their digital selves. ∎

discussion questions

1. The public opinion toward government surveillance has changed from one of support to overwhelming dissent. Explain what caused this change. How has the Internet changed the way people define privacy? Is there a clear definition of what digital privacy is? If not, then why so?

2. The "right to be alone" emphasized the idea that privacy is something that transcends the traditional sense of property, with the expectation that people could still control information about themselves even in public spaces. Explain why the "right to be alone" concept may not work in the 21st century. How have the U.S. and other countries worked to adjust privacy laws in this technological age where information is becoming increasingly digitalized and disseminated? How have recent court rulings establish the extent to which technology can be accessed before it infringes on people's privacy and violates Fourth Amendment rights?

3. The technological advancements of this era make it easier to track data from electronic devices. Explain why this is problematic, and describe the measures that certain companies have taken to counter tracking on digital identity. In addition, describe how the U.S. currently regulates different kinds of information from various sectors. Is this an effective approach? If not, then could a national and uniform privacy standard for all sectors work better?

4. Explain whether or not technology has a significant role in constructing a person's overall identity. How is technology linked to people's physical and emotional identities? How could data and information collected about people be misused? Identify consequences associated with drawing conclusions based on digital identities.

5. Identify policy options aimed at commercial data collection or use, and those for government surveillance. How could government continue to protect people's rights to privacy, and are further limits on data collection and use required? Explain why or why not. ficient organization of highly overlapping organizations, as General Alexander and his supporters have argued?

---

suggested readings

Anderson, Janna, and Lee Rainie. **Net Threats**. Washington, DC: Pew Research Center, 2014. 40 pp. Available free online: <http://www.pewinternet.org/2014/07/03/net-threats>. This study provides some insight into what the future of the Internet might be like.

Greenwald, Glenn. **No Place to Hide: Edward Snowden, the NSA, and the U.S. Surveillance State**. New York: Metropolitan Books, 2014. 272 pp. This publication documents the author's travel to Hong Kong to meet NSA contractor Edward Snowden, who entrusts the author with never-revealed information regarding the NSA and its abuses of power.

Harding, Luke. **The Snowden Files: The Inside Story of the World's Most Wanted Man**. New York: Vintage, 2014. 352 pp. This book chronicles Snowden's journey as he sought asylum from the U.S. government for leaking confidential NSA information, and the circumstances that led to his exile in Moscow.

Kiehl, Danielle, Kevin Bankston, Robyn Greene, and Robert Morgus. **Surveillance Costs: The NSA's Impact on the Economy, Internet Freedom & Cybersecurity.** Washington, DC: The New

America's Open Technology Institute, 2014. 64 pp. Available free online: <http://oti.newamerica.net/publications/policy/surveillance_costs_the_nsas_impact_on_the_economy_internet_freedom_cybersecurity>. This report analyzes effects of the NSA surveillance programs and attempts to assess their costs.

Knake, Robert K. **Internet Governance in an Age of Cyber Insecurity.** New York: Council on Foreign Relations Press, 2010. 48 pp. Available free online: <http://www.cfr.org/internet-policy/internet-governance-age-cyber-insecurity/p22832> This report examines the factors that have contributed to both the Internet's booming success as well as many cybercrime problems, and how policymakers should respond.

Singer. P.W., and Friedman, Allan. **Cybersecurity and Cyberwar: What Everyone Needs to Know.** New York: Oxford University Press, USA, 2014. 320 pp. Primer on cyberspace and its security issues, including discussion of new Chinese and U.S. military cyber units.

Warren, Samuel and Louis D. Brandeis. "The Right to Privacy." **Harvard Law Review.** Vol. IV, no. 5. 1890. Available free online: < http://groups.csail.mit.edu/mac/classes/6.805/articles/privacy/Privacy_brand_warr2.html>. The foundational text for today's legal privacy framework within the U.S.

DON'T FORGET TO VOTE!
WWW.FPA.ORG/BALLOT

KEY TO ABBREVIATIONS AND ACRONYMS FOR EACH ARTICLE NOW AVAILABLE ONLINE!

TO LEARN MORE ABOUT THIS TOPIC AND TO ACCESS WEB LINKS TO RESOURCES GO TO www.greatdecisions.org

Sectarianism in the Middle East
by Lawrence G. Potter

Sunni protesters wave Islamist flags while others chant slogans at an anti-government rally on April 26, 2013, in Fallujah, Iraq, 40 miles west of Baghdad. Iraq's Sunni minority have felt maligned by the Shi'ite-led government in Baghdad, hounded by its security forces and increasingly threatened, once again, by the militias that terrorized them during the sectarian bloodletting in 2006 and 2007. The community's anger has fueled the rampage of Islamic extremists across a third of the country, including Fallujah. (IMAGE BY © BILAL FAWZI/AP/CORBIS)

As 2014 drew to a close, much of the Middle East was in turmoil. The promise of the Arab Spring, the antigovernment revolts that broke out in many countries in early 2011, represented the challenge of a new generation demanding political reform and democracy, but remained unfulfilled. Governments and rulers were overthrown in Libya, Egypt, Yemen and Tunisia, and a serious antigovernment rebellion persists in Bahrain.

A new order has yet to arise and instability continues. Following the withdrawal of U.S. troops in 2011, political tensions rose in Iraq due to ineffective government and a Sunni insurgency led by the Islamic State (also referred to as the Islamic State in Iraq and Syria, or ISIS), which seeks to create a new caliphate. ISIS now has metastasized from Syria and taken over parts of Iraq.

To the south, the threat of political Islam represented by Hamas terrified Sunni-led states such as Egypt, Saudi Arabia and Jordan, which led to their tacit support for the Israeli assault on Gaza in summer 2014. Above all, these states considered a resurgent Shi'ism to be a major threat to regional stability, and tensions remained high between Iran and Saudi Arabia, which some regarded as carrying out proxy wars in Yemen, Syria and Iraq. It seemed clear that the post-Ottoman configuration of states put in place at the end of World War I was yielding to a new order.

LAWRENCE G. POTTER *is deputy director of Gulf/2000, a major research and documentation project on the Persian Gulf states based at Columbia University, where he also teaches. He is a longtime contributor to* Great Decisions *and published "The Persian Gulf: Tradition and Transformation" in FPA's* Headline Series *Nos. 333–334 (Fall 2011).*

The Obama administration completed a withdrawal of U.S. forces from Iraq in 2011 and, with the exception of a small residual force, was scheduled to do so in Afghanistan by the end of 2014, fulfilling campaign promises and supposedly freeing the government to focus on other issues like the "pivot" to Asia. Early in his second term, President Barack Obama outlined a pragmatic and minimalist role in the region, prioritizing the negotiation of a nuclear agreement with Iran, achieving peace between Israel and the Palestinians and assuring exports of petroleum from the Persian Gulf. However, the urgent threat to the safety of non-Muslim minorities in Iraq in August 2014 led the U.S. to resume military operations there. In conjunction with allied Arab states, the U.S. initiated air strikes on ISIS positions in Syria beginning in late September. Meanwhile, in Afghanistan, there were fears that the Afghan army would not be able to hold back the Taliban advance once the U.S. left. The continuing turmoil demanded sustained attention, and has led to a military re-engagement in the Middle East that is expected to last for years.

Why is the Middle East falling apart? The version presented by the media and pundits—as well as reflected in public discourse in the region—is that the root cause is sectarianism, above all a struggle between the Sunni and Shi'i versions of Islam. Conflicts are described as age-old and unsolvable. The ultimatum given by ISIS to the Christian and Yazidi minorities in Iraq that they convert to Islam or be slaughtered lent support for this explanation.

Religious tension provides a convenient and simple explanation for present-day conflicts, but it only paints part of the picture. A review of the history of the region shows that while there were often religious disputes, they usually did not rise to the level of warfare. Large, long-lasting empires such as that of the Ottomans (late 13th century to 1923) in Turkey and the Qajars (1794–1925) in Iran were composed of a mosaic of ethnic, religious and political groups, which was actually a factor for success. The conclusion is that the "problem of sectarianism" is something that has arisen in modern times, and is susceptible to mitigation if governments change their policies.

Indeed, many recent regional conflicts have little to do with sectarian tensions. From the Arab Spring to the conflict in Gaza, the key issue is that Middle Eastern governments refuse to reform or permit citizen participation. According to Hisham Melhem, the Washington bureau chief of Al Arabiya, an Arabic satellite channel, "The Arab world today is more violent, unstable, fragmented and driven by extremism—the extremism of the rulers and those in opposition—than at any time since the collapse of the Ottoman Empire a century ago." He continues, "the jihadists of the Islamic State, in other words, did not emerge from nowhere. They climbed out of a rotting, empty hulk—what was left of a broken-down civilization."

The issue for U.S. foreign policy is whether Washington can do anything to achieve a more peaceful region. In recent years, it has become increasingly clear that while the U.S. may be the most powerful world actor, it cannot compel other states to do its bidding or adopt its policies. Should the U.S. continue to support governments that have instigated or exploited sectarian tensions, such as in Iraq, Egypt and Bahrain, when their intransigence and repression frustrate U.S. policy aims? Should it coordinate with Iran to battle ISIS, a common foe? Obama himself declared at the UN in September 2013 that it was time to move beyond "a perpetual war footing" that set in after 9/11. The problems afflicting the Middle East, including autocratic and ineffective regimes, corrupt governments and a lack of democracy, freedom of the press and human rights, are well known. Governments, to protect themselves, have often resorted to stoking sectarian tensions in an attempt to divide and rule. But when problems are at base political, the tendency to blame them on sectarianism is misplaced. ■

The historical legacy of sectarianism

The interplay between politics and sectarian identity in the Middle East is an old one. Defining sectarianism is notoriously difficult. Sectarianism can be defined broadly to include ethnic, tribal and religious groups, and can alternatively be thought of as the politics of identity. It goes back to the idea of "sect," a group with distinctive religious, political or philosophical beliefs. Usually the term has a religious connotation; in Christendom it referred to a small group that has broken away from mainstream "orthodox" beliefs. Sectarianism has come to have a negative connotation, and the term "sectarian conflict" is often applied to religio-political struggles such as those between Protestants and Catholics in Northern Ireland, Sunni and Shi'i Muslims in Iraq, or Hindus and Muslims in India.

In the Middle East, Western writers frequently, and inaccurately, characterized Sunnis as "orthodox" Muslims and the Shi'is as "heterodox." Both Sunnis, who make up about 90% of the world's Muslims, and Shi'is, at about 10%, are large groups with innumerable subgroups. Fanar Haddad, a scholar who has studied the sectarian divide in Iraq, has concluded that the term "sectarianism" does not have a definitive meaning and regards such groups as "competing subnational mass-group identities. As such, the dynamics are in essence very similar to other such competing groups be they racial, national, ethnic or even ideological." Sectarian identities, he found, are constantly changing and being renegotiated.

Many experts who have studied sectarianism have objected to the way the concept is used in the media and foreign policy circles. "[S]ectarianism in Syria and Iraq has...often been characterized as the product of tensions raging since time immemorial and framed as the latest manifestation of an irreconcilable Sunni-Shi'i conflict, explained away by the 'ancient ethnic hatred' trope," wrote Ibrahim Marashi, an assistant professor of history at California State University. "Such interpretations make the mistake of treating sectarian communities as homogeneous entities, ignoring the often intense and sometimes violent cleavages within these communities."

The issue of sectarianism is intertwined with that of ethnicity, minorities, identity, religion and nationalism, which complicates any analysis. One question is whether sectarianism is a modern phenomenon or one that has persisted throughout history. A lack of historical research on the subject in the Middle East makes this question difficult to answer; however, a good case can be made that many of the present-day conflicts depicted by the press as existing since time immemorial, such as that between Israelis and Palestinians or Arabs and Iranians, are products of modern times.

Scholars working in recent times tend to regard sectarianism as a modern phenomenon that should not be projected back into the past. Ussama Makdisi, who reconstructed the history of sectarian identity in 19th-century Ottoman Mount Lebanon, found that "sectarianism as an idea and as a practice belongs to the realm of the modern." In Haddad's view, "an approach that insists on a sectarian or a non-sectarian Iraq misses the point: identity, sectarian or otherwise, is ambiguous both in its meaning and its salience, hence the abundance in Iraqi history of episodes of both sectarian harmony and, less commonly, sectarian division."

Throughout the history of the Middle East, while society was self-consciously Islamic, the region actually contained a mosaic of many groups, religions, languages and ethnicities. Today, most countries have heterogeneous societies, made up of multiple sectarian groups, whose borders have been carved out of multinational empires. Before the rise of the modern Middle Eastern nation-states, these groups, while sometimes clashing, managed to live together and coexist in the same space without resorting to the level of violence seen in the last few decades. In many Middle Eastern cities, minorities lived in their own quarter (*mahallah*) and largely dealt with the wider world through their own leaders. In the Ottoman Empire, each religious group had

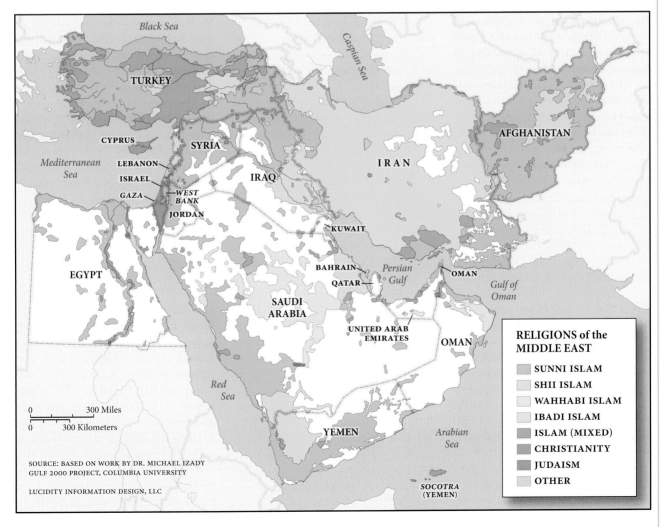

RELIGIONS of the
MIDDLE EAST

- SUNNI ISLAM
- SHII ISLAM
- WAHHABI ISLAM
- IBADI ISLAM
- ISLAM (MIXED)
- CHRISTIANITY
- JUDAISM
- OTHER

SOURCE: BASED ON WORK BY DR. MICHAEL IZADY
GULF 2000 PROJECT, COLUMBIA UNIVERSITY

LUCIDITY INFORMATION DESIGN, LLC

its own *millet* — largely self-governing religio-political communities. This may have lessened the likelihood of conflict. However, the supposedly unifying effect of Islam sometimes broke down and sectarian strife erupted.

The century of minorities

With the fall of empires in the aftermath of World War I, the nation-state became the most common political unit. The concept of minority groups emerged after the war and is linked with the idea of representative government. Because many people found themselves minorities in newly created states, laws were introduced to protect "minority rights." In a study of French Mandate Syria (1923–43), Benjamin Thomas White concludes that "in many ways, the history of the nation-state is the history of minorities: that is, the history of the processes that lead certain groups to be defined as 'minorities'." According to Anh Nga Longva, Professor of Social Anthropology at the University of Bergen, "the twentieth century has been described as the century of minorities, or more precisely, the century when concern with the need to provide a legal framework to protect minorities gained unprecedented attention."

While many ethnic groups adopted a quietist stance in the past to protect themselves, today there are powerful political and economic motivations to make their voices heard. According to Anthony D. Smith, a leading expert on nationalism at the London School of Economics, "in the modern era, *ethnie* [ethnic communities] must become politicized, must enter and remain in the political arena, and must begin to move towards nationhood, even if they have no intentions of becoming full nations themselves. That is to say, they are forced to forsake their former isolation, passivity and cultural accommodation, and become activist, mobilized and politically dynamic." In Iran, as suggested by anthropologist Lois Beck, national minorities have politicized their identities to protect their interests.

This leads to a number of questions. What is it about modern times that so often activates exclusivist sectarian identities, so that ostensibly religious or ethnic differences — as in the Balkans, Bahrain, Syria, Iraq or Afghanistan — threaten to tear countries apart? To what extent is the rise of the modern state responsible for the strengthening of sectarian identities? Is this rising "ethnicization" intrinsically linked with modernization? What are the triggering mechanisms that set off conflict? How much have major movements, such as the Islamic revival or the Arab Spring, served to obscure the continued salience of religious and ethnic cleavages? Do outside powers play a role, and how does their response color the outcome?

Historical background

World War I destroyed balance-of-power politics based on a consensus of interests as practiced in the 19th century. In Europe this was accompanied by the growth of secularism, the eclipse of religion and the rise of radical ideologies, such as Bolshevism and fascism. In the Middle East, the core of the Ottoman Empire was carved up into six new states: Turkey, Syria, Lebanon, Palestine, Iraq and Transjordan, with the later addition of Saudi Arabia and Yemen. Here, as in Asia, colonial rulers were committed to secularization and expanded the powers of formal institutions to include what had formerly been in the domain of religion, notably law and education. They did not, however, succeed in eradicating the influence of religion, particularly in two key aspects: its role in legitimizing political power and in politicizing and mobilizing the masses.

A major objective of postcolonial states was to cultivate a sense of nationalism, which was to subsume differences of religion, tribalism and ethnicity. Thus, the political priority for Iraqi governments from 1920 to 1990 was to create an Iraqi national identity that would supersede such sub-identities. The Iraqi nationalism that arose was tested and reaffirmed by the war with Iran in the 1980s, in which Iraqis fought for their country and were not swayed by the religious appeals of Ayatollah Ruhollah Khomeini, the founder of Iran's Islamic Republic.

The efforts of states to "invent traditions" to lend themselves legitimacy and create a unified national narrative and history was first pointed out by historian Eric Hobsbawm. Projects designed to invent national identities and traditions are a significant factor in the conservative Arab monarchies — Bahrain, Kuwait, Oman, Qatar, Saudi Arabia, and the United Arab Emirates–that make up the Gulf Cooperation Council (GCC), a regional organization founded in 1981. Iran and Egypt, on the other hand, retain well-established historic identities, on a par with a few other countries like China, Russia, India and Japan.

After World War II, the West faced growing anticolonial revolts. Religious leaders and groups played a key role in bringing the masses into the political process in the colonies. These leaders spearheaded opposition to colonial (often Western Christian) rule and led many of the nationalist movements. The British faced opposition from the Muslim Brotherhood in Egypt; the French battled the Islamic resistance in Algeria; and the Soviets put down a revolt by the Basmachis in Central Asia.

The political boundaries many new nations inherited from colonial administrators often bore little resemblance to geographic or demographic realities. These nascent nation-states epitomized political scientist Benedict Anderson's definition of "an imagined political community." In Africa, for example, the borders of many states are the same as those drawn at a conference of European diplomats in Berlin in 1884–85. These borders cut across tribal and ethnic groups, which continued to clash with each other after independence. The British carved up the Middle East and South Asia in such a way as to divide many peoples who might have opted to form national states, such as the Palestinians, the Kurds and the Pashtuns.

As the process of decolonization gained momentum, the newly independent states faced the problem of a loss, or at least disruption, of the political order, and in some cases, the stability provided by the old empires. The patronage of specific minority groups by colonial governments led to serious fissures in

ARCTIC OCEAN

Beaufort Sea

Queen Elizabeth
Islands

Ellesmere
Island

GREENLAND
(DENMARK)

*Baffin
Bay*

ARCTIC CIRCLE (66°33')

ALASKA
(U.S.)

Victoria
Island

Baffin
Island

*Davis
Strait*

*Denmark
Strait*

Reykjavík

Anchorage

*Great
Bear Lake*

Churchill

*Hudson
Bay*

*Labrador
Sea*

*Gulf of
Alaska* Juneau

*Great
Slave Lake*

CANADA

Vancouver

NORTH
AMERICA

*Lake
Winnipeg*

*Great
Lakes*

Montréal Québec

Seattle

Ottawa

Toronto

New York

NORTH
ATLANTIC OCEAN

NORTH
PACIFIC OCEAN

UNITED STATES

Chicago

San Francisco

Denver

St. Louis

Washington,
D.C.

Atlanta

BERMUDA
(U.K.)

AZORES
(PORTUGAL)

Los Angeles

Dallas

CANARY ISLANDS
(SPAIN)

Miami

Nassau

WESTERN SAHARA
(ADMINISTERED
BY MOROCCO)

TROPIC OF CANCER (23°27')

Monterrey

Gulf of Mexico

MEXICO

Havana

THE BAHAMAS

HONOLULU

HAWAII
(U.S.)

Mexico
City Veracruz

CUBA

HAITI

VIRGIN ISLS.
(U.S.)
BRITISH VIRGIN ISLS. (U.K.)
ANGUILLA (U.K.)
ST. KITTS AND NEVIS
ANTIGUA AND BARBUDA
GUADELOUPE (FR.)
DOMINICA
MARTINIQUE (FR.)
ST. LUCIA
BARBADOS

Nouakchott

CAPE VERDE
Praia

Dakar
SEN

ATOLL

GUATEMALA
BELMOPAN
BELIZE

JAMAICA
Kingston

Port-au-
Prince

DOMINICAN
REPUBLIC

Santo
Domingo

PUERTO RICO
(U.S.)

THE GAMBIA
Banjul
Bissau

Guatemala City
HONDURAS
San Salvador Tegucigalpa
EL SALVADOR

*Caribbean
Sea*

MONTSERRAT (U.K.)

ST. VINCENT AND
THE GRENADINES

GUINEA-BISSAU

Conakry
Freetown

REEF

PALMYRA ATOLL
(U.S.)

Managua
NICARAGUA

ARUBA (NETH.)

NETHERLANDS
ANTILLES (NETH.)

GRENADA
Port-of-Spain
TRINIDAD AND TOBAGO

SIERRA LEONE
Mon

KIRITIMATI
(CHRISTMAS ISLAND)

COSTA RICA
San
José

Panama
PANAMA

Caracas

VENEZUELA

Georgetown

Paramaribo

IS ISLAND

EQUATOR

Medellín

Bogotá

GUYANA
SURINAME

Cayenne
FRENCH GUIANA
(FR.)

Cali

COLOMBIA

GALAPAGOS ISLANDS
(ECUADOR)

Quito

ECUADOR

Manaus

Belém

MARQUESAS ISLAND
(FR. POLYNESIA)

Iquitos

BRAZIL

Recife

FRENCH POLYNESIA (FRANCE)

PERU

SOUTH
AMERICA

TUAMOTU
ARCHIPELAGO
(FR. POLYNESIA)

Lima

Cusco

SOCIETY ISLANDS
(FR. POLYNESIA)

La Paz

BOLIVIA

Brasília

Rio de
Janeiro

Sucre

TROPIC OF CAPRICORN (23°27')

TUBUAI ISLANDS
(FR. POLYNESIA)

PITCAIRN ISLANDS
(U.K.)

EASTER
ISLAND
(CHILE)

ISLA SALA
Y GÓMEZ
(CHILE)

Antofagasta

PARAGUAY

Asunción

São
Paulo

SOUTH
ATLANTIC OCEAN

CHILE

JUAN FERNÁNDEZ
ISLANDS
(CHILE)

Santiago

Buenos Aires
La Plata

URUGUAY
Montevideo

ARGENTINA

Bahía
Blanca

*SOUTH
PACIFIC OCEAN*

FALKLAND ISLANDS
(ADMINISTERED BY U.K.
CLAIMED BY ARGENTINA)

SOUTH GEORGIA AND THE
SOUTH SANDWICH ISLANDS
(ADMINISTERED BY U.K.,
CLAIMED BY ARGENTINA)

Punta Arenas

Stanley

Scotia Sea

*Drake
Passage*

SOUTH ORKNEY ISLANDS
(B.A.T.)

SOUTHERN
OCEAN

Bellingshausen Sea

Weddell Sea

Amundsen Sea

Ross Sea

*Ross
Ice Shelf*

*Ronne
Ice Shelf*

FOREIGN
POLICY
ASSOCIATION
1918

For ninety-seven years, the Foreign Policy Association has served as a catalyst for developing awareness, understanding and informed opinions on U.S. foreign policy and global issues. From mass media to grassroots organizations, the FPA promotes active civic participation in the U.S. foreign policy process, by engaging with the global public, heads of state and pre-eminent experts on foreign affairs. Founded in 1954, the FPA's flagship program Great Decisions is the largest nonpartisan public education program in the world, and provides the American public with the tools to become informed members of the global community.

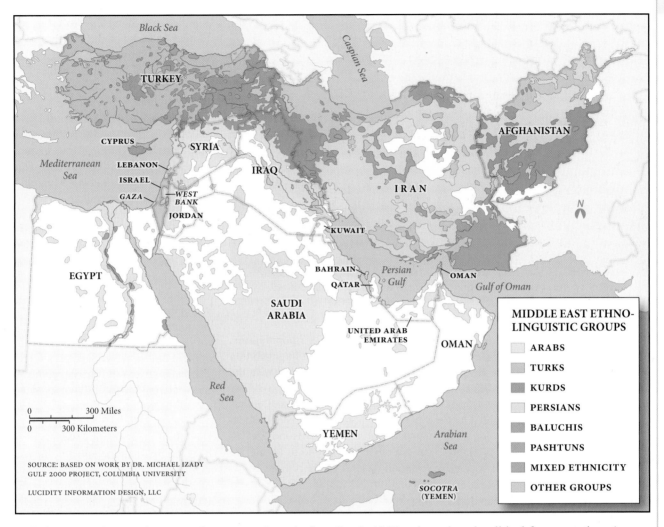

MIDDLE EAST ETHNO-LINGUISTIC GROUPS

- ARABS
- TURKS
- KURDS
- PERSIANS
- BALUCHIS
- PASHTUNS
- MIXED ETHNICITY
- OTHER GROUPS

SOURCE: BASED ON WORK BY DR. MICHAEL IZADY
GULF 2000 PROJECT, COLUMBIA UNIVERSITY

LUCIDITY INFORMATION DESIGN, LLC

societies. In Lebanon, for example, Max Weiss found that "the Lebanese Shi'i community became sectarian under French rule," which may be partly attributed to "French colonial privileging of sectarian and subnational modes of identification." Minority elites often adopted a viewpoint of their patrons on political, social and religious issues that was not shared by the majority population. After independence, minority groups formerly favored by colonial rulers—such as the Maronites in Lebanon, Sunni Arabs in Iraq and the Tamils in Sri Lanka—found their privileged status challenged by previously neglected majorities. Religion became a divisive force that diverted the new nations' energies from tackling social, political and economic issues.

With the old power systems destroyed by two world wars, there was a proliferation of new states. (The United Nations [UN], which consisted of 51 countries at its founding in 1945, today consists of 193 member states.) Many of these states lacked a coherent national identity, and people found themselves in a political centrifuge, according to political scientist Harold Isaacs. In the postwar global shakeout of power, there have been no new "larger coherences" to hold people together as in the past, he notes: "These systems [the Ottoman, Habsburg, and Romanov empires] created a certain order in which the differences and divisions were not so much submerged as held in their orbits by the gravity of the center. The force of this gravity was physical, economic, cultural and—most heavily—psychological."

While modernization has contributed to global homogeneity, paradoxically the spread of modern communications and media like Al Jazeera, the Arabic satellite channel based in Qatar, and the rapid shrinking of the globe (globalization) have caused or exacerbated political fragmentation. Access to a wider world has reinforced a sense of separateness and a need for security. By interacting with an increasingly diverse global society, the individual has become more aware of his group identity and those factors—such as religion, ethnic group, nationality, language, tribe, and history—that set him apart from others. Because impersonal governments have been unable to fulfill this need for security, there is a longing for the reassurance of community structure, traditionally supplied by religion.

Recent developments

The alienation that had begun to emerge in the 1960s sparked a religious revival in many countries in the 1970s, notably the Islamic revival in the Middle East. This led to the rise of charismatic religious and political figures such as Khomeini in Iran. Since the Iranian Revolution of 1978–79, violence has

Displaced Iraqis from the Yazidi community settle under a bridge in Dahuk, 260 miles north-west of Baghdad, Iraq, Aug. 14, 2014. ISIS militants have overrun much of the country's north and west and driven out hundreds of thousands from their homes. (IMAGE BY © KHALID MOHAMMED/AP/CORBIS)

increasingly been carried out in the name of religion in the Middle East and South Asia. The Islamic revival alarmed the U.S. and other Western countries, which previously associated Islam with stagnation and regarded it as a fatalistic faith that impeded economic and political progress. For the West, the new "political Islam" instead was associated with revolutionary activity and violence. Shi'ism became a feared ideology among Sunnis, and tensions rose

Ayatollah Khomeini waves to a crowd of enthusiastic supporters on his return to Tehran, Iran, in 1979. (IMAGE BY © MICHEL SETBOUN/CORBIS)

in Arab states with Shi'i populations.

Iran's efforts to export its revolution to the Persian Gulf coincided with the brutal Iran-Iraq war, which lasted for almost a decade (1980–88) and, in addition to the horrendous casualties and damage that resulted, poisoned political discourse and served to accelerate sectarian discord in the region. Iran's calculation that the Shi'is in southern Iraq would rally to its cause and Iraq's conviction that the Arab citizens of Khuzistan, Iran's southwest province, would welcome the Iraqi army as their liberators were both wrong. The war helped the revolutionary government in Tehran consolidate power and distracted attention from pressing social and economic problems. It was only when the leadership feared the revolution was in danger that Khomeini decided to "drink poison" by accepting the UN cease-fire proposal that had been on the table for a year.

In both Iran and Iraq, but especially the latter, the demonization of the opponent led to a stronger sense of national identity. Both waged a fierce struggle on the ideological and propaganda fronts. They invoked several broad themes: Arab against Persian, Sunni against Shi'i, and pan-Arabism against pan-Islam. Such discourse served to reinforce mutual hostility even after a cease-fire had been accepted. The hardening of negative mutual percep-

tions between Sunni and Shi'i was thus a direct outcome of the Iran-Iraq war. Frequent bickering since then over the proper name of the Gulf, whether Persian or Arabian, has continued to sour the atmosphere.

In the wake of the Gulf War of 1990–91, which evicted Iraqi forces from Kuwait, violent uprisings of Iraq's Kurds and Shi'i Arabs broke out and were brutally put down. Saddam Hussein's government, in an attempt to divide opponents, then instituted a process of "retribalization" in which subnational identities were emphasized and Sunni Arabs were firmly on top. This policy went against everything Ba'athism stood for and has contributed to the unraveling of Iraq in the post-Saddam era. A key turning point was the Shi'i revolts in southern Iraq in the spring of 1991 after the war had ended, when Saddam's forces reportedly arrived in Karbala with banners declaring "no Shi'as after today."

A Shi'i revival?

The fall of the Saddam government in 2003 led to a major change in the status of Shi'is throughout the region and enhanced the power of Iran. For the first time, Iraq had a Shi'i-led government, and Sunnis in Iraq, as well as the Persian Gulf monarchies, were on the defensive. In December 2004, King Abdullah of Jordan warned that if the new Iraqi government fell under Iranian influence, a "crescent" of Shi'i movements would emerge, threatening Sunni governments as well as posing a problem for U.S. interests. Former Egyptian President Hosni Mubarak (1981–2011), reflecting usually unstated anxieties, said in April 2006 that "Shiites are mostly always loyal to Iran and not the countries where they live." In many states the Shi'is were now perceived as a security problem, not just a religious group. Vali Nasr wrote in 2006, "by liberating and empowering Iraq's Shiite majority, the Bush administration helped launch a broad Shiite revival that will upset the sectarian balance in Iraq and the Middle East for years to come." This warning proved prescient.

Other experts disagree, noting that the Shi'is do not constitute a united bloc, and leading *ulama* (religious scholars) with rival interpretations of the faith compete for followers. The leading ayatollah in Iraq, Ali Sistani, has made clear that he does not want to introduce a form of religious government like that in Iran. The Shi'is living in Lebanon and the Arab states of the Persian Gulf are divided over their allegiance to Iran. In contrast to the oppositional role of the Shi'is in Bahrain and Saudi Arabia, in Kuwait, Qatar, Oman and the United Arab Emirates (UAE) they are largely loyal to Sunni ruling families. Laurence Louër of the Center for International Studies and Research at Sciences Po (Paris) found that in contrast to Sunni groups like Al Qaeda, Shi'i groups are focused on local and not transnational issues—a characteristic that appears to apply to ISIS as well. There is bitter rivalry between Shi'i groups in Iraq that sometimes erupts into armed conflict, such as in the Battle of Basra (2008), when the government of Nouri al-Maliki, himself a Shi'i associated with the Islamic Dawa Party, routed the Mahdi Army of influential Shiite leader Muqtada al-Sadr, which was then in control of the city.

It is risky to generalize about groups such as Sunnis or Shi'is. Such branches of Islam are too large to be meaningful indicators of behavior, which is why alarm over a rising "Shi'i crescent" is misplaced and may be confused with fear of Iranian irredentism.

Role of outsiders

Outsiders play a large role in activating and sustaining sectarian identity and are a major factor in the current conflict in Iraq and Syria. The U.S. itself played a significant role in promoting sectarian divisions after the wars to "liberate" Iraq and Afghanistan. According to Adnan Pachachi, a veteran Iraqi diplomat and politician, "perhaps the most serious mistake the United States made was to organize the new political system in Iraq on a sectarian basis." The Iraqi Governing Council appointed in July 2003 by the Coalition Provisional Authority, and the cabinet it appointed in turn, each contained thirteen Shi'i Arab members, five Sunni Arabs, five Kurds, one Turkoman, and one Christian (Assyrian, Chaldean or Armenian). Subsequent Iraqi cabinets had a similar breakdown, and excluded former Ba'athists who were Sunni. This practice, along with the identification of political parties with ethnic or religious groups, has led some to wonder whether Iraq was a viable state or could break up. Such practices mimic the sectarian structure of governance in Lebanon established in the unwritten National Pact of 1943, modified by the Taif Agreement of 1989. Under this pact, the president must be a Maronite Christian, the prime minister a Sunni Muslim and the speaker of parliament a Shi'i Muslim. ∎

The scourge of sectarianism today

S ince the Arab Spring, many governments have felt vulnerable to popular protests or interventions, either by neighboring states or transnational Islamist groups such as Al Qaeda or ISIS.

Strident sectarian rhetoric has risen to unprecedented levels, particularly since the rise of ISIS in mid-2014. The rapid spread of ISIS has raised the specter of religious intolerance and even genocide toward non-Sunnis and non-Muslims. In Iraq, the favoritism toward Shi'is by the Maliki government (which is likely to continue under his successor, Haider al-Abadi, who assumed office in September 2014) has contributed to widespread Sunni anger against it, hindering an effective response. Christians, too, have fled the country, with many taking refuge in Jordan. The situation in Syria and Iraq is so dire that even religious leaders who previously held back from intervening in politics have taken a stand. In June 2013, an influential Sunni cleric, Shaikh Yusuf al-Qaradawi—an Egyptian based in Qatar

Egyptian Coptic Christians react after taking part in a mass on Mar. 10, 2011, honoring those killed in clashes two days earlier. The Coptic Christians had gathered to protest the burning of a church in the Cairo suburbs on March 4. Violent clashes had erupted between Muslims and Coptic Christians on March 8 in Cairo leaving some 13 people dead. (IMAGE BY © AMEL PAIN/EPA/CORBIS)

with a wide media following—urged Sunni Muslims to travel to Syria and join the battle against President Bashar al-Assad. In June 2014, fearing sectarian warfare and possibly the breakup of the state, Iraq's top Shiite cleric, Ayatollah Ali Sistani, urged his followers to take up arms against ISIS.

In Egypt, under the rule of Mubarak, sectarian tension was held in check and the police generally maintained order. Mubarak was ousted in 2011 and replaced by the democratically elected president, Mohamed Morsi, in July 2013, who, in turn, was replaced by Abdel Fattah el-Sisi following a military coup in June 2014. Egypt's instability has caused the sectarian situation to deteriorate sharply. There are many religious minorities who have been targeted, including Coptic Christians, who make up an estimated 10% of the population, and Shi'ite Muslims. Copts supported the military takeover because they feared repression under the Muslim Brotherhood and believed Sisi's declarations of support for a moderate form of Islam. These promises have yet to materialize, with the government doing little to protect Copts and their churches from violence on the part of radical Islamists.

Such attacks belie the euphoria of the Tahrir Square uprisings in early 2011, which highlighted the spirit of unity of the Egyptian people and raised expectations that the government would stop employing sectarian politics to divide and rule. "The increasing Islamization of politics in post-Mubarak Egypt has badly damaged the democratic credentials of the revolution by deepening the inequities between Muslims and Christians–and creating new ones," according to Mariz Tadros, a fellow at the University of Sussex. Conflict is not only interconfessional—it has even broken out between strict Islamic groups influenced by Salafis and Wahhabis and more moderate expressions of Islam such as Sufism.

Triggers of sectarian conflict

Years of warfare have politicized identity groups, especially those based on religion and ethnicity. Leaders' manipulation of sectarian communities to sow discord and empower the government is an old strategy. According to Professor Marashi, "the ruling elites in Ba'athist Iraq and Syria consolidated their power by showering the largesse of the state on a narrow segment of society, whether it was military officers, a privileged tribe, or family...." These rulers practiced a form of patronage politics that rewarded loyalty. In Iraq the elite was Sunni; in Syria it was the Alawite religious sect, which is regarded as a form of Shi'ism. In Iraq, Haddad found that overt identification of the state with Shi'ite symbolism has sowed unease among Sunni residents and contributed to mutual hostility. He notes that one group's assertion of identity may be regarded as a provocation by the other. Thus, the prevalence in Baghdad of portraits of Shi'i imams, and flags and banners with Shi'i symbols and slogans, reflects an assertive Shi'ism that is "paradoxically a sign of both empowerment and insecurity."

In the Arab monarchies of the Persian Gulf, ruling Sunni tribal dynasties have monopolized political and economic power and excluded many residents from participation in the political process or from attaining citizenship. The lack of political institutions or an economic basis for class-based politics (due to the rentier economy) in these states makes ethnic and sectarian categories the most viable bases for political coordination, according to scholar Justin Gengler. This means that political coalitions in the Persian Gulf area will tend to form naturally along these group-based lines. Indeed, Gengler notes, "If sectarianism is to be defined as the politicization of ethnic or religious identity, then this politicization is best understood not as a *cause* of this or that political malady afflicting Persian Gulf states, but rather as an *effect* of their particular institutional characteristics."

The factors that trigger sectarian conflict, notably wars and their aftermath, are important to understand. There appears to be a pattern of challenge and response in which increased activity on the part of one group stimulates activity by another, often counter, group. The rise of the Shi'is in Iraq beginning in 2003 and the recent troubles in Bahrain have spurred Sunnis' interest in their own identity and have prompted a search for cultural symbols with which they can identify. In Lebanon, this has led to a "Sunni awakening" since 2012. Likewise, relentless government-promoted Shi'ism in Iran and Wahhabism

A Bahraini protester with her face covered and wearing a badge that reads "No Sunni No Shi'ite, I am Bahraini" takes part in a demonstration held in the Bahraini capital of Manama, March 1, 2011. (IMAGE BY © HAMAD I MOHAMMED/REUTERS/CORBIS)

in Saudi Arabia have led to greater popularity for Sufism, a mystical form of Islam, in both states.

The assessment of many experts is that the root of regional problems lies not in sectarianism, but in dysfunctional states where ruling cliques monopolize power and deny freedoms to their people. "It is the weakening of Arab states, more than sectarianism or the rise of Islamist ideologies, that has created the battlefields of the new Middle East cold war," according to Prof. Gregory Gause of Texas A & M University. "Indeed, it is the arc of state weakness and state failure running from Lebanon through Syria to Iraq that explains the current salience of sectarianism."

One of the most astute observers, Rami G. Khouri, editor-at-large of Beirut's *The Daily Star,* notes that "the capture of cities and territory across northwestern Iraq by ISIS symbolizes a common aspect of the fragmented nature of many Arab countries—the ruling party or family that runs the government is at war with well-armed nonstate actors that reflect widespread citizen discontent with the power and policies of the central state." If the current collapse of security in Iraq and Syria arises primarily from political and not religious reasons, it can be addressed with better leadership and more effective governance. ■

The U.S. response

Sectarian conflict may be the bane of today's Middle East, but it is not something that U.S. foreign policy can directly address. Because sectarianism is intertwined with the political process, Washington can influence it indirectly by putting pressure on governments. However, past attempts to reconfigure the political order by insisting on minority representation in government, such as in Iraq and Afghanistan, have not worked well. In the end, out of concern for regional security, the U.S. has opted to support longtime allies such as Iraq, Saudi Arabia and Bahrain, rather than cut ties over human-rights violations, lack of freedoms and nonrepresentative government. Getting drawn into a sectarian war is not on the U.S. agenda.

According to Gause, "The United States can do little to address the weakness of governing institutions in many Arab states....It therefore needs to take a modest approach and recall that this is not America's war....[T]he guiding principle of the American response should be to prefer order over chaos...." This means supporting the government in Iraq, engaging with Egypt, negotiating with Iran, and supporting allies like Saudi Arabia, Jordan and the GCC states.

The U.S. seems to have a permanent credibility problem in Muslim countries, as regional governments agonize over U.S. intentions and are drawn to conspiracy theories to explain events. Depending on which side it takes in local wars, the U.S. will be seen as siding with either the Sunnis or the Shi'is.

A U.S. military convoy leaves after handing over al-Asad Airbase to Iraqi troops in Anbar province, western Iraq, December 7, 2011. The U.S. military handed over control of the base, which is the largest U.S. military airbase near the Iraqi-Syrian border, to the Iraqi government as part of its withdrawal from the country at the end of the year. (IMAGE BY © MOHAMMED JALIL/EPA/CORBIS)

Ironically, in light of long-standing U.S.-Iran enmity, removing from power Saddam Hussein in Iraq and the Taliban in Afghanistan has left Iran as the regional heavyweight by default. Many Arab states are now suspicious that the U.S. seeks to cut a deal with Iran at their expense and are not in favor of normalizing Iran-U.S. relations.

The Obama administration

When Obama took office in January 2009, he inherited long-running wars in Iraq and Afghanistan, a dysfunctional state in Pakistan, a failing Arab-Israeli peace process and an inability to bring Iran's nuclear program under control. All of this was a tall order for someone eager to concentrate on domestic issues and not known for his expertise on foreign affairs.

By withdrawing the last U.S. forces from Iraq in late 2011 and by scheduling the removal of remaining troops from Afghanistan at the end of 2014 (about 10,000 U.S. forces will remain temporarily), Obama will have fulfilled campaign promises to end the two wars. After the election of President Hassan Rouhani in 2013, the U.S. and Iran initiated an unprecedented series of negotiations aimed at getting Iran to limit its nuclear program in return for sanctions relief. (At press time it was unclear if the Nov. 24, 2014, deadline would be met.) The secretary of state in Obama's second term, John Kerry, worked tirelessly to achieve peace between Israelis and Palestinians—so far without real progress—and worked mightily to achieve a cease-fire in Gaza.

However, there were setbacks with all of these issues. Many believe that the bungled U.S. occupation and withdrawal from Iraq has led to the current situation.

"The invasion of Iraq and what followed lies at the root of all that has gone wrong since [then] in that neighborhood," according to Lakhdar Brahimi, a former UN diplomat, "and the record of the United States may appear as one of the colossal blunders of recent history. It left Iran in a much stronger position than it had been in decades, and opened the door to the violence now tearing Iraq apart." This has led to deep mistrust and lack of confidence in the U.S.

Calibrating the U.S. response to the events of the Arab Spring was an early foreign policy challenge for the administration. Repeatedly, the U.S. was forced to take sides between a popular uprising demanding democracy and the autocratic rulers it had long worked with, who ensured security and stability. In the case of Tunisia, the first successful revolt, few U.S. interests were at stake and it was not difficult to cut ties to the leader. Egypt, however, was a different story. President Mubarak had been a close U.S. ally for 30 years and had kept the peace with Israel. After equivocating at first, the U.S. eventually voiced support for the demonstrators and accepted that Mubarak had to go.

However, the president's response to the spreading upheaval was inconsistent. The U.S. stood for democracy, which guided policy in Tunisia and later Egypt. In the Persian Gulf, when confronted with the uprising in Bahrain, the U.S. held back on criticism of the ruling family due to the island's strategic importance. The U.S. urged the ruling Al Khalifa family to find a peaceful solution, but this advice was disregarded. In the case of Saudi Arabia, where there were some demonstrations in Shiite areas, the U.S. was notably silent and supportive of the ruling family. The Al Saud were greatly angered at the forced departure of Mubarak and feared that the U.S. would abandon them next. While not going so far as to accept GCC claims that Iran was behind the events in Bahrain, U.S. statements did warn Iran to stop meddling or taking advantage of the turmoil there or in other Arab states.

It was Obama's decision to enter the war in Libya that was perhaps of the greatest consequence. While he refused to send ground troops, in conjunction with the North Atlantic Treaty Organization (NATO) the U.S. established a no-fly zone and participated in a bombing campaign from March to August 2011 that led to the overthrow and death of Muammar Qadhafi. This intervention, however, was a prolonged affair that has left Libya divided with a weak government. Amid a chaotic security situation, the American ambassador, J. Christopher Stevens, was assassinated on Sept. 12, 2012, in an attack on the Benghazi consulate, and the U.S. embassy in Libya was closed in July 2014.

The Obama doctrine

President Obama's approach to Middle East policy has evolved over his time in office. During his first term (2009–13), he approved hundreds of drone strikes against Al Qaeda targets in Pakistan, Yemen and Somalia. At the same time the U.S. carried out a successful cyberwar against Iran in 2009–10, disabling its computers at an enrichment plant in Natanz and setting back their nuclear program.

Unlike Bush, Obama became increasingly averse to the use of direct force. By summer 2012, despite having drawn a "red line" with Syria over the use of chemical weapons, Obama did not approve U.S. military intervention when the regime did use them against the opposition. Although Secretary of State Kerry was able to negotiate a removal of the weapons, the failure to commit military assets bitterly disappointed regional allies such as Saudi Arabia, which supported the opposition in Syria, and seriously damaged the administration's credibility.

In an address to the UN on Sept. 24, 2013, Obama laid out U.S. policy toward the Middle East for what was supposed to be the remainder of his presidency. He outlined a pragmatic and minimalist policy, which reflected a president who had been chastened by previous U.S. interventions, especially in Libya. He noted that it was time for the U.S. to shift away from a "perpetual war footing" that the U.S. had embraced since 9/11. He acknowledged that democracy should not and cannot be imposed by force—particularly relevant in Iraq and Afghanistan. The core U.S. interests, Obama declared, would be confronting external aggression against our allies, ensuring the free flow of energy, dismantling terrorist networks, and not tolerating the development or use of weapons of mass destruction. In the future, he said, U.S. diplomacy would focus on just two issues: containing Iran's nuclear program, and trying to defuse the conflict between Israel and the Palestinians. He said the U.S. would make efforts to resolve sectarian tensions in places like Iraq, Bahrain and Syria, and that he believed they could be overcome, but announced no specific policies. He added that "we understand such long-standing issues cannot be solved by outsiders; they must be addressed by Muslim communities themselves."

PARESH NATH COURTESY OF CAGLE CARTOONS

In a speech at West Point on May 28, 2014, Obama declared that "we have been through a long season of war," and indicated that there would be a higher bar in the future for U.S. military action in international crises. Regarding Syria, he said, "I made a decision that we should not put American troops into the middle of this increasingly sectarian war, and I believe it is the right decision." In his speech he tried to strike a middle road, finding a balance between isolationism and unilateralism.

However, on June 10, 2014, a resurgent ISIS, supported by disgruntled Sunnis and former Ba'athists, was able to take over Mosul, Iraq's second-largest city. With Iraq falling apart, Obama quickly reversed his promise that the U.S. was not returning to Iraq. In early November he authorized the deployment of an additional 1,500 troops to train and advise Iraqi and Kurdish forces. The gains on the ground by ISIS, and the beheadings by ISIS of American and British citizens in Syria, shocked the world, leading a coalition of Arab countries to join the U.S. and some European states in a military campaign to "degrade and ultimately defeat" ISIS. Obama promised in his address to the UN on Sept. 24, 2014, that the U.S. would dismantle the ISIS "network of death," as he ordered airstrikes on targets in Syria. However, destroying ISIS will require far more than a military strategy.

Policy options

Although the U.S. has acknowledged the importance of sectarian conflict in the Middle East, it has not proposed specific policies to address it. One of its few options is to press regional states to refrain from playing the sectarian card, which only leads to discord. Dealing with leaders the U.S. helped select and long supported, and their resistance to advice (e.g., Maliki and Hamid Karzai), has been the subject of much bitterness. (Maliki resigned as prime minister of Iraq in August 2014, and Karzai finished his term as president of Afghanistan in September 2014.) At the time of writing, it is too soon to tell

U..S. President Barack Obama attends the graduation ceremony at the United States Military Academy at West Point, New York, on May 28, 2014. (IMAGE BY © WANG LEI/XINHUA PRESS/CORBIS)

if their successors will be more amenable to U.S. pressure on domestic issues.

Pakistani journalist Ahmed Rashid suggests that the U.S. seek change through nonmilitary means: "A larger failure of Western governments is that they continue to view the collapse of Muslim states as something to be countered by military action and counterterrorism operations, rather than by creating new regional alliances and engaging Muslim leaders themselves to deal with the problem." He decries the lack of leadership in the Muslim world: "Instead of a vast public movement to condemn ISIS and other such groups, there is silence, helplessness, and hopelessness.... Rather than present Islam as a tolerant religion capable of building a modern social contract, each state blames outsiders for conspiring against it." Minorities are the most common targets, and states like Iraq and Pakistan have used them as scapegoats and may not help them when they are attacked.

The upsurge of sectarian and ethnic conflict in the Middle East is likely to continue as long as the factors that foster it persist: heated rhetoric, conflict or potential conflict, questionable political legitimacy of rulers, and a longing for security and participation that is not being met. Such tensions are being exploited by governments that seek to divide in order to rule, and in the misguided attempts by outside powers to redress sectarian discrimination. Today, human rights organizations and diasporic communities, as well as extensive online communities and bloggers, continuously shine a spotlight on abuses.

Ethnic and sectarian conflict is not inevitable. Diversity does not have to lead to conflict, and the term "sectarianism" is invoked too readily as an explanation for countless ills. Government policies have served to inflame sectarian and ethnic identities and different policies could improve the situation. States need to be persuaded that it is better for them, and will increase their security to include rather than exclude minority groups in economic, social and political life. Governments could start by toning down sectarian rhetoric, whether it is official Shi'ism in Iraq or Sunni Islam in the Arabian Peninsula.

The roots of ethnic and sectarian conflict are not obscure, and a range of confidence-building measures can easily be taken to reduce tension and avoid, manage or resolve conflict. Military force is not the solution. The U.S. has acknowledged that it cannot solve every problem in the world, and this one depends on the leadership of Muslims and people of good will. ∎

discussion questions

1. How much priority should the U.S. accord the Middle East in its foreign policy, especially in light of its reduced dependence on Gulf oil? Would it be better to "pivot" to Asia?

2. President Obama came into office resolved to end the war in Iraq and withdraw all U.S. troops, which was accomplished. Did he make a mistake in returning forces to Iraq after the rise of ISIS in the summer of 2014? Why or why not?

3. This article argues that sectarian tensions are not the root of all problems in the Middle East, even if it seems that way. Do you agree, and how do you see the situation in other countries?

4. What is the right balance the U.S. should draw between security relations and respecting human rights or aspirations for democracy in the Middle East? How did these concerns play out during the Arab Spring?

5. What do you think would be the most effective U.S. policies for tamping down sectarian tensions in the Middle East?

---

suggested readings

Abdo, Geneive. "The New Sectarianism: The Arab Uprisings and the Rebirth of the Shi'a–Sunni Divide," **Analysis Paper** No. 29. Washington, DC: Brookings Institution, Saban Center for Middle East Policy, April 2013. 66 pp. Foreign correspondent discusses why sectarianism is on the rise in Arab states, with a focus on political upheaval in Bahrain and Lebanon and the war in Syria.

Haddad, Fanar. **Sectarianism in Iraq: Antagonistic Visions of Unity.** New York: Oxford University Press, 2011. 290 pp. An ambitious work that focuses on sectarian identity and sectarian relations in Iraq, especially as expressed in symbols and popular culture. Examines the Sunni reaction to the Shi'i assertion of identity since 2003.

Longva, Anh Nga and Anne Sofie Roald, eds. **Religious Minorities in the Middle East: Domination, Self-Empowerment, Accommodation.** Leiden: Brill, 2012. 350 pp. Historically oriented study of Muslim and non-Muslim minorities that examines the contemporary situation.

Louër, Laurence. **Transnational Shia Politics: Religious and Political Networks in the Gulf.** New York: Oxford University Press, 2012. 315 pp. An analysis of the historical origins and present situation of the Shi'a that focuses on transnational networks in the Gulf, especially Kuwait, Bahrain and Saudi Arabia.

Makdisi, Ussama. **The Culture of Sectarianism: Community, History, and Violence in Nineteenth-Century Ottoman Lebanon.** Berkeley: University of California Press, 2000. 249 pp. Discusses how and why sectarian identities were constructed, and concludes sectarianism is a manifestation of modernity.

Matthiesen, Toby. **Sectarian Gulf: Bahrain, Saudi Arabia, and the Arab Spring that Wasn't.** Stanford, CA.: Stanford University Press, 2013. 186 pp. A personal account, backed up by academic research, of the rise of political sectarianism in the Gulf since 2011. Concludes that ruling families have created a sectarian Gulf to bolster their own power.

Potter, Lawrence G., ed. **Sectarian Politics in the Persian Gulf.** New York: Oxford University Press, 2014. 345 pp. The first in-depth treatment of the rise of sectarian politics in Iran, Iraq and the Gulf states. Provides a theoretical and comparative framework for understanding sectarian relations.

Maalouf, Amin. **In the Name of Identity: Violence and the Need to Belong,** trans. Barbara Bray. New York: Arcade Publishing, 2012. 164 pp. Lebanese novelist examines identity in the modern world, and the need for societies to accept multiple affiliations that have forged collective identities.

Nasr, Vali. **The Shia Revival: How Conflicts within Islam Will Shape the Future.** New York: Norton, 2007. 292 pp. An influential book that examines the historical roots of Sh'i–Sunni strife and contemporary politics in Shi'i states.

Wehrey, Frederic M. **Sectarian Politics in the Gulf: From the Iraq War to the Arab Uprisings.** New York: Columbia University Press, 2013. 304 pp. A study of religious politics in the Gulf (especially Bahrain, Kuwait and Saudi Arabia) between 2003 and 2011 based on fieldwork and primary sources.

Weiss, Max. **In the Shadow of Sectarianism: Law, Shi'ism, and the Making of Modern Lebanon.** Cambridge: Harvard University Press, 2010. 325 pp. Traces the beginning of modern Shi'i collective identity under the French Mandate in Lebanon (1923-43) based on court records.

TO LEARN MORE ABOUT THIS TOPIC AND TO ACCESS WEB LINKS TO RESOURCES GO TO www.greatdecisions.org

India Changes Course
by Barbara Crossette

Supporters throw flower petals as Bharatiya Janata Party (BJP) leader Narendra Modi rides in an open jeep on his way to file nomination papers on April 9, 2014, in Vadodra, India. (PHOTO BY KEVIN FRAYER/GETTY IMAGES)

In April and May of 2014, in the searing heat of a particularly scorching summer in India, more than 553 million people, a record 66.4% of the country's 834 million eligible voters, cast ballots in an election that profoundly changed the face of Indian politics, perhaps forever. A Hindu nationalist organization, the Bharatiya Janata Party, emerged with a clear majority in parliament, catapulting into power in New Delhi a controversial politician born in poverty who vows to put an end to bungled development and set India on a new course to greatness at home and abroad.

In its very successful election campaign, the BJP, as the party is generally known, and Narendra Modi, its leader and now prime minister of India, brought a compelling message of change to Indian voters weary and impatient with ineffective political coalitions mired in corruption, ramshackle public services and dynastic politics. Political commentators in the Indian media noted how high the participation of young people was among voters demanding

a new kind of politics. After all, their future depends on it.

There was more to this unprecedented victory for the BJP than a fed-up electorate. Powerful social and cultural forces are changing India, reflected in Indian media reports and in analyses by foreign scholars and diplomats who have followed the country's recent history closely. Restlessness has fueled populist movements such as the anti-corruption campaign of Anna Hazare, a former soldier turned civic activist, and the debut of the maverick Common Man Party of a former civil servant, Arvind Kejriwal, who seemed poised to upset traditional politics before failing to make a significant

BARBARA CROSSETTE, *a former* New York Times *bureau chief in Southeast Asia and South Asia, won the George Polk Award for coverage of the 1991 assassination of Rajiv Gandhi, a 2008 Fulbright Award for International Understanding and the 2010 Shorenstein Prize for writing on Asia. She is a member of the Foreign Policy Association Editorial Advisory Committee.*

showing in the BJP sweep of the 2014 national election.

People in rural villages as well as in metastasizing urban conglomerations with greater access to the latest communication tools and social media, used skillfully by the well financed BJP, heard the party's message down to the lowest levels of a society still divided by a punishing caste system and huge economic disparities. While voters liked the promise of reforms to make India function better—the reputation Modi brought with him from his leadership of the state of Gujarat—other messages were and still are also in circulation from zealots on the BJP's intolerant Hindu nationalist fringe. They demand a new commitment to India's Hindu roots and acceptance of an ancient sectarian history that sometimes drifts into mythology. They have little concern or respect for minority rights and religions, contrary to the tolerance enshrined in the Indian constitution.

An anti-elite mood was also evident in the electorate's spectacular rejection of the Indian National Congress, the party that had ruled India or dominated its politics for most of the nearly seven decades since independence from Britain in 1947. Until now, the party leadership has been a family preserve of the Nehru-Gandhi clan: Jawaharlal Nehru, independent India's first prime minister; Indira Gandhi, his daughter; her son, Rajiv, and his son, Rahul, who—with his mother, Sonia Gandhi, Rajiv's widow—led the Congress Party to ignominious defeat in 2014, winning only 44 parliamentary seats to the 282 of the BJP.

Political leaders of the Nehru-Gandhi dynasty and numerous other politicians have been largely cosmopolitan,

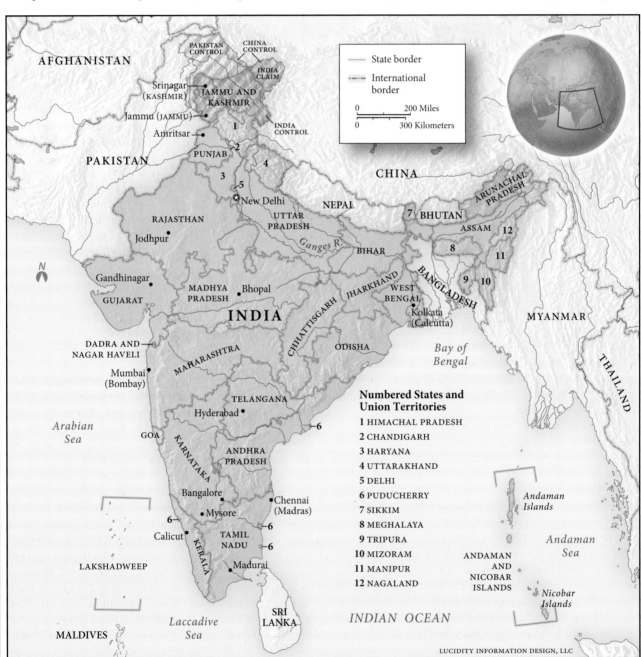

Numbered States and Union Territories

1 HIMACHAL PRADESH
2 CHANDIGARH
3 HARYANA
4 UTTARAKHAND
5 DELHI
6 PUDUCHERRY
7 SIKKIM
8 MEGHALAYA
9 TRIPURA
10 MIZORAM
11 MANIPUR
12 NAGALAND

LUCIDITY INFORMATION DESIGN, LLC

relatively secular, English-speaking, upper caste people often educated abroad or at least well traveled. To the large majority of India's 1.3 billion people, on whose votes those leaders relied, that is an alien world, not the country they traditionally call Bharat. Populist Modi, with his humble origins, appealed to them. It has become a truism in India to say that the Congress Party (and what it stands for) lost the election decisively, as much as the BJP won it.

"I think there's a sense that the time has come to get rid of the Nehrus," said Ainslie T. Embree, a professor of history emeritus at Columbia University and a lifelong scholar and writer on Indian society and politics who has served as cultural affairs counselor at the U.S. Embassy in New Delhi.

For Sanjit "Bunker" Roy, an internationally recognized, award-winning development pioneer among the rural Indian poor, this is a moment to savor. "Since 1947, Indians have not spoken out so strongly and clearly for a completely new brand of people running government," he wrote in an opinion article for *The Indian Express*. Born into privilege and educated in the most elite of Indian schools himself, Roy founded the Barefoot College in Rajasthan in 1972 to help the rural poor better their lives and communities in locally sustainable ways. Of the new Modi government, he wrote: "Mercifully, there are no ministers educated abroad. Thankfully, none of them has been brainwashed at Harvard, Stanford, Cambridge, the World Bank or the IMF."

Where India will go from this watershed moment, politically and culturally, may still be very much a question mark, said Ambassador A. Peter Burleigh, an American diplomat with extensive regional experience and knowledge of South Asia. "But I think it's really important for anybody observing India to recognize the change from the traditional Anglophone, Congress party, urban, sophisticated, highly educated India that we're used to dealing with, certainly diplomatically, and by and large in government-to-government relations and in many other relations," he said in

an interview. "The BJP in general and Mr. Modi in particular represent a different part of India."

Burleigh said there is a general sense of "We've now arrived. We won this fantastic landslide election against these Anglophone folks who are out of touch

with real India—always have been out of touch, but have managed through the manipulation of the political system to get elected most of the time. But now it's our turn. It's going to be different. And it's going to be more Indian, authentic Indian: Hindu." ■

Modi: the man and his base

The highlights of Narendra Damodardas Modi's public life are well known, celebrated by many and a cause of concern to others. He was born on September 17, 1950, in the small town of Vadnagar in Gujarat state, in a large, low-caste but not Dalit (now translated as "broken people" but formerly known as untouchable) family. As a boy, he and one of his brothers ran a tea stall at a nearby train station to supplement the family income. They were poor, but apparently not destitute; Narendra finished school – a considerable achievement even now in many parts of India—and later received a degree in political science from Gujarat University, according to the biographical information he provided to the Electoral Commission of India.

His life took a decisive turn when as a student, he joined the Rashtriya Swayamsevak Sangh (RSS), a fiercely nationalistic Hindu organization that was modeled unashamedly on European fascist movements of the 1930s. RSS members, all male and all pledged to celibacy, dress up in military-style tropical khakis and crisp white shirts to drill and parade around in formation. Their philosophy, broadly termed Hindutva, rests on the conviction that all Indians are Hindus, or should consider themselves Hindus or convert formally to Hinduism, if they want to live in India. There have been forced "reconversions" of Buddhists and Christians by extremists, and numerous assaults on Muslims. Harsh Mander, director of the Center for Equity Studies, an independent research organization in New Delhi, sees a disturbing rise in organizations manipulating Hindu passions

against Muslims. "Many corners of the country have begun to smolder in slow fires of orchestrated hate," he wrote in the *The Hindustan Times* at the end of August 2014.

The intolerant RSS fringe of the BJP does not define or represent hundreds of millions of Indians, who may support Modi more for his promises of better lives and a better nation than for his cultural and sectarian nationalism. Indians, however devout, are not on the whole extreme Hindu nationalists. Among the poor, their Hindu faith and rituals give them personal spiritual sustenance, as religions do everywhere. They may worship a favorite god or chose to pray to varying deities in the Hindu pantheon, depending on the need of the moment. Temple festivals are joyous events, and the trip of a lifetime may be a grueling trek to a distant shrine or holy river that may take weeks, or more, of hardship and sacrifice for those who have few material goods. They welcome outsiders into the humblest of homes with a generosity that is extraordinary. In this tolerance they have been, ironically, more naturally in line with secular liberals despite the huge economic and social gaps that divide them.

The RSS agenda is narrower. It wants all Indians to speak Hindi, and Modi promotes this. Hindi is a national language but not a true *lingua franca*. There are hundreds of Indian languages; 22 of them officially recognized. Many Indians do not know Hindi, or refuse to use it out of regional pride, which has made English the de facto link language in many government offices, businesses, the media and think tanks. It has served India's world class

Members of the Rashtriya Swayamsevak Sangh (RSS) stand in formation as they listen to their chief Mohan Bhagwat (unseen) during a convention of RSS workers in Indore, India, January 6, 2013. (IMAGE BY © SANJEEV GUPTA/EPA/CORBIS)

diplomatic corps well in international organizations and foreign capitals at a time when India seeks a place among the globally powerful. Yet despite these positive factors, the Modi government has ruled that applicants taking exams for civil service positions at home and abroad no longer have to answer questions posed in English.

The RSS suffered a setback under the urbane first prime minister, Jawaharlal Nehru, who termed it a "Nazi" organization after one of its former members, Nathuram Godse, assassinated Mohandas Karamchand Gandhi — the "Mahatma" — in 1948 for being soft on minorities. But it has bounced back with an estimated 4 million current members and countless part-time volunteers. As recently as August 2014, the outspoken head of the RSS, Mohan Bhagwat, unleashed a storm of controversy in a speech in eastern India, saying: "The cultural identity of all Indians is Hindutva and the present inhabitants of the country are descendants of this great culture."

An editorial in the The Hindustan Times speculated that the RSS under Bhagwat may be on "a collision course" with the Modi government. "As it is," the editorial continued, "there are fears that at least a section of the BJP is keen on changing the inclusive and secular

character of India, making it more Hindu-oriented. This would be detrimental to Mr Modi's efforts to project an image of India as a modern and progressive country…. The problem is that the BJP needs the foot soldiers of the RSS to help it win elections."

For decades, the RSS was Modi's family, as he worked his way up through its ranks to lead its Gujarat chapter before moving to the BJP, the movement's political wing. An inherently brilliant political strategist, Modi was elected chief minister of Gujarat in 2001. Indian political columnists note that before Modi's own rise to power in Delhi was complete, he had sidelined all the leaders who gave the party national prominence in the 1980s and '90s, including Atal Bihari Vajpayee, a moderate Hindu intellectual who served as prime minister briefly in 1996 and then from 1998 until 2004.

While the outlines of Modi's political career are clear, his personal life remains a fascinating mystery to many. In India, where families matter and sociability is a desired trait, Modi is a loner. In an exhaustive profile of him in the *The New Statesman* of London by William Dalrymple, the well-known India-based British historian of West and South Asia, close associates of Modi described him as an

austere vegetarian teetotaler obsessed with personal hygiene and possessing extraordinary powers of self-discipline and self-sufficiency. "And he always eats alone," someone in Modi's circle told Dalrymple. "Always." On his first official visit to the U.S. in the autumn of 2014, he didn't eat at all for the full five days because he was on a fast to mark a Hindu religious observance.

Only in the run-up to the 2014 general election did Modi acknowledge reports that he had been married as a teenager to a girl named Jashodaben. Arranged child marriages were then, and still are, common in much of India, the country with the most child brides of any nation in the world. The marriage did not last very long and did not yield any children, family members told the media. It effectively ended when the young Modi walked out of the house to go on a Himalayan pilgrimage, and never returned.

In his more public political life, Modi has surrounded himself with a close group of colleagues, many from Gujarat. One of them is a controversial former Gujarati home affairs minister, Amit Shah, who allegedly used his power to employ the law and order machinery of the state to support Modi politically. Shah, who has made numerous disparaging remarks about Muslims, was nevertheless elected president of the BJP with Modi's enthusiastic blessing.

The multifaceted picture of Modi as a Hindu nationalist, a populist born into poverty and a successful reformer with generous backing from corporate leaders, along with the enigma of his personal life, make him the center of considerable scrutiny in the media. His first address to parliament as prime minister on June 11, 2014, had a populist tone. He talked of empowering the poor by bringing 24-hour electricity, education and industry to rural people. He responded enigmatically to concerns about much-publicized abuses of Indian women by saying that it was time to "stop politicizing rape." The abuse of girls and women has become a national shame; India is considered among the worst countries in the world in which to be female.

Even the country's most disaffected and disadvantaged minority, its 174 million Muslims, "cannot be left behind in development," Modi said in his address. But there was no mention or acknowledgment of the massacre in 2002 of at least 1,000 (some reports say up to 2,000) people, mostly Muslims, in Gujarat under Modi's watch. The crisis began when 58 Hindus returning from a religious pilgrimage died in a train fire whose origin is still in dispute, but the incident resulted in a violent rampage of militant Hindus through Muslim neighborhoods. Men, women and children were slaughtered, Muslim homes, businesses, mosques and community centers were trashed and burned. The carnage was condemned worldwide. Modi's visa to travel to the U.S. was revoked in 2005; it was not reissued until after his rise to power in 2014. Concerned Indians say that Modi has rebuffed all efforts to persuade him to acknowledge if not apologize for what happened.

In that first address to parliament in June, Modi introduced the idea that he wanted to govern "on the basis of collectivity," engaging the 29 Indian states in "cooperative federalism." Later, in his Independence Day speech in August 2014, Modi fleshed out some of his thinking on building a more consen-

sual national unity. Indian states often pursue policies of their own from development planning to foreign affairs, and this has undeniably hampered expeditious decision making.

On Independence Day, Modi returned to what even critics described as a genuine concern for the poor, perhaps drawing on his own life. He promised to help the more than 75 million Indian households unable to open bank accounts or establish credit, which stifles small-scale entrepreneurship. He pledged aid to victims of caste discrimination. He said that schools would provide private toilets for girls; the absence of sanitation keeps many girls out of school across the developing world. He spoke against the illegal but widely practiced aborting of unborn girls in favor of sons, which plays a major part in the significant imbalance in the female-to-male population in India. Indian demographers warn of potential political instability in the long run if millions of young men remain unemployed and unmarriageable.

To the applause of the crowd listening to his Independence Day speech at Delhi's Red Fort, Modi announced that on October 2 he would begin a campaign to clean up the country in time for the 150th anniversary in 2019 of Mahatma Gandhi's birthday. A report in *News India Times,* a New York-based newspaper for Indian-Americans, quot-

ed him as saying that citizens must resolve "not to leave a speck of dirt in our village, city, street, area, school, temple, hospital and what have you by 2019." The income tax department was among the first government offices to get its marching orders, which will surely have bipartisan support: "There should be no dust, no old ACs, *almirahs* [cupboards] and old furniture belonging to the office lying around the corridors or common areas near staircases and no betel-leaf stained corners."

In his address, the prime minister also announced that the national Planning Commission, established in 1950 under the influence of what the BJP regards as Nehruvian Socialist (or Soviet-style) economics, was abolished, to be replaced by a council of advisers, described as a think tank, which would report directly to the prime minister's cabinet. A week later, the prime minister, an avid user of social media who avoids the mainstream press, sent out a tweet asking Indians around the country to send him their suggestions for the panel.

In another centralizing step, Modi won the support of parliament for the abolition of the current system of selecting judges wherein sitting justices chose appointees for the Supreme Court and other important benches. A six-member commission will be formed that will give the BJP government a fu-

Prime Minister Narendra Modi cleaning the premises of Mandir Marg Police Station during a surprise visit, in New Delhi on October 02, 2014. (INDIA'S PRESS INFORMATION BUREAU)

ture hand in selecting top judges. The change requires a constitutional amendment that must be approved by half the states of India.

The Modi government rejected a request from the Congress Party to be recognized as the leader of a parliamentary opposition. Congress's poor electoral showing did not automatically qualify the party for the position although it won the second-highest number of seats. At the same time, a number of Congress-appointed state governors— a partly ceremonial, partly political position—have been dismissed. In 2010 the Supreme Court ruled that governors could not be dismissed without "good and compelling reasons." The court asked Modi to show cause. Columnists are describing his philosophy as "majoritarian," a winner-take all approach.

The prime minister's moves toward a centralization of power are the focus of much political commentary. Modi came to Delhi with a history of an authoritarian—some say dictatorial—style of governance, which contributed to his ability to make many positive changes, his supporters say. Critics urge caution.

Siddharth Varadarajan, a former editor of *The Hindu,* one of the country's leading newspapers (secular despite its name), wrote in a comment for NDTV, an Indian broadcaster, that Modi's victory "represents a collective leap towards an uncertain future." Varadarajan argued that just as Modi ran a "presidential" style campaign, his style of government may also be presidential, in line with the kind of broad executive powers he held in Gujarat. Moreover, outside his inner circle the people with the greatest influence on him have been the corporate giants who financed his rise to power and whose interests he is expected to continue to protect. "While the Indian corporate sector and native and foreign investors in the stock market are justified in celebrating the arrival of a 'right wing' business-friendly government, this is not necessarily the side of 'Modinomics' that most BJP voters would like to see," Varadarajan wrote.

Modi's supporters argue that the needs of Indians might be met more rapidly by pursuing an active, personalized foreign policy on pragmatic economic grounds for the quickest results, since India needs many kinds of technical assistance and investment. Taking charge, Modi has not only focused on building new foreign economic partnerships from the start, but has also broadened India's reach geographically, starting with Japan, China and Australia.

To emphasize how much Modi's India is turning away decisively from the Nehruvian image of government, a gigantic statue of another independence leader, Vallabhbhai Patel, who opposed Nehru on critical issues, is about to be erected in Gujarat. Under Nehru, Sardar Patel (to use an honorific by which he is known) was in charge of ending the privileges and autonomy of more than 550 maharajah-ruled "princely states" of India and incorporating them into the federal union. Nehru balked on one of them, Kashmir, his Brahmin ancestral base and a region with a Muslim majority and a Hindu Maharajah. Internationally, Indian-controlled parts of Jammu and Kashmir are still not recognized universally as part of India.

The decision by Nehru to have considerable Kashmiri autonomy written into the Indian constitution (Article 370) has been excoriated by Hindu nationalists. Some BJP politicians are calling for the article's repeal and for the resettlement of Hindus, now concentrated in the Jammu region of the state, into Muslim-majority regions, where open rebellion simmers and occasionally flares. If the Modi government moves to cancel Kashmir's current constitutional status before reaching political agreement on the region's future—as the BJP demanded in its party platform for Jammu and Kashmir state elections late in November 2014—there could be more sustained violence, a temptation to Pakistan, which has supported the Indian Kashmiri rebellion.

A huge Indian army presence in Kashmir numbering in the hundreds of thousands over two decades has been accompanied by daily harassment of civilians and often unprovoked violence against Muslim boys and men, especially around the summer capital, Srinagar, and the larger Kashmir Valley. Thousands of Kashmiris have died or disappeared and hundreds of young men may have been buried in mass graves that recent exhumations are uncovering, while the Indian security services continue to be immune from prosecution on human rights violations.

Patel, who died in 1950, opposed the economic policies being adopted by Nehru under the influence of British Fabian Socialists and other leftist economists. The BJP argues strongly that these policies set India on the wrong—even disastrous—development path. Modi, speaking in 2013 in the presence of Manmohan Singh, then the prime minister in a Congress-led government, said bluntly that Patel, not Nehru, should have been India's first prime minister.

And so a foundation stone has been laid in the Gujarati town of Kevadiya for a nearly 600-foot-high statue of Patel, twice as tall as the Statue of Liberty. ■

Modi's team takes on the challenges

Prominent among the members of Modi's governing team are two veterans of national policymaking. After the spring 2014 election, Arun Jaitley was initially given the double duty of finance and defense ministries – with Modi saving the nuclear portfolio for himself, but in a large cabinet shakeup in November Jaitley relinquished the defense portfolio to Manohar Parrikar, a former state-level mister in Goa, and picked up responsibilities for corporate affairs and communications instead. Ajit Doval, the prime minister's national security adviser, is expected to influence international policies, especially in the region, with his expertise in homeland security and intelligence. The two areas of economic development and the security of India in a dangerous region are not unrelated. Extreme poverty is destabilizing, and Muslim militants are not far away. In 2014, it was revealed that some young men from the Mumbai area had joined the Islamic State militants in Syria and Iraq; one of them was killed in battle. Although the threat may never materialize, Al Qaeda has announced it will be moving into South Asia, with India as a target.

On July 10, 2014, Jaitley delivered the government's budget plans. Choosing to speak in English, perhaps because he expected a large foreign audience, he outlined a cautious and incremental approach. This did not please some influential supporters of Modi or politically neutral observers who were expecting a stronger start to Modi's term in office. Among those who thought budget reforms could have been bolder, and economic forecast less optimistic, was the Indian economist Arvind Subramanian, a fellow at the Peterson Institute for International Economics in Washington. A few months later, Subramanian, who had earlier been assistant research director of the International Monetary Fund, was named Modi's chief economic adviser, which raised hopes that more vigorous policy changes would emerge sooner or later.

In his initial budget presentation, Jaitley, a senior lawyer practicing in the Supreme Court and a former board member of the Asian Development Bank, began with an overview of the government's goals before moving to a catalogue of budget proposals and allocations. He covered the revamping of taxation and investment policies (including foreign investment in India), banking reform, the overhaul of subsidies, development of infrastructure, advances in communications, the expansion of higher education, the opening of new regional advanced medical centers and measures to help the poor rise to what he called the "neo-middle class."

"The steps that I will announce in this Budget are only the beginning of a journey towards a sustained growth of 7–8 percent or above within the next 3–4 years along with macro-economic

Indian Finance Minister Arun Jaitley (C) leaves his office to table the budget in parliament in New Delhi on July 10, 2014. (PRAKASH SINGH/AFP/GETTY IMAGES)

stabilization that includes lower levels of inflation, lesser fiscal deficit and a manageable current account deficit," he said, adding this caution: "Therefore, it would not be wise to expect everything that can be done or must be done to be in the first Budget presented within forty five days of the formation of this Government."

High on the agenda Jaitley outlined was the recent decline in the annual In-

dian economic growth rate. "Two years of sub 5% growth in the Indian economy has resulted in a challenging situation," he said. "I hope the investor community both within India and abroad would … participate in the Indian growth story with renewed vigor." He did not, however, open all doors to foreigners. "The policy of the [National Democratic Alliance] NDA Government is to promote Foreign Direct Investment (FDI) selectively in sectors where it helps the larger interest of the Indian economy," he said. Mentioning that India is now the largest buyer of defense equipment in the world, at the cost of large foreign currency outlays, and also a country that is "insurance-starved," he said that the government was prepared to make investment in India in these two areas more attractive. When Modi came to New York and Washington in the fall of 2014, he reinforced the sense that the kind of investment India wanted was for strictly Indian projects that did not necessarily promise substantial returns for foreign investors, some of whom also thought that at least a few of the development plans in infrastructure and energy were unrealistic, including a national rapid rail system and the creation of 100 "smart cities" with clean energy, safe water, modern sanitation and wireless connectivity .

In the first budget, the BJP govern-

People get on with their lives in a slum on the railway tracks on December 12, 2013, in Kolkata, India. Almost one third of the Kolkata population of more than 14 million live in slums and a further 70,000 are homeless. (PHOTO BY SAMIR HUSSEIN/GETTY IMAGES)

ment's plan for building a stronger industrial base was not backed up by concrete measures for dealing with the neglect of mass education and healthcare for millions of poor Indians who would be the workers. Also underplayed was the steadily worsening natural environment and depletion of natural resources. This perennial near-inattention by all recent governments to human progress is reflected in the United Nations Human Development Report, which in 2014 ranked India 135th among 187 nations, just ahead of countries such as Afghanistan and Myanmar as well as much of sub-Saharan Africa. The report showed India falling well behind most of Latin America and the Caribbean.

In the other four BRICS group of nations, Brazil ranks at 79, Russia at 57, China at 91, and South Africa at 118. India, with 1.3 billion people, is soon to overtake China as the world's most populous nation, but falls behind China by almost every measure of development—except, of course, in democratic politics. Almost half of Indian children are significantly malnourished and the country has the largest population of abjectly poor people in the world. The caste system, despite affirmative action programs, deepens disadvantages.

In an interview with *The Hindustan Times* in May 2014, Amartya Sen, professor of economics and philosophy at Harvard University and a Nobel Prize winner in economics who has written extensively on India, which he still calls home, addressed the importance of the human side of development. "No country in the world has achieved high rates of economic development and sustained growth of per capita income with an ill-educated and unhealthy labor force," he said. He added that India had "a substantially illiterate labor force and an extraordinarily chaotic healthcare system."

Asked for his assessment of the Modi government's ability to rise to this human challenge, Sen replied that Gujarat's record was only middling. "I am a great admirer of many things Gujarat has done, not just under Narendra Modi, but even before," he said. "But human development has not been among its better achievements." ∎

India in Asia

Under decades of Congress Party domination, India, especially during the leadership of Prime Minister Indira Gandhi, had built up a record of interference and bullying in the South Asia region. It dismembered Pakistan with the Indian Army-backed creation of Bangladesh, used ethnic political manipulation to incorporate the independent Buddhist kingdom of Sikkim, punished landlocked Nepal with blockades and other measures and continues to put subtle pressure on Bhutan, which clung to its independence as the last Buddhist kingdom in the Himalayas—and is now a democratic constitutional monarchy—but which cedes control of its foreign affairs to India. Bhutan cannot, for example, open an embassy in Washington and is expected to vote with India in international organizations, whether or not the Bhutanese agree on the issues involved.

Sri Lanka suffered the most tragic fate, as India's foreign intelligence service, the Research and Analysis Wing, known as RAW, supported a Tamil-led rebellion in the 1980s and allowed the guerrillas of the gruesomely totalitarian Liberation Tigers of Tamil Eelam to establish safe havens in the Indian state of Tamil Nadu, where they had considerable political backing. The decades-long, destructive civil war that followed between the Tamil Tigers and the Sri Lankan government led to atrocities on both sides, opened the way to Buddhist violence across the country and created a climate for thuggish politics. Sri Lankan democracy has been severely wounded.

The American diplomat A. Peter Burleigh, who was the U.S. ambassador in Sri Lanka from 1995 to 1997, said in an interview that India's relations with its neighbors are all "fraught." South Asians, he said "have a long history of both Indian over-involvement and probably under-involvement in some cases, and there is a high sensitivity on the part of all the neighbors about overweening India imposing its will on them."

Burleigh, who speaks most of the major languages of the region after years of diplomatic service in South Asia, said that the sensitivity to India varies from place to place and time to time. "But that sensitivity about Indian involvement is extremely strong, and they will all be very worried that this new, very popular, muscular central government with such a strong majority in parliament will be more able to impose India's will if it chooses to on the smaller neighbors," he said. "In their foreign policy efforts they are all busy deepening relations with China, with the U.S. if they can, with the EU [European Union], to relieve some of the pressure that Indian dominance in the region – in their perceptions—has really been a threat to them."

Pakistan has a special place in Indian policy because it s the only neighbor in South Asia big enough and well armed enough to threaten India. Both have nuclear weapons – India since its first nuclear test in 1974 and Pakistan because India's second round of explosions in 1998 led the Pakistanis to conduct tests of their own. The two nations have fought several wars and numerous skirmishes over the disputed Kashmir region, which both claim. Pakistan has supported independence for the Kashmiris on the Indian side of a "line of control" that passes for a border, often with arms and training. It has also not blocked the infiltration of Pakistan-based terrorists into India, with the most spectacular assault staged in an upscale hotel area of Mumbai in November 2008.

Tensions and fears in the region relaxed a little during a previous BJP government under Prime Minister Atal Bihari Vajpayee, though India's 1998 nuclear weapons tests took place during that time. Vajpayee, now sidelined by Prime Minister Modi, can no longer assert his moderating influence diplomatically, and Indian commentators are looking to Modi's national security adviser, Ajit Doval, for clues to Modi's intentions. Doval is described in a profile in *The Hindu* newspaper as "an acclaimed spook" with numerous successful undercover assignments over his career. The profile, written by Shashank Joshi, a research fellow of the Royal United Services Institute in London who has worked with Doval in a British-Indian working group on Afghanistan, said that the new national security adviser wants to "add muscle" to Indian intelligence agencies and put more focus on potential terrorist threats at home. He is said to be mistrustful of the U.S.

When Narendra Modi invited all the South Asian neighbors of India to his swearing in as prime minister, he seemed to be signaling better regional relations. Among those who accepted the invitation was Prime Minister Nawaz Sharif of Pakistan. There were photos of the two men looking congenial, followed by a letter soon after from Sharif expressing his "great pleasure" at meeting Modi. "I look forward to working with you in harmony to resolve all unsettled matters for the benefit of both nations" he wrote. Plans for a meeting of top foreign ministry officials from the two countries were announced.

Within a few months, however, Modi had begun to turn on Pakistan, saying it was carrying on a "proxy war" in Kashmir—not a new accusation, accepted widely as a reality in India and abroad. Soon after, Modi canceled the foreign secretaries' meeting after Pakistan's high commissioner (equivalent to an ambassador) in New Delhi, Abdul Basit, met with political leaders of a long-established Kashmiri separatist group, the Hurriyat Conference. This was also not new; the Pakistanis had met regularly in the past with representatives of the Hurryiat. The U.S. called the precipitous Indian move "unfortunate." Days later, one of the Hurriyat

leaders was arrested on charges of treason.

In the background of India's regional policy concerns is China, an enormous country that India can no longer hope to rival economically or militarily, at least in the near future, according to the prominent Indian commentator C. Raja Mohan. Writing in *The Indian Express* soon after Modi's inauguration, he said that India has to come to terms with "a significant imbalance" in the relationship. "China's [gross domestic product (GDP)] is now four times larger than that of India," he wrote. "China spends four times as much as India on defense. It is the world's second-largest economy and could soon overtake the U.S. to become number one. Beijing is the world's second-biggest military power and towers over its Asian neighbors, including India." China also attracts far more foreign investment.

Modi has been open to economic assistance from China, but keeps other options open as well. In September 2014 he visited Japan with a group of Indian industrialists, hoping to lure Japan into greater economic partnership. He sought Japanese aid in nuclear energy development, but was reported to have been stalled by conditions set by Japan that India would find unpalatable, such as adherence to international nuclear treaties. The Japanese did lift sanctions imposed on six Indian entities linked to India's 1998 nuclear tests, and pledged to increase its investments in other areas. They offered bullet-train technology to modernize the creaking Indian railway system.

A few weeks later, China's president, Xi Jinping, made an official trip to India to discuss areas of potential cooperation and steps to lower tensions between the two nations. India has no apparent reason to fear a large-scale military threat from China, but successive governments in New Delhi have been preoccupied with Chinese claims to more than 30,000 square miles in India's remote Northeast and territory in the Aksai Chin area on the Tibetan Plateau, where India lost a brief border war with China in 1962. Numerous efforts at reconciliation have failed to achieve

lasting settlements, and new skirmishes were reported even while Xi Jinping was in India saying that these problems could be resolved through dialogue.

At the same time, India, recognizing the expansion of Chinese power in the Indian Ocean region, has sought closer relationships with Southeast Asian nations to the east and the countries of the Asia-Pacific Economic Cooperation group, with 21 members around the Pacific Rim, including the U.S. India has become a leading voice in the global group of nations known as the BRICS—Brazil, Russia, India, China and South Africa—which in 2014 announced the establishment of a new international development bank to rival the World Bank. India lost its bid to house the new bank's headquarters, which will be in Shanghai, but will be responsible for its top management.

Modi, by almost all accounts, recognizes that China could be a valuable source of both investment and industrial skills for India, according to foreign policy analyst C. Raja Mohan. The prime minister will have to balance economic and security issues—and the advice of his economic and security advisers—as his relations develop not only with China, but also other East Asian nations and the immediate neighbors in the South Asian Association for Regional Cooperation, a group of eight nations, including Pakistan. ■

Indian Premier Narendra Modi (R) shakes hands with his Pakistan counterpart Nawaz Sharif prior to a meeting in New Delhi, India, May 27, 2014. (IMAGE BY © HARISH TYAGI/ EPA/CORBIS)

Indian-Americans and U.S. policy

The migration of Indians to the U.S. is a relatively recent part of the American immigration story, but they now represent the third-largest immigrant group in the U.S., after Mexicans and Chinese, with nearly 2 million Indian immigrants, or 5% of the immigrant population, up from 0.5% in 1960, census figures show. Though most arrived in the U.S. legally, many through family reunions, 2% of all the illegal immigrants in the country were also from India as of 2011. Almost a third of Indian immigrants live in two states: California and New Jersey, with a third large concentration in Illinois.

The Migration Policy Institute in Washington, DC, reported recently that as a group, Indian immigrants—many of them Gujaratis from Modi's home state—are better educated and more likely to speak English well. In American higher education, Indian student are second in numbers to Chinese students. Indians hold jobs in information technology and various management positions, are more likely to own homes than any other people in the country,

and are less likely to live in poverty than the general population, native or immigrant. They have also built successful careers in the arts, academia, the law and medicine, among other professions. Many are rich, and among them there are big donors to Modi, for whom they staged a huge theatrical rally in Madison Square Garden when the prime minister was in New York to speak to the UN in September 2014.

Sunil Adam is chief editor of the largest Indian-American media group, based in New York, which publishes the weekly *News India Times*, a source of information from India and around the world of particular interest to Indian readers. Adam has watched the evolution of Indian-American life closely and has identified some changes in the composition of Indian communities that mirror social and political developments in India, particularly the increase in non-elite migrants from small towns and rural areas. The first wave of Indian migrants, many of them in the professions, was followed by an influx of students in the 1960s and then the beginning of a

surge of arrivals in the 1970s from Gujarat. Many Gujaratis quickly became successful in the retail economy. In the 1990s, a "dot.com boom" took off, Adam said, attracting Indians to centers of American technology.

Though these various immigrant groups were diverse they could find common cause in support of India, he said, "Gujarati businesses, followed by American companies lobbying for Indian professionals, eventually meshing with the clout of immigrant tech entrepreneurs" built up one of the most influential lobbies in Washington.

"The current influence of the Indian-American community," Adam said, "can be clearly related to the change of image of the average Indian in the U.S. thanks to the dot-com boom. "This has given a lot of impetus to Indian-Americans to step out of their shadows and say, OK, we've got something going here and we should use that to influence things. Indians are never shy of taking credit for a civilization of greatness. So Indians started organizing."

They found models in the American Israel Public Affairs Committee (AIPAC) and other pro-Israeli groups. The collapse of the Soviet Union, and India's initial loss of a reliable Russian partner, helped cement ties to Israel after years of pro-Palestinian policies. "The opening up of India and the business opportunities that Americans suddenly discovered there in the 1990s also led to the political lobbying by American corporations on behalf of India," Adam said. "They took help from Indian-Americans, particularly those Indian-Americans who looked to Israel and their lobbying tactics," Those Indians saw that they could use their economic clout to advance both their influence in the U.S. and also the cause of Indo-U.S. relations, Adam added, contributing across party lines to both Democrats and Republicans.

In recent years, Indian-Americans and the Modi governments, first in Gujarat and then at the national level, have found other powerful public relations tools. Pro-India caucuses have formed in the U.S. Congress, in the House of Representatives in 1993 and in the Sen-

Supporters of Prime Minister Narendra Modi crowd the streets outside Madison Square Garden in New York City after Modi gave a speech there during a reception by the Indian community in honor of his visit to the U.S., Sept. 28, 2014. (IMAGE BY © JASON DECROW/AP/CORBIS)

ate (organized by Hillary Clinton) in 2004. Public relations firms and lobbying organizations hired by India and Indian-Americans employ former American ambassadors to India, whose names might carry weight in Washington and abroad. Frank G. Wisner, an experienced diplomat in Asia and the Middle East and ambassador to India from 1994 to 1997, is an international affairs adviser to Patton Boggs and a board member of the U.S.-India Business Council. Tim Roemer, a former Representative in Congress from Indiana and ambassador from 2009 to 2011, works for APCO Worldwide. Robert Blackwill, ambassador from 2001 to 2003, is a senior counselor for international business at the DCI Group.

Former American ambassadors to many countries are frequently sought after for their experience and informed analysis by universities, research organizations, foreign policy think tanks and the media, but to do public relations work on behalf of a country where they once served disturbs many other diplomats, who say that ambassadors should not be lobbyists for those countries and there should be a ban on former ambassadors doing such work.

The positive portrait of India that public relations firms, professional lobbyists and Indian-Americans alone or in organizations they have formed appears to have obscured other less positive aspects of Indian-American influence. The concept of Hindutva is strong in some Indian-American communities and Hindu temples, and caste discrimination follows lower-caste migrants and Dalits to the U.S. The reach of Hindu nationalists in the U.S. is not widely or easily recognized by non-Indians.

Ainslie T. Embree, a cultural historian, recalled that in 2008, when Romila Thapar, India's most celebrated historian of the ancient Indian world, was named a winner of the million-dollar Kluge Prize for Lifetime Achievement in the Study of Humanity by the Library of Congress (which she shared with Peter Robert Lamont Brown, an author of books on late antiquity in the Middle East and beyond) Thapar

Indian Dalit women shout slogans during a protest against a gang-rape of four Dalit girls in Haryana's Hisar district, as they gather outside the residence of Haryana Chief Minister Bhupinder Singh Hooda in New Delhi, India, May 11, 2014. (IMAGE BY © TSERING TOPGYAL/AP/CORBIS)

became the target of an ultimately unsuccessful campaign mounted by Indian-Americans to have the award rescinded. Still, the Library of Congress hailed her secular scholarship in its citation: "Thapar's relentless striving for historical truth—independent of the superimposition of vacillating, fashionable theories of current sociopolitical conditions—is a landmark in the global writing of history."

American academics and writers have experienced similar assaults. "People they especially attack are Americans teaching Indian studies," Embree said, adding that many of them are women. "The great example is Wendy Doniger." In 2010, a book by Doniger, *The Hindus: An Alternative History* was published in India and won two Indian awards for the author, a distinguished professor of religion at the University of Chicago. But it also attracted the attention of Dina Nath Batra, a retired Indian headmaster and RSS member, who filed civil and criminal suits against Penguin Books India, the Indian publisher, demanding that the book be withdrawn. After years of legal wrangling, Penguin Books India agreed to cease publication and pulp remaining copies of the book, sparking an outcry from Indian intellectuals. Doniger, telling her story in *The New York Review of Books*

noted wryly that the pulping wasn't necessary; Indian booksellers had apparently already bought the remaining stock.

The stories of Indian-Americans whose lives do not fit the dot.com image of wealth and success may get more attention in India than in the American media. In 2014, *Elle India* published a chilling essay by the Indian-American artist Thenmozhi Soundararajan titled "Still I Rise." She told how she learned that she was a Dalit as a child in California, and became aware that her Tamil parents had fled South India to escape caste prejudice. She described her "coming out" at 19 years old and the consequences she faced at the University of California, Berkeley. "All of the Indian professors on campus were upper caste… and all, except one, refused to advise me on projects and blacklisted my work," she wrote. "I stopped getting invited to South Asian events. These are some of the structural manifestations of caste in the diaspora. Once you're out, you're…out."

The *Elle* essay followed an article that she had written for another Indian publication, *Outlook*, two years earlier. Entitled "The Black Indians," she said it received messages of support from all over the world, as well as "a good number of death threats from conservative Hindus." ∎

India and the U.S.: starting over

There have been a number of issues on which the U.S. and India have differed in recent years, well before the Modi government came to power. Nevertheless, this fundamental political shift in India does offer the possibility of new initiatives on both sides in what an American diplomat described as "an enabling atmosphere."

Initial contacts between Prime Minister Modi and American officials have been disappointing, however, with both sides hewing to often-stated positions for the most part. Ambassador Burleigh, who as *chargé d'affaires* in 2011–12 was head of the U.S. Embassy in New Delhi, enumerated some of the outstanding areas of concern to the American government. He mentioned patent issues involving the transfer of sensitive technologies to India for which American exporters want better legal protection. There are also disputes over the overstaying of visas in the U.S. by employees of Indian information technology companies, which transfer Indians who are admitted legally for specific jobs to other positions "intended to avoid the core of our visa regulations," he said, adding the American government has gone to court over these practices and won cases that led to expulsions.

"Quality control in India's pharmaceuticals is a gigantic problem now," he said. "More than half of the generic drugs imported into the U.S. are made in India." Recently imports from big Indian pharmaceutical companies have been banned by the Food and Drug Administration because of contamination or unacceptable quality. American pharmaceutical companies say that India has been hostile to recognizing and enforcing intellectual property rights, invalidating patents on innovative American drugs and supplanting them with Indian copies or slightly altered versions to make them classifiable as new for patent purposes. As in other areas, U.S. drug companies have trouble with "an unpredictable regulatory environment," Rod Hunter, senior vice president of the Pharmaceutical Research and Manufacturers of America, wrote in *The Hindustan Times* in September 2014.

Disputes such as these reflect the larger question of how to bring India into more active cooperation with a host of international bodies and agreements, from climate change to trade and nuclear nonproliferation.

On July 28, 2014, in a speech at the Washington-based Center for American Progress in advance of talks in New Delhi with the new Indian government, Secretary of State John Kerry, aware that India was threatening to stall a new World Trade Organization (WTO) agreement on trade and customs liberalization, said pointedly: "So as we work with our trading partners around the world to advance trade and investment liberalization, India has a decision to make about where it fits in the global trading system. India's willingness to support a rules-based trading order and fulfill its obligations will help to welcome greater investment from the U.S. and from elsewhere around the world." Three days later, while Kerry was in New Delhi, India blocked the WTO accord, which had taken years to negotiate. India demanded a separate agreement protecting its subsidized and warehoused food stocks from freer trade and when its demand was not met, the Modi government vetoed the accord. In November 2014, the U.S. and India were reported to have reached a compromise allowing the Indians to opt out of some provisions, which may enable the trade liberalization agreement to go forward,.

As for climate change negotiations, India, the world's third largest carbon emitter after China and the U.S., announced in September that that it will not be bound by international emissions agreements setting national targets since it relies on coal for energy and will continue to rely on coal for decades to come.

India and U.S. population density compared

2014:

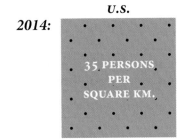

U.S.
35 PERSONS PER SQUARE KM.

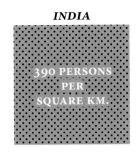

INDIA
390 PERSONS PER SQUARE KM.

2050 (projected):

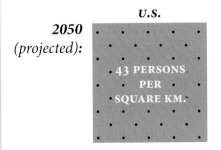

U.S.
43 PERSONS PER SQUARE KM.

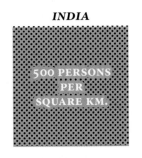

INDIA
500 PERSONS PER SQUARE KM.

NOTE: INDIA ACCOUNTS FOR ABOUT 1/5 OF ANNUAL WORLD POPULATION GROWTH

LUCIDITY INFORMATION DESIGN, LLC

In looking for common ground with India, American officials have identified energy development as a win-win issue, with India facing dire power shortages and American companies ready to invest in expanding civil nuclear energy production. But a huge hurdle was thrown up by India in 2010, putting into question the fate of a 2005 agreement that gave India—one of the very few countries with nuclear weapons that refuse to sign international nonproliferation treaties—the right to buy civilian nuclear equipment, against the advice of leading American nuclear experts and numerous other governments. Among the beneficiaries of this extraordinary decision were to be American energy companies and suppliers of civilian nuclear equipment.

Devesh Kapur, director of the Center for the Advanced study of India at the University of Pennsylvania, writing in December 2013 in *The Economic Times* of India, analyzed a steady deterioration in relations between the two countries, symbolized by the diplomatic dispute over an Indian consular officer in New York arrested for bringing a servant into the county under fraudulent circumstances and substantially underpaying her. Kapur suggested this was only a manifestation of something deeper.

"The root of the current crisis," Kapur wrote, "is the unraveling of the India-U.S. nuclear deal, once hailed as transformative and now the poster child of aborted hopes and bitter recriminations. U.S. business lobbies, NRIs [non-resident Indians; i.e., Indians living abroad] and the Indian government worked with the U.S. government and lobbied extremely hard for an agreement against the teeth of opposition from the non-proliferation lobby and patronizing liberals far more comfortable with a nuclear China than India. But instead of running with an amazing breakthrough, a weak Indian [Congress party] government fumbled, passing a nuclear liability law that no other country had and no international supplier could ever agree to."

The 2010 liability law essentially demanded that any foreign company seeking to build a nuclear facility in

President Barack Obama shakes hands with Indian Prime Minister Narendra Modi, Tuesday, Sept. 30, 2014, in the Oval Office of the White House in Washington, DC. (IMAGE BY © EVAN VUCCI/AP/CORBIS)

India would be responsible in perpetuity (and without a monetary cap) for any accident that might take place there, even if the company was being run entirely by an Indian staff. "U.S. business, which saw as its reward only headaches and few opportunities in India, had become embittered," Kapur wrote. Modi, with his large parliamentary majority, has not taken steps to repeal the troublesome law. American policymakers are stymied, while Prime Minister Modi looks for companies in other countries, most recently Japan and Australia, to invest in India's energy development.

When Prime Minister Modi came to Washington in late September for his first meeting with President Obama, a flurry of Indian-American initiatives emerged. Most, however, were renewals of ongoing or still aspirational projects from economic cooperation and energy development to partnerships in defense, high technology and space.

None of the big issues blocking closer ties with India—the attempted sabotage by India of the WTO trade liberalization treaty, the roadblock to civilian nuclear trade or the need for a global consensus on climate change

—were settled. Speaking at the United Nations earlier, Modi reached into Hindu Vedic philosophy for keys to a universal humanity, and suggested that more yoga could deter environmental destruction and climate change.

Modi's visit to the U.S., even his meetings with President Obama, did not get the extensive mainstream media coverage that it did in India, but commentators and editorial writers on both sides, while expressing optimism about the range of subjects discussed, also noted the overriding but unspoken issues not on the active agenda and agreed that there is much more work to be done.

"At the very least, this visit restored a degree of confidence to a neglected relationship," Jayant Prasad, a career Indian ambassador who is now a fellow at the Center for Advanced Study of India at Penn, wrote in *The Hindu*. "Notwithstanding shared values and interests, the real traction in India-U.S. relations lies ahead, perhaps with a new U.S. President just over two years away, as India begins to realize its economic potential and augments all aspects of what the Chinese describe as a comprehensive national power." ■

discussion questions

1. India and the U.S. are often described by their respective leaders as "natural partners" with shared democratic values. Do you agree and, if so, why? If you disagree, explain the reasons.

2. What are the most important challenges the government of Prime Minister Modi faces? What kind of help does he want or need from other nations?

3. Do relations with the U.S. look brighter now that there is more interaction between American and Indian officials? What issues are still unresolved?

4. Why does India, a democracy and a rising economic power, rank so low in global measures of human development, often at the levels of Sub-Saharan Africa and well behind China?

5. What factors caused the almost total political collapse of India's oldest and traditionally strongest political party, the Indian National Congress (INC)? Will social changes in the country and the presence of a very large youth population make it harder for Congress to return to power anytime soon?

suggested readings

Dalrymple, William. "Narendra Modi: Man of the Masses," London: **The New Statesman,** May 12, 2014. <http://www.newstatesman.com/politics/2014/05/narendra-modi-man-masses>. Dalrymple profiles Modi, his rise to power and mass appeal in this article.

Department of State. Country Reports on Human Rights Practices for 2013: India. <http://www.state.gov/documents/organization/220604.pdf >. An exhaustive survey prepared and documented by the UN Embassy in New Delhi, as required by Congress.

Doniger, Wendy. "India: Censorship by the Batra Brigade." **The New York Review of Books.** May 8, 2014. <http://www.nybooks.com/articles/archives/2014/may/08/india-censorship-batra-brigade/>. Doniger, the author of the award-winning book **The Hindus: An Alternative History,** details her side of the story in the controversy surrounding the book.

Madan, T.N. **Modern Myths, Locked Minds: Secularism and Fundamentalism in India.** Second edition. New Delhi: Oxford University Press, 2009. See Chapter Seven, pp 203–232: "The Hindu Religious Tradition: Revivalism and Fundamentalism," on several centuries of debate within Hinduism between reformers and nationalists over the nature of the religion and its place in Indian society. It includes an illuminating section on Mahatma Gandhi's views on being a Hindu.

Mishra, Pankaj. "The Gujarat massacre: New India's blood rite," an opinion article published by **The Guardian** newspaper: London: March 14, 2012. <http://www.theguardian.com/commentisfree/2012/mar/14/new-india-gujarat-massacre/>

McDermott, Rachel Fell, Leonard A. Gordon, Ainslie T. Embree, Frances W. Pritchett and Dennis Dalton eds. "The Plight Of Indian Women." **Sources of Indian Traditions,** Vol. 2, third edition, New York: Columbia University Press, 2014. A letter by Pandita Ramabai Sarasvati to a former British governor of Bengal in the 19th century—an account of women's lives that still resonates in India.

Soundararajan, Thenmozhi. "Still I Rise." **Elle India,** 2014. <http://elle.in/magazine/still-i-rise/>. Soundararajan, an Indian-American who learned she was a Dalit in fifth grade, discusses her experiences with being branded "untouchable."

DON'T FORGET TO VOTE!
WWW.FPA.ORG/BALLOT

KEY TO ABBREVIATIONS AND ACRONYMS FOR EACH ARTICLE NOW AVAILABLE ONLINE!

TO LEARN MORE ABOUT THIS TOPIC AND TO ACCESS WEB LINKS TO RESOURCES GO TO www.greatdecisions.org

The U.S. and Africa:
The rise and fall of Obamamania
by Adekeye Adebajo

Nigerians celebrate U.S. President-elect Senator Barack Obama's (D-IL) historic White House victory in Lagos November 5, 2008. People across Africa sang and danced with joy on Wednesday as the Illinois senator they see as one of their own became the first black U.S. president. (© AKINTUNDE AKINLEYE/REUTERS/CORBIS)

When Barack Obama was elected the first black U.S. president in 2008, a wave of "Obamamania" swept across the African continent. In South Africa, former president Nelson Mandela (1919–2013) noted: "Your victory has demonstrated that no person anywhere in the world should not dare to dream of wanting to change the world for a better place"; the country's then president, Kgalema Motlanthe, opined, "Your election...carries with it hope for millions...of people of...African descent both in Africa and in the diaspora." In Nigeria, Umaru Yar'Adua, the late Nigerian president, noted: "Obama's election has finally broken the greatest barrier of prejudice in human history. For us in Nigeria, we have a great lesson to draw from this

historic event." And in Kenya, Obama's father's homeland, President Mwai Kibaki said: "The victory of Senator Obama is our own victory because of his roots here in Kenya. As a country, we are full of pride for his success." Indeed, Kenya,

ADEKEYE ADEBAJO *has been Executive Director of the Centre for Conflict Resolution (CCR) in Cape Town, South Africa, since 2003. He served on UN missions in South Africa, Western Sahara and Iraq. Dr. Adebajo is the author of four books:* Building Peace in West Africa; Liberia's Civil War; The Curse of Berlin: Africa After the Cold War; *and* UN Peacekeeping in Africa: From the Suez Crisis to the Sudan Conflicts. *He is co-editor or editor of eight books, on managing global conflicts, the United Nations, the European Union, West African security, South Africa's and Nigeria's foreign policies in Africa and Nobel Peace laureates of African descent. He obtained his doctorate from Oxford University in England, where he studied as a Rhodes Scholar.*

The author wishes to thank Bill Minter and Steve Weissman for extremely useful comments on an earlier draft of this essay.

declared a public holiday to mark the occasion.

By the time Obama visited South Africa, Senegal and Tanzania in June/July 2013—four years after a brief visit to Egypt and Ghana in the summer of 2009—the "Cinderella syndrome" had worn off. The president was far from the "messiah" for a U.S.-Africa policy he had once been touted as. Despite Obama's Kenyan ancestry, he has had other pressing policy priorities as president, including a recession, health-care reform, two ongoing wars in the Middle East and South Asia, and a rapidly rising China. U.S. policy toward Africa also still continues to lack consistent congressional support; the Congressional Black Caucus (CBC) had one senator out of 100, and a mere 42 out of 435 members in the U.S. House of Representatives as of October 2014. Despite its limited membership though, the CBC has sometimes been able to build coalitions for taking action in specific African cases.

Obama visited Kenya, South Africa and Darfuri refugees in Chad as a U.S. senator in 2006. In his ancestral homeland of Kenya, he was enthusiastically received like a rock star and returning "son of the soil." His condemnation of human-rights abuses and corruption in Africa was widely applauded. As a 19-year-old student at Occidental College in the U.S., Obama had raised his political consciousness by taking part in anti-apartheid demonstrations. He even adopted Mandela as a hero.

I went to listen to Obama speak in Cape Town on his senatorial safari in August 2006, during a visit in which he met fellow Nobel peace laureate and former Cape Town archbishop, Desmond Tutu, and criticized then-president Thabo Mbeki's AIDS policies. During his speech, Obama noted the influence of Mahatma Gandhi and Martin Luther King, Jr., on the anti-apartheid struggle and called for South Africa and the U.S. to assist poorer countries to "build a vibrant civil society." Still, he seemed like a machine politician—he dodged difficult questions, sometimes giving vacuous responses.

Obama's rise to the presidency,

Sarah Hussein Obama, 86, the grandmother of Presidential candidate Barak Obama, holds a photo of her grandson as she awaits the results of Super Tuesday's primary February 5, 2008, in Kogelo, Kenya. (PHOTO PAULA BRONSTEIN/GETTY IMAGES)

however, produced some of the most eloquent and inspirational performances given by any recent politician. His soaring, often biblical, campaign oratory offered a vision of a better, even renewed America, channeling prophets like King and Robert F. Kennedy, who had preceded him. He provided hope and succour to a U.S. on the brink of a recession and mired in two seemingly endless wars that was desperately in need of both. Obama appeared to have a profound sense of justice and empathy. By speaking for those typically invisible to mainstream American politicians, he sought to "give voice to the voiceless, and power to the powerless."

Dreams from our ancestors

In understanding the symbolism of Barack Obama for the African continent, it is essential to revisit his African heritage. His elegant 1995 memoir, *Dreams from My Father,* describes a painful quest for identity triggered by the death of his arrogant and impulsive, albeit determined, Kenyan father in a car crash in 1982. His father had left his family when Obama was only two years old. Obama met his father

only one other time, when he was ten years old. Yet he still idolized his father. Barack Hussein Obama, Sr., who went from being a goat herder as a boy to a student at Harvard University, inspiring Obama to study at his father's alma mater. Barack's father—a civil servant in Kenya—died in penury, as an alcoholic and abuser who had failed to fulfil both his personal ambitions and his family responsibilities. Obama was determined to avoid these flaws, and his firm resolve to become president of the U.S. was borne out of a desire to fulfil the personal ambitions that his father had tragically failed to realize.

Obama identifies with Africa, as is evident from his journey of self-discovery to Kenya as a 26-year old. "The pain I felt was my father's pain. My questions were my brothers' questions. Their struggle, my birthright," he wrote in *Dreams from My Father.* But his father's legacy was also a heavy burden that the young, sensitive Obama struggled to comprehend. He was caught in a cultural limbo, feeling neither wholly American nor wholly African, neither wholly black nor wholly white. On his way to his ancestral continent, Obama toured historic sites in Europe and made the startling observation: "It wasn't that Europe wasn't beautiful…. It just wasn't mine. I felt as if I were living out someone else's romance; the incompleteness of my own history stood between me and the sites I saw like a hard pane of glass." Obama described himself as a "Westerner not entirely at home in the West, an African on his way to a land full of strangers." None of the previous 43 American presidents of European ancestry could have uttered such words. That was what made Obama's ascent to the White House so phenomenal, and of such great interest to Africa.

But like many African-Americans, Obama had a somewhat romanticized view of Africa, which, he notes, "had become an idea more than an actual place, a new promised land, full of ancient traditions and sweeping vistas, noble struggles and talking drums." Once in Kenya, Obama felt his father's seemingly ubiquitous presence. He is nostalgic about the life and times of Obama Sr., seeking to recreate a mythical past that he so badly needed to understand and be a part of. It is with great trepidation and anxiety that Obama approached this visit, as if fearing that his long quest for identity in America would once again be frustrated. Having struggled to become an African-American in order to overcome his painful, fatherless childhood, it is as if he now wants to don the robes of an African identity in order to reconnect with his ancestral homeland. In Kenya, Obama meets and enjoys the extravagant hospitality and warmth of his large extended Kenyan family. He speaks a bit of his native Luo and learns about the corruption and ethnic tensions of Kenyan politics. He rides in *matatus* (rickety taxis) and goes on safari, where he discovers and appreciates the beauty of the historical site of the biblical Garden of Eden. He eats goat curry and ugali (corn meal). He identifies with, and makes connections between, black Americans in Chicago ghettoes and Kenyans in dirt-poor Nairobi shantytowns, and is appalled by the continuing, pernicious socio-economic impact of British colonialism on Kenya.

In a final scene in his ancestral rural hometown of Siaya, Obama breaks down and cries by his father's grave. He is finally "home," writing—perhaps a bit sentimentally—about no longer feeling watched, and not having awkward questions raised about his name or his hair. He had read about Dedan Kimathi, the great Kenyan liberation fighter during the Mau Mau struggle against British colonialism in the 1950s, and could now put a place to the legendary names he had learned about in America.

But Obama has sometimes been guilty of reinforcing stereotypes of the continent similar to those that he condemned in his 1995 memoir. In his 2006 book, *The Audacity of Hope*, Obama talks about Africa in broad-brushed, Afro-pessimistic strokes: "There are times when considering the plight of Africa—the millions racked by AIDS, the constant droughts and famines, the dictatorships, the pervasive corruption, the brutality of twelve-year-old guerril-

las who know nothing but war, wielding machetes or AK-47s—I find myself plunged into cynicism and despair."

It is important to note that Africa seems to represent the lowest priority in the implementation of U.S. foreign policy around the world. The president is rarely directly involved in making Africa policy, which has normally been delegated to the level of assistant secretary of state. The departments of State, Commerce and Defense, as well as the

U.S. Agency for International Development (USAID), do not always pursue coherent or coordinated strategies in Africa. Nevertheless, policy is still carried out in the name of the president, and on issues such as counterterrorism and peacekeeping, Obama often gets directly involved. With these caveats in mind, any analysis of Africa policy must still include the important role of the first American president of African descent. ∎

Four pillars of U.S. Africa policy

Since he became president in 2009, the four pillars of Obama's Africa policy have been to support democratic governance, help manage conflicts, foster economic growth and development, and increase access to quality health and education. However, the administration's rhetoric has often not been matched by action on the ground. Obama has continued several of George W. Bush's (2001–09) most questionable policies. These have militarized American engagement with the continent: "Extraordinary rendition" of terror suspects abroad has continued; 4,000 American military personnel remain in Djibouti to

track terrorists; autocratic regimes in oil-rich Equatorial Guinea, as well as Egypt, Morocco and Ethiopia remain U.S. allies or clients; and officials from the Germany-based U.S. Africa Command (africom) continue to roam the continent. The Obama administration has relied heavily on armed drone strikes in Somalia and Libya as a counterterrorism measure, and these have been responsible for countless civilian casualties and tend to perpetuate anti-Americanism in the region. Surveillance drones have also been used in Mali and Nigeria. At least 100 U.S. Special Forces (soldiers) are operating inside Somalia.

U.S. President Barack Obama delivers remarks after touring Cape Coast Castle in Cape Coast, Ghana, July 11, 2009. (IMAGE BY © SHAWN THEW/EPA/CORBIS)

Obama's non-Gandhian promotion of democratic governance

Six months into his tenure, Obama's visit to the Ghanaian capital of Accra in July 2009 was a 24-hour sojourn that marked the first trip to sub-Saharan Africa by America's first black president. This followed a brief stopover in Egypt a month earlier. In Accra, Obama delivered a major address to the Ghanaian parliament on development and democracy, in which he stressed the interdependence of Africa with the rest of the world, declaring: "The 21st century will be shaped by what happens not just in Rome or Moscow or Washington, but by what happens in Accra as well." He argued that Africans should acknowledge "agency" in resolving the continent's own problems, noting "Africa's future is up to Africans." He also recognized the historical "Curse of Berlin" (which refers to the 1884–85 Conference of Berlin, where a group of mostly European states partitioned Africa): "Yes, a colonial map that made little sense helped to breed conflict. The West has often approached Africa as a patron and source of resources rather than a partner."

Obama emphasized his strong personal ties to Africa by referencing his father's Kenyan background three times and observing: "I have the blood of Africa within me." His message was one of "good governance," although his earlier praise of deceased tyrant of oil-rich Gabon, Omar Bongo, as a peacemaker in June 2009 and his embrace of Arab autocrats appeared to contradict this. He encouraged increased opportunity, better health policy (announcing a $63 billion plan to combat AIDS and malaria), and conflict resolution. The essence of Obama's speech was that Africa needed "strong institutions," not "strongmen." He concluded with a reminder that the continued pursuit of the American civil rights struggle of Martin Luther King, Jr., was inspired by his attendance at Ghana's independence celebrations in 1957.

In Ghana, Obama also visited the Cape Coast Castle, a former slave post with suffocating dungeons from which human cargo was transported to Europe and the Americas. The first black U.S. president visiting the site of a tragic and sordid historical monument to a trade in which an estimated 20 million Africans perished was a particularly poignant image. To parts of America's black community, it revived feelings that Obama was not a "real" African-American— his ancestors, namely his father, came to America willingly by plane in order to study, not forcibly by ship from Africa to be used as slave labor.

Some Africans complained that Obama's early presidential visits to Africa resembled refueling stops on the way to or from more strategic destinations. Kenyans and Nigerians were peeved that he chose to go to Ghana before visiting them. Obama's aides, however, insisted that the Ghana trip was linked to the Group of Eight (G8) summit that the president attended in Italy in the same week, at which issues of critical importance to Africa—food security, climate change, world trade and the global financial crisis—were discussed. The idea was to use Ghana—which held five multiparty elections between 1992 and 2008—as a role model of democratic governance and civil society in promoting development in Africa. The choice of Ghana was also strategic: The country is expected to become a major oil exporter. Recently, about two-thirds of U.S. trade with Africa has been with oil-rich Nigeria, Angola and Gabon.

Egypt

The 2011 revolution in Egypt presented an early test of Obama's Accra commitment to back "strong institutions, not strongmen." Beginning in late January, thousands of peaceful protestors took to the streets and toppled the mummified 30-year dictatorship of American-backed autocrat Hosni Mubarak. After Mubarak resigned in February, Obama praised the "moral force of nonviolence" and reminisced about "Gandhi leading his people down the path of justice."

Mahatma Gandhi's Satyagraha ("soul force") nonviolent methods had, of course, been honed fighting discrimination against South Africa's Indian community. Gandhi had lived in the country for 21 years until 1914, and he returned to his homeland to use nonviolent methods to end British rule in 1947. In his statement on events in Egypt, Obama also quoted King, his fellow Nobel peace laureate and disciple of Gandhian nonviolence, who had noted after attending Kwame Nkrumah's inauguration as prime minister of Ghana in 1957 that "[t]here is something in the soul that cries out for freedom."

Two years prior to Egypt's revolution, in June 2009, Obama delivered a speech in Cairo in which he spoke out forcefully for democratic values in Islamic countries, a powerful message that was somewhat diluted when he stated "each nation gives life to this principle in its own way." This was in stark contrast to his unequivocal support for democratic governance in his Accra speech a month later. Obama's rhetoric supported democracy strongly in sub-Saharan Africa, but his actions demonstrated a preference for autocratic stability over democratic freedom in the Arab world. As Lebanese-American intellectual Fouad Ajami observed: "The Arab liberals were quick to read Barack Obama, and they gave up on him. They saw his comfort with the autocracies, his eagerness to 'engage' and conciliate the dictators."

The Obama administration continued to provide Mubarak's Egypt with $1.5 billion a year. When democratically elected president Mohamed Morsi, an Islamist member of the Muslim Brotherhood, was removed from power in July 2013 by a military coup led by General Abdel Fattah el-Sisi, the Obama administration refused publicly to refer to the change of government as a coup d'état. Even after at least 1,000 Muslim Brotherhood members were killed, the administration made sure that Congress did not halt its support to the Egyptian army, which is required by law after a military coup. Although prior to the coup the administration had threatened "consequences" against any attempt to depose an elected government, the administration's subsequent response was to call for yet another "democratic" transition, not a restoration of the old order. These actions only fueled el-Sisi's political bravado and continuing corruption in the country.

In October 2014, *The New York Times* Editorial Board called for a halt to the delivery of $650 million worth of tanks and fighter planes to Egypt, noting that the country was "in many ways more repressive than it was during the darkest periods of the reign of deposed strongman Hosni Mubarak." The newspaper accused el-Sisi of rigging an election, curbing demonstrations, muzzling the media and civil society, and reportedly using U.S.-built tanks to shell civilian areas in Sinai. Egypt, however, never stopped receiving its $1.5 billion annually in American assistance, while all 49 sub-Saharan African countries combined shared $6.7 billion in 2014.

Despite the pretty poetry heard during the 2008 presidential campaign, Obama has so far ruled in pragmatic prose. He is a dyed-in-the-wool politician, cut from the same cloth as his Democratic Party predecessor, Bill Clinton (1993–2001). Both men demonstrated a willingness to sacrifice core principles at the altar of political survival. Just before Tunisia's Zine el-Abidine Ben Ali's 23-year rule was cut short by a popular uprising in January 2011, Obama's administration had approved $12 million in military aid to the regime. Not wanting for America to be caught again on the wrong side of history, Obama belatedly threw in his lot with the Egyptian people a few months later. Obama has now clearly decided to support a "strongman" in Cairo rather than help to build "strong institutions."

Kenya

Johnnie Carson, the former U.S. ambassador to Kenya, Zimbabwe and Uganda, intervened in Kenya's March 2013 election by seeming to urge Kenyans not to vote for Uhuru Kenyatta and William Ruto, who had both been charged with, but not convicted of, crimes against humanity by the International Criminal Court (ICC). A month before the polls, Carson threatened that "actions have consequences," contradicting Obama's statement days before that the U.S. would not favor any candidate in the

Sudanese President Omar al-Bashir gestures as he addresses his supporters, during a visit in Heglig, Sudan, April 23, 2012. (IMAGE BY © STR/EPA/CORBIS)

forthcoming election. This interference in the sovereign responsibility of Kenyan citizens is believed to have contributed to swaying the closely fought presidential vote in favor of Kenyatta.

Pax Americana trumps Pax Africana

Moving from democratic governance to the security field, American security interests have trumped promoting democracy and African security priorities. By 2013, the U.S. africom cost $300 million a year, with 100 training programs and exercises in 35 African countries. The command was involved in the North Atlantic Treaty Organization (NATO) campaign in Libya between March and October 2011, and is currently combating piracy and oil bunkering (theft) on the Gulf of Guinea, as well as fighting narco-trafficking in West Africa. U.S. Special Forces have also been deployed to the Great Lakes region of Africa to hunt Ugandan warlord Joseph Kony. Washington did provide $355 million to the 22,000-strong African Union (AU) peacekeeping mission in Somalia (AMISOM); however, many African armies continue to complain that they need more help with logistics and equipment, and not counterterrorism training. In post-conflict Liberia, the U.S. also led efforts

to train a 2,000-strong national army and national police force. But since 2006 the government of Ellen Johnson Sirleaf has struggled to receive concrete donor assistance to complete its critical security-sector reform efforts.

In the Horn of Africa, Obama appointed General Scott Gration as his special envoy to Sudan in March 2009. Though the U.S. president and many of his officials vowed to be tough on the regime of Omar al-Bashir in Khartoum, discordant voices have been heard. Former Secretary of State Hillary Clinton and Gration favored accommodation with Khartoum; Susan Rice— then the U.S. permanent representative at the United Nations (UN), who had reportedly opposed action against the perpetrators of genocide in Rwanda in 1994 while serving on Bill Clinton's National Security Council—called for stronger action. Gration was widely seen as out of his depth and not conversant with the intricacies of the treacherous Sudanese landscape. In June 2009, Senator Russ Feingold (D-WI), chair of the U.S. Senate subcommittee on African affairs, along with six other senators, wrote to Obama warning him that Khartoum had been an untrustworthy ally in the past and that pressure, such as a willingness to impose sanctions, was needed to deal with the regime. Princeton Lyman, a former U.S. ambassador to South Africa and Nigeria, was dispatched to Sudan in 2010, and soon replaced Gration as special envoy to Sudan. In October 2010 Washington chaired talks on Abyei in Addis Ababa, Ethiopia, demonstrating a willingness to remain involved in the peace process.

Four months earlier, Obama had signed into law the "Lord's Resistance Army (LRA) Disarmament and Northern Uganda Recovery Act," making it American policy to kill or capture Kony and to defeat his rebellion in northern Uganda. One year prior, in 2009, Gration had met in Khartoum and Juba with Sudanese and South Sudanese officials to help determine the deadlines for elections, referenda, popular consultations and border demarcation in preparation for a referendum on South Sudanese independence in 2011. By September 2010 Clinton had already begun talking about the "inevitable" secession of South Sudan. During the UN General Assembly in New York in the same month, Obama met with Sudanese vice-president, Ali Osman Taha, and president of South Sudan, Salva Kiir. Throughout the meeting Obama insisted that the Comprehensive Peace Agreement (CPA) be fully implemented in a timely fashion. Two months later, then-Senator John Kerry (D-MA),

traveled to Khartoum and informed al-Bashir that Washington would remove Sudan from its list of state sponsors of terrorism if he allowed a referendum to take place in the south in January 2011, a promise on which the U.S. would later renege. Washington also promised the restoration of diplomatic relations and an annulment of part of Sudan's $40 billion external debt, but as of this writing neither promise had been fulfilled.

In West Africa, the Obama administration played an important role in Mali and Nigeria, focused largely on counterterrorism. Throughout 2012, Washington consistently warned against a premature deployment of an African-led International Support Mission in Mali (AFISMA), doubting its capacity to rout Islamist and Tuareg militias in the north. The U.S. proposed a two-step process for AFISMA to train the Malian army before engaging in peacekeeping activities. Washington spent $41 million between 2009 and 2012 on training the military in Mali, including a future putschist, Captain Amadou Sanogo. Prior to the Malian coup in March 2012, the U.S. shifted resources from Mali to Mauritania and Niger because it felt that Mali's military brass were not in line with American interests, specifically on counterterrorism and antinarcotics. Hence, even after a French-led

intervention in Mali in January 2013, Washington remained wary of supporting the Malian army and AFISMA. It is also critical to note that it was the sophisticated weaponry from Muammar Qadhafi's Libya that had enabled radical Islamists—who had been fighting in that country during the NATO-led campaign—to destabilize northern Mali.

In the end, Washington provided logistical support to France's deployment in Mali. By 2013, the Obama administration had deployed drones to Niger to track militants in Mali, and a small number of soldiers to operate on the ground. The U.S. further pressured Algeria, which has historically been wary of French influence in the region, to back an African-led military intervention in Mali, following a visit by Secretary of State Hillary Clinton to Algiers in October 2012.

A real disappointment of Obama's presidency for Africa is that he has continued to support, rather than challenge, French neocolonial actions in Mali, Côte d'Ivoire, the Central African Republic (CAR) and Libya. Obama could have lent greater support to regional efforts through the UN in all four cases by supporting early deployment of AFISMA in Mali, bolstering the Economic Community of West African States (ecowas)-initiated UN mission in Côte d'Ivoire, accelerating the "rehatting" of the Economic Community of Central African States (eccas) mission into a UN-sponsored one in CAR, and supporting AU mediation and the deployment of a UN peacekeeping force in Libya.

Nigeria, a country that has traditionally provided the U.S. with about 10 percent of its oil, was an important part of U.S. counterterrorism activities in Africa. The Nigerian government under Goodluck Jonathan, however, demonstrated rank incompetence and callous indifference in tackling the terrorist group Boko Haram—incompetence that became abundantly clear after the militant group kidnapped 276 schoolgirls in April 2014. As of October 2014, the group had killed over 13,000 Nigerian civilians since 2009. The Nigerian army has struggled with equipment, logistical and other capabilities, and the $6 bil-

Nigerian staff of Kaduna Polytechnic protest over the abducted Chibok school girls in Kaduna, Nigeria, June 2, 2014. (IMAGE BY © STR/EPA/CORBIS)

lion annual security budget that Abuja claimed to be spending, was clearly not reaching the army. Washington began providing Jonathan's government with surveillance and intelligence assistance in its battle against Boko Haram in May 2014, in part due to its links to Islamists in Mali and Somalia.

Libya

In an August 2014 interview with *The New York Times,* Obama described the aftermath of NATO's Libya intervention in 2011 as his "biggest foreign policy regret," noting that "there has to be a much more aggressive effort to rebuild societies that didn't have any civic traditions." The intervention was spearheaded by France and Britain; the U.S. "led from behind." Libya reinforced the view that the Obama administration still considered parts of Africa as European "spheres of influence," to be largely managed by two medium-sized European former Great Powers. In the UN Security Council, Britain and France have been the most hyperactive members, drafting all the resolutions concerning 11 of 15 African cases on the council agenda, with the U.S. "holding the pen" in two other African cases.

That the AU could not implement its peace plan in Libya in 2011 was due largely to the refusal of the rebel National Transitional Council (NTC) to negotiate with Qadhafi's regime, as well as to NATO's adoption of a military approach to resolving the crisis. Obama was, however, able to convince the leaders of Africa's two aspiring hegemons — Nigeria and South Africa — to vote for the intervention on the Security Council. (South Africa later regretted the decision, and became a vociferous critic of the abuse of a resolution intended to protect civilians becoming a pursuit of a "regime change" agenda.) Washington informed AU officials in April 2011 that any cease-fire in Libya would be contingent on Qadhafi's departure from power. Along with France and Britain, the U.S. encouraged the NTC's intransigence, even as AU mediators — led by South African president Jacob Zuma — shuttled back and forth between both parties. Having at first

denied an agenda of "regime change," Obama finally conceded in October 2011 that "we…had to make sure that Muammar Qadhafi didn't stay there…. Qadhafi had more American blood on his hands than any individual other than Osama bin Laden."

The AU was denied a chance to implement its March 2011 "road map" and a July 2011 "Framework Agreement" calling for a cease-fire, transition to democracy and deployment of a UN peacekeeping force. The Western-led Libya Contact Group subverted AU mediation efforts by declaring that it would deal only with UN Special Envoy Abdel Elah al-Khatib, who, unlike AU mediators, had never met Qadhafi, nor presented a comprehensive peace proposal to both parties. Out of NATO's 28 members, only eight countries agreed to take part in the bombing raids in Libya. Germany not only abstained from the UN Security Council resolution that sanctioned the NATO attacks — it also declined to contribute to the military mission. Poland, too, refused to join the intervention, critizing it as driven by a thirst for Libyan oil.

Following Qadhafi's assassination in his hometown of Sirte in October 2011, a myth developed in American policy circles that NTC horsemen had ridden into Tripoli to establish a new dawn of multiparty democracy. This was most eloquently expressed by Susan Rice, the U.S. permanent representative to the UN at the time, who noted that the NATO mission had put Libya back on a path to freedom: "This closes what I think history will judge to be a proud chapter in the Security Council's history." Nothing could have been further from the truth.

Murmurings about the NTC's nepotism and corruption were already growing louder within months of Qadhafi's ouster. That the assassination of the NTC's military commander, Abdel Fattah Younes, still remains unexplained three years later, suggests that the revolution had started to implode even before it had had a chance to consolidate its power. The massacre of scores of black African migrants by NTC forces further damaged a regime that callously

Libyan leader Muammar Qadhafi stands outside his tent during his meeting with the African delegation, who arrived in Libya to try to negotiate a truce between Qadhafi's forces and rebels seeking to oust him, April 10, 2011, in Tripoli, Libya. (PHOTO BY XINHUA/GAMMA-RAPHO VIA GETTY IMAGES)

disregarded the principle of "responsibility to protect" — the justification for the NATO intervention that had put them in power. All the Western posse seemed to care about was restoring credibility in the region following the fall of Western-backed autocrats in Egypt and Tunisia. The challenges of post-conflict reconstruction and stability were not properly addressed. Qadhafi was the glue that had held this motley crew of secularists, Islamists and ethnic-based factions together. With his demise and with growing chaos in Libya dominated by local warlords, military strongmen and Islamists, Afghanistan and Iraq may well be the future that awaits post-Qadhafi Libya. Indeed, by October 2014, Libya had become a powder keg divided between two rival governments in Tripoli and Tobruk, and political assassinations continued unabated.

On a more positive note, the Obama administration has consistently supported UN peacekeeping in Africa, providing 28% of the UN's assessed contributions in this area (though Washington underfunded UN peacekeeping by $350 million in its FY2014 budget) and backing the creation of new peacekeeping missions in Mali and the CAR. The Obama administration also contributed generously to humanitarian crises in South Sudan and CAR in 2014.

Supporting the socioeconomic pillars

In the socioeconomic sphere, Obama's New Alliance for Food Security and Nutrition, launched in 2012, sought to create about 650,000 jobs and benefit over 5 million small-holder farmers. By August 2014, however, only 37,000 jobs had been created, though 3 million small-holder farmers had reportedly been reached. Civil society critics argued that the program has so far benefited large foreign agribusiness at the expense of African small-holders. They accused the project of forcing African governments to change laws in favor of foreign investors, and noted the lack of effective monitoring and accountability mechanisms in the program to measure their impact on hunger and poverty.

In education, various U.S. programs sought to improve early-grade reading for 500,000 children in Nigeria, deliver emergency education to 150,000 children in South Sudan, and provide scholarships and other support to girls in Liberia, the Democratic Republic of the Congo (DRC), Mozambique, Tanzania and Côte d'Ivoire. Obama also inaugurated a Young African Leaders Initiative, wherein 500 young African leaders under the age of 35 are provided with six weeks of intensive executive leadership training, networking and skill building by being embedded within organizations focusing on business and entrepreneurship, civic leadership, and/or public management. The program also secures internship placements in African private and public institutions. Some $10 million is provided by the U.S. government for building businesses and social enterprises and enhancing nongovernmental organisations (NGOs) in Africa.

In the area of public health, Obama cut AIDS funding to Africa by $214 million in 2012, somewhat undermining one of the few successes of U.S. policy toward the continent under the previous Bush administration. Bush had spent $18.8 billion through the President's Emergency Plan for AIDS Relief (PEPFAR), which provided treatment to 1.7 million people and care to 6.6 million AIDS patients between 2003 and 2008. The Obama administration, however, increased the number of people receiving treatment for AIDS from 1.7 million in 2008 to 6.7 million by 2013, and provided testing and counseling to over 12.8 million pregnant women that same year. The president's request for FY2015, nevertheless, proposed a $300 million cut to the Global Fund to Fight AIDS, Tuberculosis, and Malaria, although generous funding was still requested ($8 billion, down from $8.4 billion in 2014).

In October 2014, Obama's administration began deploying a 3,000-strong military contingent to build health facilities in Liberia and Senegal to treat victims of Ebola, a disease that had killed over 5,000 people in Liberia, Sierra Leone and Guinea. Obama also urged Japan and the West to provide a more urgent and generous response to the crisis. How successfully the Ebola crisis is managed could contribute greatly to determining the legacy of Obama's Africa policy. ∎

The 2014 U.S.-Africa summit

In August 2014 President Obama hosted over 40 African leaders in Washington, DC, in the first ever U.S.-Africa summit. However, the meeting was effectively a talking shop unlikely to produce concrete results.

In hosting this summit, the U.S. was merely catching up with China, Japan, France and the EU, all of which convene periodic meetings with African leaders. There was a sense that Washington was particularly concerned about Beijing's growing presence on the continent, which has made China Africa's largest bilateral trading partner with over $200 billion in commerce. The summit focused on investment, peace and regional stability and governance. A U.S.-Africa Business Forum was also convened. Other sideline events included fora with youth, faith-based, and civil society groups; there were also sessions on trade, women, health, food security and wildlife trafficking.

As the presidential motorcades swept down Pennsylvania Avenue and Africa's flamboyant first ladies paraded their haute couture, the summit was dogged by controversy. There were damaging allegations of Obama treating African leaders like supplicant "tribal chiefs" being summoned to Washington to pay obeisance to America's "commander-in-chief." Unlike other African summits with Japan and China, Obama refused to have any bilateral meetings with the 40 African leaders. Following much criticism, Vice President Joe Biden agreed to meet with the leaders of South Africa and Nigeria.

In a further breach of protocol, American cabinet ministers were asked to host African leaders at private dinners without Obama's presence. Leaders from Zimbabwe, Sudan and Eritrea were excluded from the summit for not being in "good standing" with Washington, even as autocrats from Gambia, Burkina Faso, Equatorial Guinea, Congo-Brazzaville and Chad made the guest list.

There were other discordant notes. Senegal's Macky Sall and Tanzania's Jakaya Kikwete criticized the American media for continuing to stereotype Africa. Sudanese billionaire, Mo Ibrahim, berated U.S. companies for dodging taxes in their African operations. Hundreds of demonstrators protested against the leaders of Ethiopia and the DRC. Even the meal that Obama hosted for his African guests was not at the level of an official state dinner.

Part of the problem of past African summits with external powers like China is that the continent's leaders have failed to define their own interests. The U.S. summit followed a similar ignominious pattern. The gathering saw pledges of $14 billion from America's private sector. Obama's "Power

Africa," which pledged $7 billion of government funding but included only 6 out of 54 African countries, also un-convincingly promised to provide electricity to 20 million Africans two years after Obama would have left office. Only $285 million had been specifically allocated to this project by March 2014. An African Peacekeeping Rapid Response Partnership (aprrp) was announced with a price tag of only $110 million. As with any such bazaars, Africans should sensibly adopt the mantra "buyer beware," as these investments are unlikely to materialize. Leaders should instead insist on the American saying: "Show me the money!" The fact that no substantive final document was produced from the 2014 Washington summit was the clearest sign that the gathering represented a triumph of symbolism over substance.

Strident opponents in certain corners of the U.S. government, media and general public have clearly affected the president's ability to deliver on many promises to Africa. The control of both houses of Congress by the Republicans after the November 2014 elections will make this challenge even more difficult.

Concluding reflections

As Obama prepared to send more troops to Afghanistan, word came through in October 2009 that he had been awarded the Nobel Peace Prize. As previously noted, some of his early foreign policy actions unfortunately followed in the hawkish footsteps of his predecessor, George W. Bush: Obama ordered targeted strikes on suspected terrorists, averaging one drone strike every four days versus Bush's average of one strike every 40 days. Bush ordered about 50 drone strikes in eight years; Obama ordered 400 strikes in four-and-a-half years.

Some have been forced to ask whether Obama's foreign policy could come to represent "Bush with a smile." Stung by criticisms from conservative, prejudiced "birthers" that he was not born in the U.S., Obama almost seems determined to prove that he is more American than anyone. His perpetual

U.S. President Barack Obama (front center) joins other leaders during the family photo at the US-Africa Leaders Summit, at the State Department in Washington DC, August 6, 2014.
(IMAGE BY © MICHAEL REYNOLDS/EPA/CORBIS)

quest for identity and the need to belong and be accepted as an American sometimes appears to be driving his martial fervor.

Moving forward, it is important that pro-Africa lobbyists work closely with legislators in the U.S. Congress, as well as NGOs, as they did in order to sanction apartheid South Africa in the 1980s. The tens of thousands of highly educated Africans in America need to be mobilized to build a viable constituency for Africa. Obama should also substantively and consistently support UN peacekeeping in Africa, as well as work to strengthen African regional organizations. The U.S. needs to eliminate deleterious agricultural subsidies to farmers and allow free access to its markets for Africa's agricultural products. Doing so would take advantage of the potential trade with an African market of over 1 billion consumers with a fast-growing middle class. U.S. exports to Africa tripled from $7 billion in 2001 to $21 billion in 2011, though 75 percent of American imports from Africa still consisted of oil, while the African Growth and Opportunity Act (AGOA) accounted for only 2% of U.S. trade.

One of the most important recent developments in U.S. policy toward Africa is that, for the first time since 1973, Nigeria—traditionally one of the top five U.S. oil suppliers—did not export oil to the U.S. between July

and September 2014. America's shale revolution has put the U.S. on a path to overtake Saudi Arabia as the world's largest producer of petroleum by December 2014. The drop in U.S. oil imports has also affected Algeria, Libya and Angola, which could have serious implications for African oil exporters, who would be forced to diversfy supplies to Asia, and also could allow the U.S. to promote democracy more consistently in these countries.

That Obama's first lengthy visit to Africa occurred in June/July 2013, one year after his reelection, underlined the continuing low priority of the continent for U.S. foreign policy. There remains a lingering suspicion that the U.S. president mainly views Africa as "Europe's backyard" that is to be left to old colonial powers, France and Britain, to fix. As an individual, Obama remains popular throughout Africa, where many are proud that one of their own sits in the most powerful office in the world. However, the early luster of Obamamania has faded as Africans began to realize that even a powerful leader with close family ties to the continent cannot reverse five-and-a-half decades of "malign neglect."

The tragedy of this tale is that the enduring continuity of U.S. foreign policy has trumped the early idealism of an extraordinary individual of African ancestry. ∎

discussion questions

1. Why was the African continent swept by a wave of "Obamamania" following Barack Obama's election as U.S. president in 2008? Why is Obama's African ancestry important to his engagement with Africa? Were the expectations that Obama would transform U.S. Africa policy unrealistic? Why has this optimism now diminished?

2. What more can be done by the U.S. government to support democracy, peacekeeping, and socioeconomic development in Africa? Is the U.S.-Africa summit likely to be a mechanism for promoting stronger U.S.-Africa relations? What impact might the reduction in U.S. oil imports have on democracy-promotion and American commitment to the continent?

3. Why does U.S. policy toward Africa continue to be dominated by a focus on the "war against terror"? Have African security interests been undermined by American security priorities?

4. Why has the Obama administration promoted democratic governance in Africa so inconsistently? Is there a difference between democracy promotion in North Africa and in sub-Saharan Africa?

5. Has the U.S. supported peacekeeping in Africa effectively enough? Has the Obama administration deferred too much to French interests in authorizing and backing some of these missions?

6. What have been the main achievements of the Obama administration in the areas of health, education and socioeconomic development in Africa? Will the fight against Ebola divert resources from tackling HIV/AIDS, tuberculosis, and malaria? Will the Young African Leaders Initiative produce transformative results?

7. What is likely to be the lasting legacy of the Obama administration in Africa? How can a broad and effective Africa lobby be built in Congress, the humanitarian community and civil society in the U.S.?

---

suggested readings

Adebajo, Adekeye. **The Curse of Berlin: Africa After the Cold War.** New York: Columbia University Press, 2010. 414pp. The book assesses the key challenges involving security, hegemony, and unity in post-Cold War Africa, including U.S. policy toward Africa and Obama's significance and role in the continent.

Adebajo, Adekeye (ed.). **Africa's Peacemakers: Nobel Peace Laureates of African Descent.** London: Zed Books, 2013. 330 pp. The book assesses the 14 Nobel peace laureates of African descent, including three chapters that examine Barack Obama's Nobel peace prize within the context of other laureates and great Pan-Africans.

Anyaso, Claudia E. (ed.). **Fifty Years of U.S. Africa Policy.** Washington, DC: Association for Diplomatic Studies and Training, 2011. (paperback). Reflective essays from the U.S. Assistant Secretaries for African Affairs in the State Department between 1958 and 2008.

Clough, Michael. **Free at Last? U.S. Policy Toward Africa and the End of the Cold War.** New York, Council on Foreign Relations Press, 1992. The book analyzes past U.S. foreign policy choices toward Africa, raises the issue of Africa's diminishing significance to American interests and describes how it can be fixed by prioritizing promotion of democracy and economic development.

Lewis, Peter M. **Nigeria: Assessing Risks to Stability.** Washington, DC: Center for Strategic and International Studies, 2011. (PDF). Detailed assessment of security challenges in Nigeria.

Mendell, David. Obama: **From Promise to Power.** New York: HarperCollins, 2007. 406 pp. An insightful biography by an Obama "insider."

Obama, Barack. **Dreams from My Father: A Story of Race and Inheritance.** New York: Three Rivers, 1995, 453 pp. Barack Obama's memoir of a painful quest for identity in America and Africa.

Schraeder, Peter J. **United States Foreign Policy toward Africa: Incrementalism, Crisis and Change.** Cambridge: Cambridge University Press, 1994. 376 pp. This book offers comprehensive analyses of U.S. foreign policy toward Africa since World War II.

Weissman, Stephen R. "In Syria, Unlearned Lessons From Libya." **In These Times**, April 19, 2013. (online). Solid analysis of the complex dynamics and difficulties of unsuccessful peacemaking efforts in Libya.

TO LEARN MORE ABOUT THIS TOPIC AND TO ACCESS WEB LINKS TO RESOURCES GO TO www.greatdecisions.org

Syria's refugee crisis
by Rochelle Davis

Rmaining residents of the besieged Yarmouk camp near Damascus, Syria, wait to receive food aid distributed by the UN Relief and Works Agency (UNRWA), the first aid allowed in after four months of total closure, on Jan. 31, 2014. (REUTERS /HANDOUT /LANDOV)

Over three years after the popular uprising against the government of Bashar al-Assad, the number of official Syrian refugees registered with the United Nations High Commission for Refugees (UNHCR) hit 3 million in August 2014. Combined with the estimated 6 to 9 million internally displaced persons (IDPs) inside Syria, nearly half of Syria's population of 22 million have lost or fled from their homes. Upwards of 200,000 people have been killed since the March 2011 uprising degraded into a full-scale civil war. Syrian refugee camps are regularly in the news, but house only 16% of the refugees—the remainder live with and among local communities in the surrounding countries of Iraq, Jordan, Lebanon and Turkey.

Syria is now largely divided. What was once a mid-to-low-income country with rich farmlands and an established manufacturing base has witnessed its major urban neighborhoods and infrastructure gutted. The Assad regime maintains rule over Damascus, the still-functioning capital. Assad's troops have fought to maintain control of the western part of the country: the corridor to Lebanon, the road north connecting Damascus to all of the major cities and the Mediterranean coastline. Control of the remainder of the country has shifted between the regime, militias (such as the Free Syrian Army, or FSA and local groups), and extremist groups, such as the Al Qaeda-linked al-Nusra Front and the Islamic State (also known as the Islamic State in Iraq and Syria, or ISIS).

ROCHELLE DAVIS *is an associate professor of Anthropology in the Center for Contemporary Arab Studies, School of Foreign Service, Georgetown University. Her book,* Palestinian Village Histories: Geographies of the Displaced *(Stanford University Press, 2011), was co-winner of the Middle East Studies Association's Albert Hourani Book Award. Her current research focuses on Iraqi, Syrian and Palestinian refugees and war.*

Dividing Syrians into two camps—regime and anti-regime—is too simple. Some Syrians participate in the fighting out of belief or because they are conscripted, some stay and support family members on the battlefields, and others try and avoid all engagement with any authority or oppositional movement. Some Syrians remain committed to nonviolent action, struggling against the regime and the militant opposition, and in particular against the oppositional Islamist jihadi groups. Many more flee with their families to areas they perceive to be safe, whether inside or outside the country. Most Syrians today find it difficult to champion a side, and instead lament the destruction of the country and their lives and livelihoods.

In large part, mass migration has occurred because Syrians' lives have been dominated by violence for the past three years, whether from the regime, anti-regime militias or jihadi militants. Ongoing violence and insecurity have resulted in the breakdown of general services and infrastructure. To an extent, the surrounding countries have kept their borders open to Syrians fleeing from the war-torn country at significant costs to their own citizens. The influx of refugees to Syria's neighbors means strained funds for service provisions, development, the community's social fabric, the local economy and national security. Though the refugees' presence is not all negative, the influx of such large numbers affects everyone in material and nonmaterial ways. ∎

Before the uprising

Syria gained independence in 1946. The country shifted between brief periods of civilian and military rule until a 1963 coup d'état put the Ba'ath party in power. Struggles among the party's leadership continued until Hafez al-Assad became president in 1971, a post he held until death.

The one-party political system and the Emergency Laws of 1963 ensured strict crackdowns on any type of political organizing, and violence at the hands of secret police caused many to fear their government. Following Assad's death in 2000, his son, Bashar, took control of the government and became president. At first, Bashar's rule was welcomed as an economic and political opening, but only a select urban elite was given privileged access to economic invest-

AUTHOR'S NOTE: *The research for this work was funded by Georgetown University's Global Human Development Initiative and conducted with Abbie Taylor, Research Associate at the Institute for the Study of International Migration, Georgetown University. I have benefitted from conversations with no fewer than 100 people: Syrians, Palestinians, Jordanians, Lebanese, Turks, and local and international aid workers. I am also grateful to the insights of two colleagues, Abbie Taylor and Asli Ilgit, with whom I have published similar work before. Traces of their analysis, ideas, and writing appear in this essay. While this is a work in progress by virtue of the subject and the shifting political arena, all errors are my own. Interviews quoted in this essay were conducted during May–June 2013 and March 2014.*

ment opportunities, resulting in uneven economic development that amplified basic structural inequalities.

A drought from 2006 to 2010 furthered the economic divide and forced around 300,000 Syrians to leave their rural homes and find work in regional urban centers. According to journalist and scholar Francesca de Châtel, figures from 2004 show that the northeastern regions of Aleppo, Deir ez-Zor, Hassakeh, Idlib and Raqqa accounted for 58.1% of the country's rural and urban poverty.

And the ever-present security regime remained entrenched. "Our biggest problem was that all of the people were afraid of the security forces," a taxi driver from the Damascus suburbs explained. "We were scared to speak about the state, or anything related to politics."

Knowing the political and socioeconomic history of modern Syria is crucial to understanding why the uprising started, how the regime decided to respond and the differences in refugees that started flowing out of the country in June 2011. It should come as no surprise that Syrians living under repression and inequality in provincial cities like Homs, Hama and Dara'a started the March 2011 uprising and its calls for greater freedom. "A person was not able to say a word—all we could do was get enough bread to survive and thank God for it. Bribes and patrimonialism, these things were our daily lives—it was something natural like eating and drinking and breathing. Unfortunately, we got used to it and we didn't ever

question it," said one 24-year-old man from Dara'a. Built on a long history of resisting state policies, it was citizens disenfranchised by government cronyism, and those displaced by the drought, who went out to the streets in unprecedented numbers to call for change.

Urban areas echoed, amplified and organized those initial calls for freedom. The widespread nature of peaceful demonstrations mirrored earlier Arab Spring movements in Tunisia, Egypt, Yemen, Libya and Bahrain. The Syrian government responded to these demonstrations in their traditional way: widespread arrests, interrogations and torture, paid informants, secret police and the use of live ammunition to kill and dissuade protesters in the streets. The people remained in the streets, though, and began organizing ways to counter the regime.

"The young people developed their struggle from their local society and their own resistance to the system. We witnessed the faithful and faithless together," a person on the ground in Syria said. "But the elite of the dissident political movements held back from embracing this youth movement. I heard them say, 'Don't the people know how awful the regime is? Why did they revolt against it?' It was as if they were blaming the people for inciting the regime against them."

As the uprising continued, the regime announced a number of concessions, such as releasing political prisoners, lifting the emergency laws and agreeing to hold talks in an effort to begin a formal dialogue. Still, violent crackdowns on any form of anti-government expression continued. Over 300 members of the government party resigned in April 2011 due to a sustained military assault on the southern city of Dara'a. By June, estimates were that 1,400 people had been killed and over 10,000 arrested, and in July and August, military assaults began across almost all parts of Syria.

The FSA was created in summer 2011 by defectors from the Syrian army. An expatriate political movement emerged as well but remained ineffectual and regularly changed its leaders and mission. Meanwhile, the Syrian regime maintained control of most of the country through 2012, but diverting resources to crush the uprising meant that other governmental responsibilities were neglected. In the first year of the uprising, agriculture, food subsidies and poverty assistance programs inside Syria dwindled in favor of military priorities, and sanctions weakened already limited state services. The U.S. trade and economic sanctions, like the Syria Accountability Act of 2004, were tightened. The European Union (EU), the Arab League and Turkey implemented sanctions that limited oil the Syrian regime could export, forcing Assad to draw from Syria's hard currency reserves. On the ground, reports indicated that the army found it increasingly difficult to keep its machinery and weapons working and faced increasingly low morale. Many Syrians outside Damascus and Aleppo were distanced from the government's once all-encompassing services and had to find their own basic supplies. In areas under rebel control, services such as water, electricity, health care, education and government employment came to an abrupt end. Trade came close to a standstill.

Outside influences have complicated the situation inside Syria. The Syrian government has received economic and military support from Iran, Russia and Hezbollah, the Lebanese Shi'a political/military group. Various groups of opposition fighters have received assistance from regional Arab governments and the U.S. has provided nonlethal aid to the FSA. Extremist Islamists receive aid from states and wealthy patrons in the region. As the situation deteriorated, the U.S. formed a coalition to bomb ISIS fighters and began supplying weapons and training to moderate rebels. ∎

From uprising to refugee movement

The regime's attacks during 2011 pushed a small, steady flow of Syrians out of their homes to other parts of the country. Refugees also began trickling across borders to Turkey and Jordan. Another factor that pushed Syrians out of their homes was the opposition militias' lack of organization and discipline. Those who fled reported stealing, looting and other extortionate behavior in rebel-controlled areas. This may have been because these fighters had no bases, little financial or material support and no nearby families to provide for them.

In September 2011, Turkey began setting up refugee camps: six along its southeastern border for over 7,000 Syrians. By the end of that year, Turkey was the largest refugee host. Refugees continued crossing the border to Lebanon, Turkey and Jordan, and each country tried new policies for addressing the refugee presence and local needs.

First-wave refugees often fled across borders and used connections they had prior to the conflict. The tens of thousands who fled into Hatay province in southern Turkey and into northern Jor-

A giant Syrian flag is held by the crowd during a protest against President Bashar al-Assad in the city center of Hama, July 29, 2011. Syrians in their thousands took to the streets nationwide for the 17th consecutive Friday to demand an end to Assad's 11-year rule. (IMAGE BY © HO/REUTERS/CORBIS)

dan most often stayed with relatives. In Lebanon, Syrians used labor relations (Lebanon has long had a huge Syrian migrant labor population) and connections made hosting Lebanese during Israeli attacks in 2006. In addition, the long history of Syrian involvement in Lebanon from the late 1970s has played a factor in why people go to Lebanon and how Lebanese respond to Syrians. The refugees brought with them some of their assets, and may have even had valid passports and a sense that this move was temporary. Whatever the host country, those fleeing in this wave would often move back home when the fighting died

Syrian President Bashar Al-Assad addresses the parliament in Damascus, Syria, March 30, 2011. Bashar Al-Assad delivered his first address to the nation since the unprecedented dissent erupted two weeks ago. (PHOTO BY XINHUA/GAMMA-RAPHO VIA GETTY IMAGES)

down, or certain family members would move back and others would stay.

But many others had made political choices that meant that their ability to return was only possible if Assad fell. "In order for the country to stabilize, they have to hold Bashar al-Assad accountable for his crimes that he committed to his people and land," explained a 45-year-old man from the Idlib area. "If the world had held Hafez al-Assad accountable for his crimes when he killed 20,000 people in Hama in 1982, then Bashar al-Assad wouldn't dare to kill his people these days. But because he saw his dad do this once, he's doing whatever he wants right now. But because he saw his dad do this once, he's doing whatever he wants right now."

Jordan addressed the first wave of Syrian refugees in the way it had responded to Iraqi refugees since 2006, allowing them access to both governmental and nongovernmental services. The Jordanian government set up temporary refugee centers near its northern border, something not done for Iraqi refugees who came in the tens of thousands in 2006–09, many of whom remain. But most of the Syrian refugees found places to stay with relatives in the northern border towns and villages.

A former radio broadcaster in his 50s described his decision to flee as one of principle. "When the revolution started, I empathized with the people of Dara'a who rose up for their dignity and for the sake of their children who were arrested and tortured only because of silly graffiti on the walls," he said. "Like usual, those of us in the media remained silent about the media lies we were asked to read and the injustice to our people. As it went on and on, I was ashamed to say that I was working for them. I didn't know what I should do with the truth, but the only thing that made me stay with them was my financial situation. Frankly, I have nothing except that salary to live from. But despite all those difficulties, I couldn't stay with them, and I decided to defect from this despicable gang. I came here with my family to Jordan because I have relatives here, and they can help me until I find a job."

Second wave

The second wave of Syrian refugees started crossing the borders daily in spring 2012. Numbers reached over 450,000 total refugees by the end of the year and around 2.5 million—over 10% of the population—were displaced inside the country. March and April marked a particularly severe exodus, which took place following a number of Syrian regime offensives. (Turkey recorded over 23,000 refugees arriving in April alone.) All countries kept their borders open, though periodic closures of Turkish border crossings meant that refugees amassed in areas close to the border, and Turkey often sent supplies to them across the border.

In the northeast of Syria, the area with the largest number of Kurds, the uprising against the regime allowed for the more open development of Kurdish political relations with other Kurds in Turkey and Iraq. Syrian Kurds, who had long been repressed by the Syrian government, suddenly found themselves freer than ever before after regime forces withdrew from the northeast part of the country in July 2012. For a brief time until 2014, Kurds organized militias and local councils, which allowed them to keep the area's infrastructure functioning. Resources in the area include a number of dams on the Tigres and Euphrates rivers and oil-drilling facilities. The land is also home to rich agriculture and mercantile communities like Hassakeh, Raqqa and Deir ez-Zor. But fighting in the area forced refugees to begin moving to Iraq. Refugee flows continued until the present, particularly because of the rise of ISIS in Syria, but the group's spread into Iraq has caused internal displacement there as well.

As refugees increased into the tens of thousands, Jordan requested that the

Syrian refugees are seen at the Al Za'atari refugee camp in the Jordanian city of Mafraq, near the border with Syria, on Aug. 6, 2012. The camp is one of many set up along the border between Jordan and Syria under the management of the United Nations High Commissioner for Refugees (UNHCR) and with the help of local charity groups. (IMAGE BY © MOHAMMAD ABU GHOSH/XINHUA PRESS/CORBIS)

Example of Yarmouk Camp for Palestinian Refugees in Syria

Yarmouk refugee camp is a southern suburb of Damascus and had hosted the largest collective of Palestinian refugees in Syria, with a population of around 160,000 with a similar number of Syrians. Palestinians in Syria, most of whose families have been there since 1948, have many rights that Syrian citizens do but carry identity cards and travel documents marking them as Palestinians. At the beginning of the uprising in Syria, the Palestinian political and civic leadership worked to maintain Yarmouk as a neutral space. One faction among the Palestinian political factions—specifically the Popular Front for the Liberation of Palestine-General Command (PFLP-GC), led by Ahmad Jibril—took the side of the Assad regime, often acting as its arm in the camp. Hamas, on the other hand, tried to remain neutral and then finally declared itself in support of the "heroic Syrian people" in early 2012 and the leadership went into exile.

Early in the uprising, the camp served as hosts to the displaced from nearby as fighting shifted in the suburbs around Damascus. There were repeated calls from civil society to

host refugees, and they saw this as their opportunity to repay the generosity of their Syrian hosts. In December 2012, opposition fighters entered the camp, using it as a base to attack regime forces in the area around the camp. In the following months, fighting largely destroyed the camp, which still remains under siege. Most of the residents fled to nearby areas, and because they are Palestinians, they are unable to travel outside of Syria. Jordan has closed its borders to any Palestinian from Syria, and Lebanon has severe restrictions. A lucky few have found refuge with relatives in Europe. On Oct. 21, 2014, U.S. Ambassador to the UN Samantha Powers described Yarmouk at a Security Council session:

One community subjected to the Assad regime's merciless attacks has been Palestinians in the refugee camp of Yarmouk, which the regime has sealed since July 2013. The 18,000 residents who remain there have been relying on untreated groundwater and a single well for drinking water for nearly a month. Just yesterday, a spokesman for unrwa issued a statement that began: 'UNRWA was not cleared to distribute humanitarian assistance in Yarmouk today, 20th of October.' The day before, unrwa's statement began: 'unrwa was not cleared to distribute humanitarian assistance in Yarmouk today, 19 October.' unrwa notes that since July this year, there has been a steady and significant decline in the quantity of food and other essential items, such as medicine, that the Agency has been able to offer to the Palestinians in Yarmouk. That on any day—let alone so many days—the Assad regime is not allowing aid to flow to the Palestinians suffering in Yarmouk shows extreme cruelty. The international community must be more vocal in its condemnation of these unspeakable tactics. And when the Syrian government hails its leadership on behalf of the Palestinian people, they should be reminded by all of us of the people living in Yarmouk.

CARTOON BY LATUFF, HTTP://LATUFFCARTOONS.WORDPRESS.COM/TAG/YARMOUK/

unhcr open the Za'atari refugee camp in July 2012. Lebanon and Turkey also started receiving many more refugees and other countries, such as Armenia, Egypt and Libya, also began to receive people fleeing violence.

This second wave trickled out of Syria as services like hospitals and clinics were attacked or failed, schools that hosted displaced persons could not muster classes for children, and neighborhoods morphed into battlegrounds between government forces and the armed opposition. The second wave included more people who feared being labeled an enemy of the regime or opposition, or whose homes had been destroyed. Most did not have the same family or trade connections in host countries as those in the first wave.

They often came without much preparation and were in immediate need of financial and material support, which required a stronger response from both government and nongovernmental organizations (NGOs), especially in Turkey, Jordan and, later, Lebanon.

Gender and age played a significant role in the second wave. The decision by adult males to fight the Assad government meant that their families could become targets of the security apparatus of the regime. Family members of at least some of those men fighting against the regime in the FSA or other groups thus moved outside of Syria for their own safety.

Another group of refugees consisted of thousands of men, many of whom were unmarried and had refused to fight

for either the regime or the rebels. They fled to other countries to continue their education, find work or avoid the draft. A good portion of this group were from the educated middle classes in Damascus and Aleppo who may or may not have supported the uprising but, by virtue of their gender and age, were likely going to be forced to be involved. These men, as well as women who were activists, often traveled alone or with a brother or sister. Once outside Syria, they now either provide support for those back home (particularly if they landed jobs in the Persian Gulf) or need support from those back home (particularly if they managed to find places to study). In all but the most well-off families, the refugees struggle to find places to live and resources to support them. In addition, the Syrian lira has dropped in value (it is currently at 162 Syrian pounds to the dollar, whereas before the uprising started it was 45 Syrian pounds to the dollar) and hard currency is costly and difficult to find.

Third wave

The beginning of 2013 marked a turning point in the refugee flow—thousands of refugees streamed over the border each day. By the end of that year almost 2 million Syrians had registered as refugees, overwhelming host countries and aid organizations.

The major reason for the movement was the increase in the areas and types of fighting and the subsequent solidification of areas into government controlled and non-government controlled (whether under local councils, FSA, other militias, or jihadist groups). The destructive internal dynamics of areas under regime and rebel control caused even more to flee. From the perspective of a refugee, three primary causes were: (1) the destruction from the regime's widespread campaign to take back parts of the country, (2) the area where they lived was taken over by a group hostile to the refugee's beliefs or activities, (3) they fled for fear of the security apparatus.

One characteristic of this period was that people who were IDPs became refugees. For example, people had fled from conflicts in villages surrounding a larger urban center to safe parts of that urban center. Then, when that area in the city was attacked, they had few options of where to find shelter again. Their resilience depleted by hardship and fear, they often chose to cross borders to another country, giving up the stability of all that they had known in Syria, for safety in a foreign country. It was estimated that most refugees arriving in this wave had moved three to five times before becoming refugees.

During this period, the overt intervention of outside forces—Russian and Iranian funding and logistical support to the regime, money given to militia leaders from wealthy Persian Gulf individuals, foreign fighters joining the opposition (particularly from Iraq), and U.S. and others' nonlethal support to the rebels—made it much clearer that Syria had become a battlefield on which larger battles were being fought. In particular, 2013 saw sectarian loyalties become a framework through which actions were launched or interpreted. Hezbollah—a Lebanese Shi'a political party and militia supported by Shi'a-majority Iran—joined the side of the Syrian regime in May of 2013, fighting intensified against the FSA, resulting in the regime retaking many areas and punishing the inhabitants, resulting in more refugees. The increased strength of Jabhat al-Nusra, an Islamist jihadi militia that eventually declared itself part of Al Qaeda, allowed many to characterize the fight against the regime and its Hezbollah proxies as sectarian. Jabhat al-Nusra fights in the name of Sunni Islam, and it declared itself fighting against "the Shi'a"—in other words, the Alawi President Assad and Hezbollah. Gone was any discussion of "the people" or "freedom."

Fourth wave

The fourth wave of refugees started in 2014 and has two major characteristics: (1) refugees from the jihadi militias growing control of territory, the creation of the Islamic State (ISIS), and the establishment of salafi/jihadi forms of governance over territory achieved through their desire and willingness to use violence; and (2) refugees beginning to seek new lives beyond the surrounding countries.

In Iraq and Syria, the rise of ISIS, which eliminates opposition through mass and well-publicized executions and harsh repression, has resulted in a steady flow of refugees fleeing areas where the group has taken or is likely to take control. Throughout the spring and summer of 2014, families of targeted Syrians—such as local leaders, militias and FSA members—were fleeing rebel-controlled areas across borders to safety. In September and October alone, over 190,000 Syrians, the vast majority Kurds from the northeast, crossed into Turkey. The U.S. decision to bomb ISIS targets and Turkey's decision to let Kurdish fighters carry arms against ISIS are significant political decisions with unclear outcomes.

Since the conflict began, some refugees have sought more permanent solutions, either through work permits or third-country asylum, beyond the initial host countries. In 2014, more and more refugees adopted the attitude that they cannot return to Syria and their lives there have been lost. The talk among refugees about resettlement reflects the shift from "we will return to Syria" to "we have to make our lives somewhere else." With the passage of time, their children not in schools and adults jobless, and the utter destruction of the Syria that they knew, people realize they are not going back soon and that they are not able to create "normal" lives in the host countries. ∎

ISIS fighters carry their weapons during a parade at the Syrian town of Tel Abyad, near the border with Turkey January 2, 2014. (IMAGE BY © STRINGER/REUTERS/CORBIS)

International response

In August 2012, as Turkey was poised to host more than 100,000 Syrian refugees, the country repeated its calls for a safe zone for Syrians facing "humanitarian disaster" and appealed to the UN to establish those camps inside Syria. While that issue was not addressed, the UN Security Council approved a resolution in July 2014 that would allow aid convoys to go into rebel-held areas without the approval of the Syrian government. Prior to this date, the UN only provided aid to the Syrian regime in Damascus, wanting to appease the Syrian government and not jeopardize the lives of people living under government control. However, this meant that aid was not reaching rebel-held territory. In addition, the Syrian regime withheld assistance to areas it wanted to punish.

Humanitarian aid to refugees outside of Syria is provided from two main sources. The most comprehensive and well known is the unhcr's interagency approach: seeking funding by working with host governments, coordinating donations and providing registration and cash assistance services. The process is transparent and NGOs and development organizations across the world participate in the process. Turkey funds and runs its own refugee registration and management, but also participates in parts of the interagency approach.

The second source of aid to refugees is through local charities, municipalities, political groups and unknown actors. While little information exists about these groups or their accountability, much of their funding comes from abroad as charitable or individual donations and many are religiously based, usually Christian and Muslim. In Lebanon, a lack of government oversight allows these players to operate with a free hand; however, in Jordan they must register with the government.

Three years into the crisis, there is a "layering of humanitarian experience" in which large international aid organizations move around host countries, responding to refugee needs within a large system, while local organizations

A newly arrived Syrian refugee boy smiles at an Emirati Red Crescent worker upon his arrival with his family to the new Jordanian-Emirati refugee camp, Mrajeeb al-Fhood, in Zarqa, Jordan, Apr. 10, 2013. (IMAGE BY © MOHAMMAD HANNON/ /AP/CORBIS)

provide services in a specific area. One example of this "layering" is drawing upon local staff members in host countries who have had extensive experience in humanitarian aid provision from other recent crises.

Like the refugees, the international community is realizing Syrians may not be able to return home soon and cannot settle permanently in neighbor countries with dwindling resources. UNHCR has already asked countries to extend the number of refugees allowed for asylum. As of June 2014, 22 countries have agreed to resettle Syrians but only in the hundreds and low thousands. The exception is Germany, which agreed to accept 25,000.

Most importantly, the lack of funding for refugees is creating increasing hardships among the refugees, who lack even the most basic foodstuffs. The unhcr Regional Response Plan guides and coordinates funding requests and funding for NGOs (and semi-NGOS), and only half of the $3.7 billion dollar appeal has received commitments to date.

Host countries:

The countries surrounding Syria and beyond have allowed Syrians to cross their borders to find safety, and this magnanimity has meant the difference between life and death for Syrians. Bordering countries, Turkey, Iraq, Jordan and Lebanon (but not Israel), have for the most part kept their borders open, created national bodies to address the issues, and worked with international agencies and local groups to alleviate the difficult economic and health situations of displaced Syrians. In late 2014, however, most of these countries have started de facto closing their borders. Syrians continue to attempt to cross all of these borders illegally—not through legal border crossings. Many have had to do this because they cannot leave Syria legally, in particular men who are seen to be "of military age" (between 18 and 52). Thus, because they avoid official Syrian border crossings, they then enter the neighboring countries without registering a presence.

Each host country has a different approach to how it deals with "legal" versus "illegal" non-nationals. In Turkey and Jordan, they must register with the government before being able to access services. In Lebanon, if they register and want to stay legally in the country, they need to pay $200 per person for

Kurdish refugee children from the Syrian town of Kobani sit behind a fence in a camp in the southeastern town of Suruc on the Turkish-Syrian border, Oct. 19, 2014. (IMAGE BY © KAI PFAFFENBACH/REUTERS/CORBIS)

a permit that lasts for one year. This sum is close to impossible for many individuals and even harder for those with families.

The people living in those host countries have been exceptionally generous in their embrace of Syrians. Without a doubt there are governmental policies that keep Syrians out, and political and military figures, along with neighbors who are vicious or exploitative. But these cases tend to be either exceptions to general rules or smaller trends among a larger sense of goodwill toward the refugees as people in need. However, more and more citizens of host countries are expressing the tension, competition for services and resources, and challenges they face due to the huge numbers of refugees.

TURKEY: Through mid-2012, Syrians came to Turkey to escape immediate attack and returned home after the threat passed. As violence spread and refugees stopped going home, the government took on financial and logistical management of the refugee populations under its Disaster and Emergency Management Presidency (AFAD).

Two historical elements influence Turkey's refugee policies. After hundreds of thousands of Iraqi Kurds crossed into eastern Turkey in 1991 following the first Gulf War, the Turkish government, the U.S. and the UN pushed for the successful implementation of a "safe haven" in northern Iraq. As a result, 400,000 Kurds left Turkey and returned to Iraq, where they were provided protection and aid. While this ensured protection and assistance for the refugees, many in Turkey felt it came at a high price. They argued the semi-autonomous Kurdish state would be used to train Kurdistan Workers' Party (PKK) militants to fight for independence in Turkey. Similar concerns about the role of Syrian Kurds and the possible growth of militant Kurdish organizations in Syria have arisen.

Another issue complicating Turkey's response to the crisis is who they consider to be refugees. Past agreements allowed Syrians with passports to cross into Turkey and not be considered a refugee. Turkish border authorities initially let Syrians with passports or valid travel documents enter the country, and those without such documents were taken to nearby refugee camps established by AFAD. At the end of 2012, there were 170,000 refugees (up from 9,000 in early 2012), with the vast majority in 14 camps, and an estimated 60,000 Syrians not in camps. Syrians who registered with AFAD, whether inside or outside the camp, could get access to basic services. Turkish refugee camps have been called "model camps" for their provisions and administration, but they come at a considerable cost to the Turkish government.

When large numbers of Syrians poured into the country in 2013 and 2014, there were no longer places in the camps for incoming refugees, and the population outside camps quickly increased tenfold. These legal and social service arrangements have recently changed. "A new law governing migration to Turkey went into effect in April 2014. It provides, for the first time, a

Syrian refugees wait guarded by a Turkish soldier at the Syrian-Turkish border near Sanliurfa, Turkey, Sept. 27, 2014. (IMAGE BY © SEDAT SUNA/EPA/CORBIS)

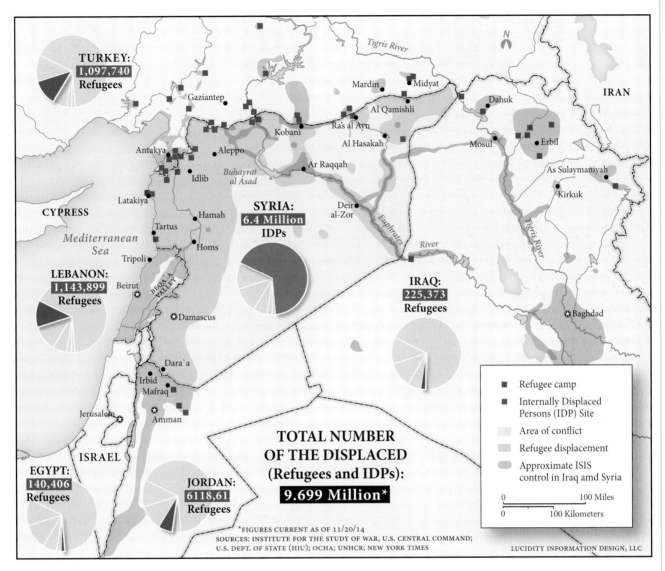

TURKEY:
1,097,740
Refugees

Tigris River

Mardin •Midyat

Gaziantep

Dahuk

IRAN

Al Qamishli

Ra's al Ayn

Kobani

Al Hasakah

Mosul •Erbil

Antakya •Aleppo

Ar Raqqah

As Sulaymaniyah

Idlib

Buhayrat
al Asad

Kirkuk

Latakiya

Deir
al-Zor

Euphrates

CYPRESS

Hamah

SYRIA:
6.4 Million
IDPs

River

Tartus

Mediterranean
Sea

Homs

Tripoli

IRAQ:
225,373
Refugees

LEBANON:
1,143,899
Refugees

Beirut

BEQA'A
VALLEY

☉Baghdad

✪Damascus

Dara'a

■ Refugee camp

Irbid
Mafraq

■ Internally Displaced
Persons (IDP) Site

Jerusalem

Area of conflict

Amman

Refugee displacement

ISRAEL

TOTAL NUMBER
OF THE DISPLACED
(Refugees and IDPs):
9.699 Million*

Approximate ISIS
control in Iraq amd Syria

EGYPT:
140,406
Refugees

JORDAN:
6118,61
Refugees

0   100 Miles

0   100 Kilometers

*FIGURES CURRENT AS OF 11/20/14

SOURCES: INSTITUTE FOR THE STUDY OF WAR, U.S. CENTRAL COMMAND;
U.S. DEPT. OF STATE (HIU); OCHA; UNHCR; NEW YORK TIMES

LUCIDITY INFORMATION DESIGN, LLC

legal basis for temporary protection. [New temporary protection papers] will provide exemption from fees for primary and emergency health care and the respective treatment and medication, the right to psychosocial services, the right to education for children aged 33 months and above, the possibility to apply for work permits in certain sectors and regions, and access to other services," Noga Malkin and Nick Danforth wrote in an article published by the Middle East Research and Information Project.

Local and national politics also play a role in where Syrian refugees can get permits to live. Some think the reason Syrian refugees are not given permits to live in Hatay province is because of tensions with the Arabic-speaking Alawi residents who live there and are

Turkish citizens. (Turkey acquired the Hatay territory in 1938). "[B]y denying Syrian refugees residence permits in Hatay, the AKP (Turkish social conservative Justice and Development Party, whose members include the president and prime minister) is playing a constructive role in trying to minimize the risk that Syria's sectarian tensions will spill over into Turkey," Malkin and Danforth said.

As of October 2014, the total number of refugees in Turkey is over 1 million. This is partly due to a recent 20% increase, when almost 200,000 Kurdish Syrians fled ISIS attacks.

JORDAN: Jordan began receiving refugees in spring 2011 when the Syrian regime attacked the southern city of Dara'a and surrounding areas. Here, as in Turkey, strong family and mercan-

tile ties made it easier for those fleeing Syria to find places to stay with connections across the border. Syria's southern border and Jordan's northern border divide an area called the Hauran, which has centuries of historical connections among people living there. Despite borders drawn on a map, those who live in Hauran continued crossborder labor, trade, family, marriage and other relations through the present. For the first months, the majority of Syrians remained in the towns and villages in the north.

Jordan's experience as a host for hundreds of thousands of Iraqi refugees following the 2003 U.S.-led invasion of Iraq shaped its response to the arrival of Syrians. Working with the unhcr and a strong INGO/NGO presence, it advocated for continued and modified policies and practices that were developed for Iraqi refugees, including direct cash assistance rather than food aid, incorporation of refugees into health care networks and public schools.

As more refugees entered the country, two things happened. First, Jordan asked the unhcr to set up the Za'atari refugee camp in an area close to the border. Second, in late 2012, it refused to allow any of the Palestinians in Syria (approximately 500,000) to enter Jordan, While some had crossed into Jordan before this time and were detained in the Cyber City refugee camp, as of May 2013, there were over 6,600 Palestinian refugees from Syria registered with unrwa in Jordan, though the actual number is thought to be slightly higher due to a reluctance to make themselves known to unrwa and the Jordanian authorities. It has also become much harder for single men to cross into Jordan, thus pushing men to bring their families with them.

Like Turkey, Jordan is a country that prefers a strong, centralized response. Jordanian officials are intent on making sure that every refugee is registered both with unhcr and within its own system for security reasons, particularly because of the rise in jihadi groups. Without such registration, Syrians cannot access any of the services for refugees, and without prior school records, children have been excluded from education opportunities.

Jordan's Za'atari Camp, with a population around 80,000, is now the country's fifth largest city and all services are provided to camp residents. The vast majority of Syrians registered and unregistered are dispersed among the local population. This means that Jordan, especially in the north, has absorbed more than 530,000 people, just under 10% of the total Jordanian population.

LEBANON: Lebanon received a trickle of refugees starting in 2011, and they numbered less than 6,000 in early 2012. In 2013 and 2014, however, the number of Lebanese refugees increased exponentially, from 130,000 in 2013 to 1 million as of May 2014. Parts of the country are still recovering from its own civil war (1975–90), as well as Israeli airstrikes in 2006 that destroyed major parts of the country's electrical, transportation and water infrastructure. The main issue in the last 10 years has been Lebanon's weak and ineffectual government, which is not strong enough to plan, guide or provide services or hold others accountable. As a result, the UN is reluctant to provide funds to the Lebanese government and has chosen instead to work with and through NGOs. Meanwhile, the Lebanese government has been unable to find donors and was considering loans in the form of credit fund management from the World Bank to meet refugee needs.

Lebanon's tumultuous history influences Lebanese attitudes toward Syrians. A Syrian military presence and occupation of Lebanon from 1976 to 2005 makes Lebanese wary of Syrians. At the same time, Syrians have long provided migrant labor in agriculture and service sectors and have extensive knowledge of the country. Some Syrian families are sheltering with Lebanese hosts who fled to Syria during the 2006 Israeli airstrikes. Adding to the complexity is the relationship between the Syrian regime

A Syrian Kurdish woman and a child, having fled from the clashes between ISIS and armed groups in Ayn al-Arab (Kobani), wait in Arbat Refugee Camp in Sulaymaniyah, Iraq on Oct. 15, 2014. (PHOTO BY FERIQ FEREC/ANADOLU AGENCY/GETTY IMAGES)

and Hezbollah, which is part of the Lebanese government and which entered the fighting in Syria on the side of the Syrian regime in May 2013.

Lebanon's high cost of living is a deterrent for many refugees, despite the fact that they are able to work illegally. In this rich agricultural area, Syrians are a cheap source of agricultural labor. In the Beqa'a Valley, most of the informal camps are run by a *shaweesh*, an intermediary between the landowner and Syrians. The shaweesh takes money for rent, charges for electricity and water and may take a cut of any aid they receive. One Syrian family reportedly paid 800,000 Lebanese Lira ($570) per year for the tent, 35,000/month ($25) in electricity and an additional charge for access to the communal water tap. Outhouses serve as toilets for the group of 40 tents, and waste goes into the irrigation canal. In southern Lebanon, the refugees are registered by municipalities and Hezbollah, in an attempt to keep them organized, and they find empty flats and refurbished spaces for them.

IRAQ: The majority of Syrian refugees fleeing to Iraq are Kurds who have moved in large numbers to the Kurdistan Regional Government (KRG, Iraqi Kurdistan in northern Iraq). A small number of Syrian refugees are in other parts of the country. Refugees in the KRG now number 220,000, and they fall under the mandate of the Iraqi Department of Displacement and Migration (DDM). UNHCR administers 12 refugee camps in areas governed by the KRG, and these camps house 50% of the refugees. Because the KRG gives Syrians residency permits and allows them to work, the demography of this refugee community is different than in other host countries. In particular, the population of men over the age of 17 is much higher than other places and much larger compared to other demographics—men over the age of 17 account for 35.2% of the refugee population.

The camps in the KRG have developed over time, but unevenly. Refugees who are not part of a camp live in urban centers. Although these refugees have access to medical services and education, the KRG's infrastructure is overwhelmed. As in Lebanon and Jordan, the influx of refugees has had tremendous negative effects on the poor, who compete with them for low-cost housing, jobs and government services. In addition, Syria was a host to Iraqi refugees, and as of 2011 well over 100,000 were registered with the unhcr. Because of the fighting in Syria, many Iraqis have returned to Iraq, but those numbers have been impossible to document.

EGYPT: Egypt's refugee policy has changed significantly in the aftermath of its 2013 coup d'état. From 2011 to 2013, Syrians could enter, live legally and study at university in Egypt, resulting in over 100,000 finding refuge there. A large number of them were men and women of university age. However, as of July 2013, Syrians seeking refuge in Egypt had to acquire security authorization before doing so. Even those who were already registered have been rounded up and detained, including refugees registered with the UN. Egypt has also served as a launching point for smugglers taking boats filled with Syrians, Palestinians and others across the Mediterranean to Europe.

Policy options

In the previously mentioned five countries, host now to over 3 million refugees, governments, local communities and humanitarian aid will need to develop ways to support them and provide self-sufficiency. Yet in Lebanon, Syrians make up almost 25% of the total population, and in Jordan, 10%. This is equivalent of adding 30 million to 65 million people to the U.S. homeless population in a span of three years. Syrians, who rose up against the indignities of the Assad regime, are growing tired of displacement and the need for support, and an uncertain future. Instead of being defined as refugees, they would rather be in their homes farming their land, running shops, treating patients, teaching children and raising families. Aid has come in huge numbers but still is not enough. The UNHCR said it has received only $1.9 billion of the $3.7 billion it determined

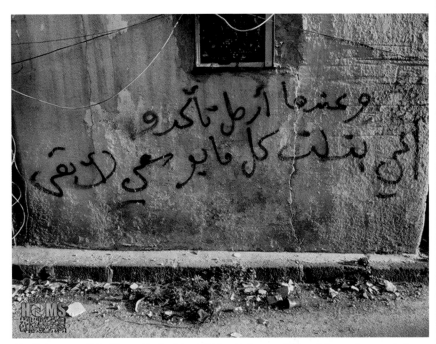

Graffiti on a wall in Homs, Syria, May 2014, which says, "When I leave, be sure to know that I did everything I could to stay." (PHOTOGRAPH BY HOMS MEDIA FIELD FACEBOOK PAGE)

would be needed to adequately cover supplies, resulting in significant food program cuts in October 2014.

The U.S. government has provided $2.8 billion in humanitarian aid to displaced Syrians since March 2011. Much of this aid—from USAID and the State Department's Bureau of Population, Refugees, and Migration—has been crucial to the survival of refugees and IDPs. In addition, the U.S. has provided hundreds of millions of dollars in nonlethal aid to the Syrian opposition, as well as lethal support through the Department of Defense and CIA.

A call for third-country asylum is growing louder in the international community, and some say western nations can do more. The U.S. admitted only 31 Syrian asylum seekers in the 2014 fiscal year, bringing the total to 90 since 2011. In addition, the U.S. has repeatedly renewed the availability of Temporary Protected Status for Syrian passport holders and residents within the U.S., which allows them to renew U.S. visas and not have to return to Syria. Thousands of others have been given visas to come to the U.S. through family requests or other means; however, these are considered temporary and not asylum cases. The U.S. accepts

around 60,000 refugees each year from around the world—the largest number of any one country. The Obama administration has committed to raising the number of Syrians approved for permanent resettlement, and is in the process of reviewing 4,000 applications. But no one country, or even all of the countries together, should need to resettle millions of Syrians.

The solutions for refugees are few. Most want to return to Syria, which is only possible if the fighting ends or if protected areas are created in Syrian territory, as was done in northern Iraq after the 1991 conflict. The different players and sects involved in the conflict makes enforcing such an area difficult, and no one seems eager to provide security. Host countries cannot support refugees forever, and without international aid, the point will come where Turkey, Jordan and Lebanon reach a critical mass for the amount of refugees they are able to absorb and support. Helping refugees deserves immediate attention from the global community, but this is still a band-aid solution. The real answer is ending the conflict and giving Syrians a country free of violent intimidation and repression to go home to. ∎

discussion questions

1. As Syria's neighbors struggle to support their growing refugee populations, there are growing calls for the U.S. and other Western nations to do more other than provide aid. Should the U.S. grant asylum to more Syrian refugees?

2. How can the international community ensure that Syrian refugee children receive an education so they can be productive members of society when the conflict is over? Is there a risk that the crisis will give birth to a "lost generation" of Syrians?

3. How likely do you think it is that Turkey, Lebanon or Jordan will feel they have reached a critical mass of refugees at some point and close their borders? What should the reaction of the international community be in that case? And how can the international com-munity support these three countries so as to limit the likelihood that they will become overwhelmed?

4. Suffering from years of conflict and poverty, are Syrian refugees at an increased risk of seeing radical Islamic groups as their most promising future? Should tackling Syria's refugee crisis be seen as a national security priority for U.S. lawmakers as well?

5. Lebanon's democracy was structured to carefully balance its Sunni, Shi'a and Christian populations. Will an influx of refugees disrupt this balance and create tensions in Lebanon?

6. Think of other refugee crises that have faced the Middle East in the past, such as the Iraqi or Palestinian refugee crises. What lessons should the U.S. and the international community draw from these other crises? What did the U.S. and the international community do well? What went wrong? And how can the U.S. and international community apply these lessons to the current Syrian refugee crisis?

suggested readings

de Chatel, Francesca. "The Role of Drought and Climate Change in the Syrian Uprising: Untangling the Triggers of the Revolution." **Middle Eastern Studies,** Vol. 50, Iss. 4, 2014. A ground-breaking study of the environmental and administrative crises that preceded and led to the uprising.

Haddad, Bassam. "Syria's Curious Dilemma" in **Middle East Report,** No. 236 (Fall, 2005), pp. 4–13. A short piece explaining the political and economic changes under Bashar al-Assad.

Halasa, Malu, Omareen, Zaher, and Mahfoud, Nawara. **Syria Speaks: Art and Culture from the Frontline.** London : Saqi Books, 2014. This book features the work of over 50 artists and writers who challenge the culture of violence in Syria.

Hashemi, Nader, and Postel, Danny. **The Syria Dilemma.** Cambridge: The MIT Press, 2013. 272 pp. This book raises the question of whether or not humanitarian intervention should occur in Syria, with input from experts, theorists, human rights activists and scholars.

Hokayem, Emile. **Syria's Uprising and the Fracturing of the Levant.** Abingdon: Routledge, 2013. 211 pp. This book delves into the transformation of Syria's former peaceful uprising into current civil war, and how turbulent events in the country will affect the future of the Eastern Mediterranean.

Lesch, David W. Syria: **The Fall of the House of Assad.** New Haven: Yale University Press, 2012. 288 pp. This book explores the leadership of Syrian President Bashar al-Assad, his ruthless tyranny in response to the Arab Spring events, as well as the causes leading to the Syrian uprising.

Pipher, Mary. **The Middle of Everywhere: Helping Refugees Enter the American Community**. Boston, MA. 2003. 416 pp. $12.71 (paper). This book covers the refugee story a lot closer to home for Americans. Refugees arrive in the U.S. daily and face assimilation and the task of seeking asylum to begin their new life. The stories of refugees who experienced just that are told in moving detail.

Tobin, Sarah A., Ekaterina Anderson, and Lisa Jenkins. **The Syrian Refugee Crisis and Lessons from the Iraqi Refugee Experience.** Boston: Institute for Iraqi Studies, 2013. 58 pp. Available free online: <http://www.bu.edu/iis/files/2013/05/Syrian-Refugee-Report-v-5.1.pdf>. This report, taken from an Institute for Iraqi Studies workshop, documents the disaster resulting from the displacement of many Syrians as they fled their homes, similar to that of the very recent Iraqi refugee crisis.

Wedeen, Lisa. **Ambiguities of Domination: Politics, Rhetoric, and Symbols in Contemporary Syria.** Chicago: University of Chicago Press, 1999. A classic study, both political and ethnographic, of the ways in which the authoritarian regime of Hafez al-Assad maintained control and manufactured consent.

Wieland, Carsten. **Syria—A Decade of Lost Chances: Repression and Revolution from Damascus Spring to Arab Spring.** Seattle: Cune Press, 2012. Discussing politics, society, religion, and economy, this book examines Bashar al-Asad's ten-year rule

TO LEARN MORE ABOUT THIS TOPIC AND TO ACCESS WEB LINKS TO RESOURCES GO TO www.greatdecisions.org

Human trafficking:
A serious challenge to humanity
by Joseph Chamie

Haris (bonded laborers) who were recently freed from a private jail of landlord Imam Bakhsh Mangrio, protest outside Hyderabad Press Club in Hyderabad, Pakistan, against the oppression of the said landlord on May 15, 2012. (IMAGE BY © RAJPUT YASIR/DEMOTIX/CORBIS)

Human trafficking in its many diverse forms constitutes a serious challenge to humanity, affecting millions of woman and men, as well as girls and boys, in numerous countries irrespective of region and development level. Effectively addressing human trafficking is a growing priority for governments and international and national agencies, with global and regional agreements coordinating policies and programs aimed at combating and eliminating all forms of trafficking in persons. In addition to the serious direct consequences borne by trafficked persons, human trafficking violates international and national laws, undermines universally recognized fundamental human rights and individual freedoms, negatively impacts families and communities, and fuels criminal activities and traffickers with billions of dollars in profits.

Human trafficking may occur within a country or across borders. As its full impact is largely hidden, human trafficking is difficult to assess and analyze accurately and comprehensively. Trafficked persons frequently find themselves in fearful, dangerous or illegal circumstances, making them reluctant to report crimes, cooperate with law enforcement authorities in the identification and prosecution of traffickers and to seek out needed medical care and social services. Moreover, as trafficked persons transported across interna-

JOSEPH CHAMIE *recently retired as research director of the Center for Migration Studies in New York and as editor of the International Migration Review. He was formerly the director of the United Nations Population Division, having worked at the UN on population issues for more than a quarter century. He has written numerous population studies for the UN—as well as under his own name—on growth, fertility, estimates and projections, international migration and population and development policy. He is a member of the Council on Foreign Relations and a trustee of the Migration Policy Institute.*

Defendants walk into court to stand trial for kidney trafficking in Hangzhou, capital of east China's Zhejiang Province, Feb. 21, 2013. (IMAGE BY © JU HUANZONG/XINHUA PRESS/CORBIS)

tional borders often lack proper residence and employment status and are generally unaware of their individual rights, they avoid encounters with police and immigration officials fearing possible arrest, incarceration and deportation. Also, any travel and identity documents that trafficked persons may possess are frequently confiscated and held by traffickers in order to manipulate, control and coerce their victims.

Defining, measuring and analyzing the extent and impact of human trafficking are central challenges for governments, organizations, researchers and activists. Considerable descriptive writing, anecdotal reporting and media coverage have been done on trafficking, especially regarding sexual exploitation. However, the systematic collection of comparable data, preparation of meaningful statistics and compilation of reliable evidence on the basic dimensions and characteristics of human trafficking remain problematic. In addition to being underreported to government authorities, human trafficking in many instances involves various overseas jurisdictions and violates a myriad of laws relating to different government agencies, including immigration, labor, slavery, servitude, marriage and family, health and medicine, child abuse, prostitution and sexual exploitation.

As noted above, it is widely recognized that the levels and trends of people trafficked globally are extremely difficult to measure. International and

national reports on human trafficking acknowledge and caution readers that it is impossible to accurately determine the scale of trafficking persons using only official criminal justice statistics, with estimates of trafficked persons varying greatly. Accordingly, the 2014 U.S. report on human trafficking included an explicit warning to reporters and the broader media to be careful when doing stories using numbers of human trafficking and advised to pursue individual stories of survival, new government initiatives, or innovative research efforts until better data are available.

It is also widely agreed that the numbers of victims reported to authorities and assisted by agencies represent a small fraction of the actual numbers trafficked. Nevertheless, while the officially reported information on human trafficking is limited, varying greatly in reporting coverage by region and cannot be used to generate solid global estimates of the number of trafficked persons, the available information and estimate techniques do shed some light on and are perhaps indicative of the patterns, flows and occurrences of human trafficking, as well as how the police, prosecutors and courts are responding to trafficking cases.

According to the most recent biennial report in 2012 prepared by the United Nations Office on Drugs and Crime, at least 136 different nationalities were trafficked and detected in 118

different countries between 2007 and 2010. Also, about 460 distinct trafficking flows worldwide were identified during that time. The trafficking victims can be found in the world's restaurants, fisheries, brothels, farms and homes, shops and work sites, as well as among many other sectors of society.

Estimates of humans trafficked vary from 4 million to 27 million. Recent International Labor Office (ILO) estimates of victims of forced labor, including sexual exploitation, put the global number at approximately 21 million. While the precise number of victims of forced labor as a result of human trafficking is not known, it is estimated at no less than 2.5 million.

The statistics on human trafficking presented below are based on data from 132 countries compiled by the UN Office on Drugs and Crime and published in their 2012 biennial report, *Global Report on Trafficking in Persons*. The large majority of the data, 88%, are from national institutions, with non-government and international government organizations representing 7% and 5% of the sources, respectively. The statistics are based on information on approximately 55,000 victims and 50,000 offenders detected globally over the period from August 2010 to August 2012.

The reliance on officially reported data of human trafficking has a number of important limitations. The data, for example, are not compiled for research but for administrative purposes to record enforcement efforts. Also, the data on victims tend to overrepresent trafficking for sexual exploitation and underrepresent the prevalence of forced labor trafficking. Another important bias concerns the availability of information, which varies greatly among regions. For example, the data are fewer and weaker for Africa than for Europe and the Americas. Consequently, the uneven reporting of detected human trafficking victims and offenders is likely to result in unreliable estimates for certain regions as well as inaccurate comparisons of differences in human trafficking levels and trends both globally and regionally. ∎

Complexities of trafficking

Worldwide sexual exploitation is the most commonly identified form of human trafficking at approximately 58%, followed by forced labor at about 36% (Figure 1). As sexual exploitation is more frequently reported or detected by authorities than other forms of human trafficking, it has become the most statistically documented type of trafficking.

The more frequent reporting is also likely due to the difficulties in distinguishing between trafficking for sexual exploitation and prostitution, with the two widely believed to be synonymous. In addition, some studies have found that countries with legalized prostitution are associated with higher human trafficking inflows than countries where prostitution is prohibited. The effect of legalizing prostitution does not seem to outweigh the substitution effect, that is, where legal sex workers are preferred over illegal workers. While legalizing prostitution may have beneficial effects on the working conditions of prostitutes and others legally employed in the sex industry, legalization appears to increase the market for sexual human trafficking.

In addition to commercial prostitution and sexual exploitation, which tends to attract media attention and the concern of the public, human trafficking occurs for other purposes. An important and widespread purpose is for forced labor. In addition to trafficking at construction sites, bonded domestic work in homes and child labor in shops and factories, forced labor is also encountered at massage parlors, bars and similar enterprises that provide sexual services. Human trafficking also includes fraudulent or forced marriages, forced begging, illegal child adoption, forced child armed combatants and the trade of human organs, such as kidneys.

Among the underlying factors making people vulnerable to human trafficking are poverty, unemployment, lack of socioeconomic opportunities, gender-based violence, discrimination and marginalization. Harmful social practices, such as female illiteracy, barring basic education, child marriage and parental/spousal neglect and abandonment, make women and girls especially vulnerable to traffickers.

In addition to children, two especially vulnerable groups are would-be migrants and undocumented migrants. Those seeking employment abroad are frequently so desperate or eager to secure overseas work that they do not or are unable to properly evaluate job offers or the legitimacy of the recruitment firms. Also migrants who are unlawfully residing in a country are vulnerable to exploitation and abuse, often taking on dangerous and difficult employment without proper compensation and legal protection.

Trafficking is also greatly facilitated by worldwide demands for cheap, compliant labor as well as the low risk and high profits made by criminal groups from human trafficking. As a result of such factors, trafficked persons are often victims of exploitation and mistreatment, including debt bondage, torture, unlawful confinement and rape, and threats and violence against them, their families and friends.

A major underlying reason for illegal migration and why so many rely on human smuggling—which subsequently may evolve into trafficking in persons—is that the supply of potential migrants wishing to go abroad greatly exceeds the demand for migrants in immigrant receiving countries. While every year countries are receiving millions of immigrants of their choosing, the pool of potential immigrants—many who are likely not to qualify for legal immigration—is many times larger.

Important differences exist between trafficking and smuggling. First, while human smuggling may be dangerous or degrading, it involves the consent of the person being smuggled. In contrast, a trafficking victim has either never consented or if he or she has initially consented, that consent has been rendered meaningless by the coercive, deceptive or abusive action of the traffickers or the victim was a child. Second, migrant smuggling generally ends with the migrants' arrival at their destination, whereas trafficking involves the continuing exploitation of the victim. Third, smuggling is transnational, whereas trafficking may occur within a country. Fourth, while smuggling profits are derived from the transportation and facilitation of the illegal entry into another country, trafficking profits are derived from exploitation.

Despite these notable differences, it is frequently difficult to determine whether a case is human trafficking or human smuggling. In practice, distinguishing between consent and coercion is a difficult and complex undertaking, especially given the poverty, desperation and vulnerability of many migrants. Some migrants, for instance, might have started their journey by agreeing to be smuggled into a country illegally, but later find themselves deceived, coerced or forced into an exploitative situation.

Figure 1

Forms of exploitation for all detected trafficking victims worldwide, 2010

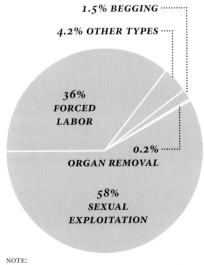

1.5% BEGGING

4.2% OTHER TYPES

36% FORCED LABOR

0.2% ORGAN REMOVAL

58% SEXUAL EXPLOITATION

NOTE:
DUE TO ROUNDING, FIGURES DO NOT TOTAL 100%

LUCIDITY INFORMATION DESIGN, LLC

Figure 2

Share of total number of detected victims, by region: 2007–2010

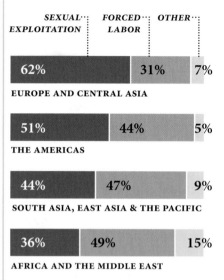

SEXUAL EXPLOITATION   FORCED LABOR   OTHER

EUROPE AND CENTRAL ASIA — 62%   31%   7%

THE AMERICAS — 51%   44%   5%

SOUTH ASIA, EAST ASIA & THE PACIFIC — 44%   47%   9%

AFRICA AND THE MIDDLE EAST — 36%   49%   15%

LUCIDITY INFORMATION DESIGN, LLC

The migrants may be forced to work for extraordinarily low wages for lengthy periods of time in order to pay for their transportation.

Also, the same criminals may both smuggle and traffic persons, using similar routes and methods of transport. Furthermore, migrant smuggling often results in ensuing benefits for human traffickers, as smuggled migrants are particularly vulnerable to being subsequently trafficked and exploited.

Although forced labor represented slightly more than a third of detected human trafficking in 2010, it is double the level reported four years ago. This increase may reflect recent changes in national legislation as well as in public awareness, which is increasingly recognizing forced labor as an important form of human trafficking. Consequently the detected increase in the proportion of human trafficking for forced labor likely reflects improved detection by authorities and public concern about trafficked forced labor.

Various other forms of exploitation, including forced marriage, human organ removal, child begging and child war combatants, are by and large underreported and accounted for about 6% of the total number of detected cases. Trafficking for begging and the removal of human organs represented 1.5% and 0.2% of all detected cases globally, respectively.

Regional variations

The distribution of the forms of human trafficking exploitation based on detected cases varies considerably by region (Figure 2). More cases of sexual exploitation than forced labor were detected in Europe and Central Asia and the Americas. In contrast, Africa and the Middle East, as well as South and East Asia and the Pacific, detected more cases of forced labor than sexual exploitation.

During the period 2007–10, close to half of the human trafficking victims detected globally were trafficked across national borders within their region of origin (Figure 3). The remaining detected human trafficking cases were divided roughly equally, 27% for transcontinental and 24% for domestic, i.e., within a country. Also, irrespective of region or subregion, people are generally trafficked from relatively poorer areas to comparatively richer ones.

Among the regions, the Middle East reported the highest proportion of trafficked persons from other regions, 70%. Nearly all the detected human traffick-

Figure 3

Distribution of domestic, regional and transcontinental human trafficking, 2007–2010

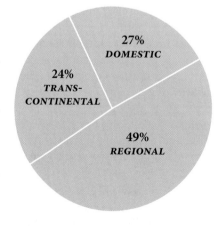

27% DOMESTIC

24% TRANS-CONTINENTAL

49% REGIONAL

LUCIDITY INFORMATION DESIGN, LLC

Figure 4

Human trafficking victims, by sex: circa 2010

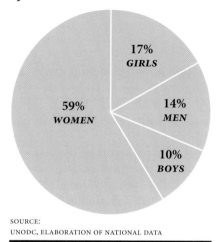

17% GIRLS

14% MEN

59% WOMEN

10% BOYS

SOURCE:
UNODC, ELABORATION OF NATIONAL DATA

LUCIDITY INFORMATION DESIGN, LLC

ing flows originating in Africa are either intraregional—with Africa and the Middle East as their destination—or to Western Europe. Also, trafficked persons from the largest number of origin countries were detected in Western and Central Europe. The most prominent transnational flow globally originated in East Asia, with East Asian victims detected in large numbers in various nations around the world.

It is estimated that women account for nearly 60% of all trafficking victims detected globally, with women and girls together representing 75% of the detected victims. (Figure 4) Also, roughly one-quarter of all trafficked persons detected globally are children and of every three child victims, two are girls and one is a boy.

One of the most worrying trends in human trafficking is the increase in child victims. Whereas about a decade ago 20% of all detected victims were children, more recent estimates have found that it has increased to 27%. Again in this instance, caution is warranted as it is uncertain whether this is a genuine increase or simply the result of improved reporting of trafficked children.

As observed earlier with the types of human trafficking, trafficking in children also varies greatly by region (Figure 5). For the period 2007–10, children accounted for approximately

Figure 5

Share of detected child victims, by region: 2007–2010

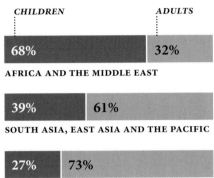

CHILDREN · · · · · · · · · · · · · · · · · · ADULTS

| 68% | 32% |

AFRICA AND THE MIDDLE EAST

| 39% | 61% |

SOUTH ASIA, EAST ASIA AND THE PACIFIC

| 27% | 73% |

GLOBAL

| 27% | 73% |

THE AMERICAS

| 16% | 84% |

EUROPE AND CENTRAL ASIA

LUCIDITY INFORMATION DESIGN, LLC

of those prosecuted and/or convicted for trafficking in persons. However, the participation of women in human trafficking is higher than for most other crimes. While by and large women's criminal rates are below 15% of the total for all crimes, women offenders represent about a third of prosecutions and convictions for trafficking in persons.

The compiled data also indicate that women's involvement in human trafficking is more frequent in recruitment for sexual exploitation and in the trafficking of girls. Some studies find that woman traffickers are typically in low-level positions of human trafficking networks and tend to be more exposed to being detected and prosecuted than men.

The proportions of men and women prosecuted and convicted for trafficking in persons vary considerably by region (Figure 7, on next page). In the Eastern Europe and Central Asia regions, the large majority of those prosecuted and convicted are women, 62% and 77%, respectively. In contrast, in the Africa and Middle East regions the proportions of women among those prosecuted and convicted are substantially lower, 17% and 21%, respectively.

Again, it is important to keep in mind that the law enforcement statis-

Figure 6

Recorded convictions per year: 2007–2010

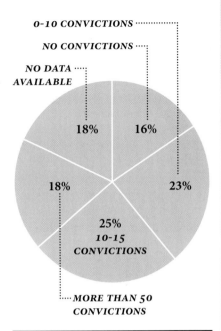

0-10 CONVICTIONS · · · · · · · · · · · · · ·

NO CONVICTIONS · · · · ·

NO DATA · · · ·
AVAILABLE

18% 16%

18% 23%

25%
10-15
CONVICTIONS

· · · · · MORE THAN 50
CONVICTIONS

LUCIDITY INFORMATION DESIGN, LLC

tics on human trafficking may not be representative of the actual situation in regions and countries. In many developing countries, for example, the capacities of police and legal authorities are often limited, resulting in an under-

16% of the trafficked persons in Europe and Central Asia. Markedly higher are the proportions for the Americas at 27%—roughly the global average—and about 40% for South and East Asia and the Pacific. The highest proportion of trafficked children, at nearly 70%, was recorded for Africa and the Middle East. Also, the most conspicuous child trafficking globally originates from East Asia, with East Asian victims found in 64 countries in all regions of the world.

With respect to prosecutions and convictions for human trafficking, the numbers are generally very low. Between 2007 and 2010, 16% of the 132 countries covered did not record a single conviction and 18% of the countries had no data available. Also among the remaining countries, 23% recorded between 1 and 10 convictions for human trafficking per year, 25% between 10 to 50 convictions and 18% more than 50 convictions per year. (Figure 6)

Statistics based on recorded information from more than 50 countries during the period 2007–10 indicates that men account for about two-thirds

Migrant workers from Myanmar clean fishing nets aboard a trawler after a fishing trip in the Gulf of Thailand in Samut Sakhon Province, west of Bangkok, Thailand. (IMAGE BY © SAKCHAI LALIT/AP/CORBIS)

estimation of human trafficking. Also, national laws and enforcement efforts, as well as the concerns of the public may focus on different forms of human trafficking that are viewed as particularly problematic for the country.

Individual nations and regions have adopted laws and policies in the past aimed at limiting human trafficking, particularly regarding slavery, forced labor and sexual exploitation. However, it is only since the early 2000s that UN member states decided collectively to confront directly and decisively human trafficking in its many forms. Progress in reducing human trafficking globally will require intensified national resolve and concerted international cooperation and collaboration. In particular, increased efforts are needed to: a.) undertake quantitative research as well as in-depth qualitative studies; b.) raise public understanding and awareness of human trafficking's criminal nature; c.) encourage needed changes in norms, attitudes and behavior towards human trafficking in many parts of the world; and d.) pursue and prosecute human traffickers. ■

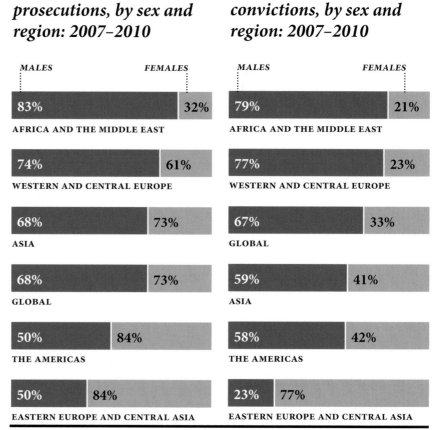

Figure 7

Human trafficking prosecutions, by sex and region: 2007–2010

MALES   FEMALES

83%   32%
AFRICA AND THE MIDDLE EAST

74%   61%
WESTERN AND CENTRAL EUROPE

68%   73%
ASIA

68%   73%
GLOBAL

50%   84%
THE AMERICAS

50%   84%
EASTERN EUROPE AND CENTRAL ASIA

Human trafficking convictions, by sex and region: 2007–2010

MALES   FEMALES

79%   21%
AFRICA AND THE MIDDLE EAST

77%   23%
WESTERN AND CENTRAL EUROPE

67%   33%
GLOBAL

59%   41%
ASIA

58%   42%
THE AMERICAS

23%   77%
EASTERN EUROPE AND CENTRAL ASIA

LUCIDITY INFORMATION DESIGN, LLC

Taking action against trafficking

Human trafficking has existed throughout human history in virtually all societies with varying success by authorities to suppress it. Slavery and forced labor in particular were not uncommon in the past and are well documented throughout the ages. For example, the ancient societies of China, Egypt, India and Mesopotamia as well as the Greek and Roman empires, used trafficked slaves and forced labor to develop their economies and expand their influence and power.

Also, less than 200 years ago, slavery and involuntary labor were practiced throughout the British, French, Spanish and other European empires. In the U.S., slavery was practiced until 1865 when Congress abolished it, freeing some 4 million slaves, or approxi-

mately 13% of the American population, at that time.

In the modern era, international pressures to combat trafficking, especially of women and children, began with the growing social reform movements in Europe and the U.S. at the close of the 19th century. Following an international convention held just at the start of the 20th century, 12 countries ratified the International Agreement for the Suppression of the White Slave Traffic in 1904. Among other things, each of the contracting governments agreed to establish an authority charged with the coordination of all information relating to "…the procuring of women or girls for immoral purposes abroad." The governments also agreed that these authorities are empowered to correspond directly

with similar bodies in each of the other contracting states. In 1910 this international agreement was further enhanced with the protocol, which strengthened international mechanisms and cooperation to suppress the white slave traffic.

With financing by John D. Rockefeller, one of the earliest attempts to investigate and publicize the extent of human trafficking internationally was carried out by the American Bureau of Social Hygiene. A committee of the bureau, established in 1923, investigated human trafficking in 28 countries, interviewing approximately 5,000 informants. Its final report, which took two years to complete, is considered the first formal international study of trafficking in women and children to be issued by an official governmental body.

With its establishment in 1919, the League of Nations took on the international role of coordinating legislation addressing the trafficking of women and children. An important League of

Nations initiative was the 1926 Slavery Convention, or the Convention to Suppress the Slave Trade and Slavery, which is considered a milestone in banning global slavery. Among other things, the convention codified definitions, rules and articles aimed at the suppression of slavery and the slave trade. Slavery, for example, was defined as "the status or condition of a person over whom any or all of the powers attaching to the right of ownership are exercised." Shortly thereafter, the Forced Labour Convention of 1930 addressed forced or compulsory labor by banning debt bondage serfdom, and child servitude, as well as early and servile marriage.

The establishment of the UN in 1945 led to the international adoption of important treaties, conventions and agreements relating to human trafficking. For example, in 1948 member states of the UN General Assembly adopted the Universal Declaration of Human Rights, which explicitly banned slavery: "No one shall be held in slavery or servitude; slavery and the slave trade shall be prohibited in all their forms" (Article 4). In addition, the declaration addressed two other notable forms of human trafficking: forced labor, "Everyone has the right to work, to free choice of employment, to just and favourable conditions of work and to protection against unemployment" (Article 23), and forced marriage, "Marriage shall be entered into only with the free and full consent of the intending spouses" (Article 16).

In 1949 the Convention for the Suppression of the Traffic in Persons and Exploitation of Prostitution of Others was also adopted. Building upon the Slavery Convention of 1926, the UN adopted in 1956 the Supplementary Convention on the Abolition of Slavery, the Slave Trade and Institutions and Practices similar to Slavery. Parties to the Supplementary Convention committed their countries to abolishing debt bondage, serfdom, servile marriage and child servitude.

These early and subsequent efforts by both nations and regional organizations led to the landmark adoption in 2000 of the "United Nations Protocol to Prevent, Suppress and Punish Trafficking in Persons, Especially Women and Children, Supplementing the United Nations Convention Against Transnational Organized Crime"—also called the Palermo Protocol—which came into force in December 2003. Currently, 164 countries have ratified the Palermo Protocol, with more than 130 countries having enacted national legislation criminalizing human trafficking,

The Palermo Protocol is a global, legally binding instrument on human trafficking and the only one with an internationally agreed upon definition of trafficking in persons. In fact, the Palermo Protocol established the first definition of human trafficking in international law:

"… the recruitment, transportation, transfer, harbouring or receipt of persons, by means of the threat or use of force or other forms of coercion, of abduction, of fraud, of deception, of the abuse of power or of a position of vulnerability or of the giving or receiving of payments or benefits to achieve the consent of a person having control over another person, for the purpose of exploitation. Exploitation shall include, at a minimum, the exploitation of the prostitution of others or other forms of sexual exploitation, forced labour or services, slavery or practices similar to slavery, servitude or the removal of organs, …The recruitment, transportation, transfer, harbouring or receipt of a child for the purpose of exploitation shall be considered "trafficking in persons" even if this does not involve any of the means set forth in subparagraph (a) of this article…" (Art. 3, par. a).

According to the Palermo Protocol definition, human trafficking has three basic components. The first component is the act or what is done, that is the recruitment, transportation, transfer, harboring or receipt of persons. The second component is the means or how it is done, for example, the threat or use of force, coercion, abduction, fraud, deception, abuse of power or vulnerability, or giving payments or benefits to a person in control of the victim. The third basic component of human trafficking is the purpose or why the trafficking is being done, that is for the purpose of exploitation, including the prostitution of others, sexual exploitation, forced labor, slavery or similar practices and the forced removal of human organs.

One of the Palermo Protocol's major goals is to facilitate international cooperation in investigating and prosecuting such trafficking. The definition and elaboration of human trafficking in the Palermo Protocol is aimed at ensuring international consistency and consensus. Another is to protect and assist human trafficking victims with full respect for their rights as established in the Universal Declaration of Human Rights.

In 2010, 10 years after the adoption of the Palermo Protocol, UN member states renewed their commitment to the fight against trafficking in persons when the General Assembly adopted the United Nations Global Plan of Action to Combat Trafficking in Persons. This plan of action, which commits nations to a multidisciplinary and integrated approach to end trafficking in persons, stresses an overall strategy that respects human rights and nondiscrimination in the broader context of development, peace and security.

The plan includes action widely referred to as the "4 Ps": 1.) Prevention of trafficking in persons; 2.) Protection and assistance to the victims of trafficking in persons; 3.) Prosecution of crimes of trafficking in persons; and 4.) Partnerships strengthening against trafficking in persons. With the intention to support implementation of the Palermo Protocol, the plan of action focuses on helping countries reinforce their commitments and obligations to combat trafficking using comprehensive, coordinated and consistent responses, at the national, regional and international levels.

The plan also called for the establishment of the UN Voluntary Trust Fund for Victims of Trafficking in Persons, Especially Women and Children. In addition the plan requested the UN secretary-general to strengthen the capacity of the UN Office on Drugs and Crime to collect information and report biennially on patterns and flows of trafficking in persons at the national, regional and international levels and share best practices and lessons learned from various initiatives and mechanisms.

Domestic legislation

As a result of the Palermo Protocol, an increasing number of governments have adopted or amended their laws in order to criminalize and prosecute human traffickers and provide aid and protection to the trafficked victims. Article 5 of the Palermo Protocol requires that human trafficking be criminalized in domestic legislation. National legislation would also include criminalization of: 1.) attempts to commit human trafficking offense; 2.) participation as an accomplice; and 3.) organizing or directing others to commit trafficking. National laws would also utilize the broad definition of trafficking prescribed in the Palermo Protocol, thereby permitting effective responses to a variety of trafficking offenses occurring across and within national borders.

Domestic legislation does not need to follow precisely the language of the protocol. National laws are expected to be adapted in accordance with domestic legal systems to give effect to the concepts contained in the protocol. However, national legislative definitions should be dynamic and flexible in order to respond effectively to trafficking that: 1.) occurs both across borders and within a country; 2.) includes a wide range of exploitative purposes; 3.) victimizes children, women and men; and 4.) takes place with or without the participation of organized crime groups.

In the last few years, country laws and national jurisdictions have expanded the application of trafficking legislation. This expansion has resulted in the inclusion of phenomena that existed long before the Palermo Protocol, such as forced marriages, illegal child adoptions and child begging or the use of children to commit petty crimes. To ascertain whether a particular circumstance constitutes trafficking in persons, consideration is needed of both the definition of trafficking in the Palermo Protocol and the constituent elements of the criminal offense, as defined by relevant national legislation.

For purposes of illustration, brief descriptions of national laws and efforts are presented below for the 28 member countries of the European Union, U.S., Russian Federation, China, India, Saudi Arabia, Nigeria and Brazil.

European Union

The EU is particularly concerned with the effects of human trafficking on women and children and has focused its actions on protecting these groups from exploitation. According to the EU legislation, exploitation should include, as a minimum: 1.) the exploitation for prostitution or other forms of sexual exploitation; 2.) forced labor or services, including begging, slavery or practices similar to slavery, servitude; and 3.) exploitation for criminal activities, including the forced removal of organs. Moreover, exploitation is considered to exist when a constraint has been exerted on a person—by means of threat or use of force, abduction, fraud, deception, etc.—whether or not the victim has given his or her consent. If the victim is a child, below 18 years of age, the acts are automatically considered human trafficking irrespective of whether constraints have been exerted on the child.

According to recent EU directives on human trafficking, the maximum penalty for these offenses is at least five years of imprisonment and ten years when the victim is a child, the crime was done in the framework of a criminal organization, serious violence was used, or the victim was seriously harmed. Also, with the aim of preventing human trafficking, the EU Directive requests its member states to: 1.) discourage demand for human trafficking through education and training; 2.) lead information and awareness-raising campaigns; 3.) train officials likely to assist victims of trafficking; and 4.) take the necessary measures to criminalize the use of services, sexual or other, of a person who is a victim of trafficking.

United States

The U.S. has also been active domestically and internationally in addressing human trafficking, which is deemed a great assault on basic human freedoms. In addition to dismantling trafficking networks and aiding survivors in rebuilding their lives, the U.S. aims to address the underlying forces pushing many people into exploitation. Among other things, meaningful steps include creating legitimate jobs, halting the exploitation of children and empowering both girls and boys with the same chances to pursue their goals.

The first comprehensive U.S. federal law to address trafficking in persons was the Trafficking Victims Protection Act of 2000, which was reauthorized in 2003, 2005 and 2008. The law focused on three major aspects of human trafficking: prevention, protection and prosecution and considers commercial sexual exploitation and labor trafficking as severe forms of trafficking in persons. Also in accordance with the act, the U.S. is working to combat trafficking in persons globally. Each year the U.S. State Department publishes a report with data, analyses and national assessments concerning human trafficking worldwide, especially highlighting countries that do not fully comply with the minimum standards and are not making significant efforts to suppress trafficking.

Russian Federation

In the Russian Federation human trafficking evolved into a serious concern following the collapse of the Soviet Union as a result of difficult economic and social circumstances in the newly independent nations. High levels of unemployment, poverty, weak law enforcement and limited social welfare institutions contributed to increasing levels of human trafficking, especially forced labor and sexual exploitation.

In addition to signing on to international conventions and agreements on human trafficking, the Russian Federation has passed national legislation that prohibits human trafficking, particularly for purposes of sexual exploitation, forced labor and trade in children for adoption. Russian criminal laws also permit the prosecution and conviction of traffickers. The prescribed punishments for human trafficking crimes are imprisonment up to five years, with penalties up to 15 years for serious offenses. In addition, penalties may include asset forfeiture, permitting authorities to confiscate the financial assets of convicted traffickers.

China

In the world's largest countries, China and India, human trafficking became a major concern for governmental authorities relatively recently. In 2007 the Chinese government adopted a national plan of action to combat trafficking of women and children. The plan aims to prevent and suppress criminal activities relating to the trafficking of women and children, safeguard the legal rights and interests of children and provide aid and care for human trafficking victims. China also has increased inspections at labor sites, updated its criminal codes with increased penalties for human trafficking, set up hotlines and shelters for victims and cooperates with international agencies and other nations for law enforcement coordination on human trafficking.

India

Like China, India is attempting to combat human trafficking in its various forms, including forced labor especially of children, sexual exploitation, forced marriage and begging. Domestically the Indian government has adopted various types of human trafficking legislation and acts that aim to prevent commercial sexual exploitation and bonded/forced labor. In addition to penalties of imprisonment of seven, ten or more years for human trafficking, India is also pushing national media campaigns against child labor.

Also, human trafficking of Indians outside India, although illegal, remains a major problem for the country. In response to the trafficking of women, India requires governmental clearance on the emigration of women aged less than 30 years as domestic help to several countries in order to check the possibility of their sexual exploitation. In addition, Indian officials are traveling abroad and negotiating with various countries to ensure that Indian workers are being correctly compensated and properly treated by their employers.

Saudi Arabia

In Saudi Arabia the government has relatively recently adopted a tougher policy on human trafficking. The country has banned all forms of human trafficking and announced that it will spare no effort to prevent and punish all types of human trafficking criminal offenses, especially with regard to women, children and persons with special needs. It has also established programs within its Human Rights Commission to coordinate efforts to combat human trafficking.

The Saudi laws have been made explicit with regard to the illegal dimensions of human trafficking and include coercion of a person; threat, deception, deceit or abduction; misuse of position, influence or authority against a person; taking advantage of their weakness, or giving or receiving money or enticements to gain the approval of a person for sexual acts, work, coercive service, begging, slavery, practices similar to slavery, organ removal or performance of medical tests on a person. The penalties for human trafficking have also been made more severe, including imprisonment up to 15 years and fines in excess of a quarter of a million dollars.

Nigeria

Human trafficking in Nigeria is a major concern of the government, especially in light of the recent abduction of nearly 300 girls in the northern part of the country. The Nigerian government has indicated that it complies with the standards stipulated in the Palermo Protocol for the elimination of trafficking and has adopted legislation prohibiting all forms of human trafficking.

Nigeria has also stepped up its efforts and resources to prosecute trafficking offenders and has increased the penalties for trafficking. The laws prescribe five years of imprisonment for labor trafficking, ten years for trafficking of children for begging, and ten years or more for sex trafficking.

The Nigerian government also reports that it is providing assistance and care to the human trafficking victims. In addition, governmental programs have been established to raise the public's awareness and understanding of human trafficking and enlist their cooperation in combating it. The programs aim to sensitize vulnerable people, identify the methods and deceptions traffickers use to lure victims and warn parents of potential trafficking threats to their children.

In this photo taken July 12, 2012, Leila Mohamed, 13, cleans utensils at the home of a family she works for in Mogadishu, Somalia, as part of nonstop daily labor to earn her living.
(IMAGE BY © FARAH ABDI WARSAMEH/ /AP/CORBIS)

Brazil

As has been the case in many other countries, Brazil has recently adopted more stringent antihuman trafficking measures, especially with regard to slave/forced labor and commercial sexual exploitation. Under Brazilian law, slave labor is labor performed during exhausting days, in degrading working conditions or involving debt bondage. Also, although prostitution is legal in Brazil for persons aged 18 years or older, the country is confronting the problem of sex-trafficked children.

Brazilian laws prohibit most forms of human trafficking recognized by international agreements. In recent years the penal code on human trafficking has been strengthened and toughened. In addition to having prohibited slavery, forced labor and commercial sexual exploitation, the new codes criminalize the illegal adoption of children and forced organ extraction. Penalties for human trafficking generally vary from three to eight years of imprisonment, with sentences increased up to twelve years when the victim is a child.

In addition to increased domestic work site inspections for forced slave/labor violations, the Brazilian government has announced tougher border controls, establishing more new control centers in key border towns that will aim to combat trafficking and aid foreign trafficking victims. Also in cooperation with the neighboring countries of Argentina and Paraguay, the government has established a migrant's assistance center in the tri-border area. ∎

Perspectives and challenges

During the past two decades, considerable progress has been made in addressing the global problem of human trafficking. Since the Palermo Protocol came into force in 2003, 134 countries have criminalized human trafficking consistent with the principles and recommendations of the Protocol.

Currently, 164 countries are signatories or have ratified the Palermo Protocol. Among the nearly two-dozen member states that have not yet become signatories to the Palermo Protocol are Afghanistan, Bangladesh, Iran, Nepal, North Korea, Pakistan, Singapore and Yemen.

Global awareness and understanding of human trafficking have also increased markedly over the past few years. Global inventories, national reports and research studies have been published, with international agencies, governments and non-governmental organizations compiling and analyzing detected trafficking cases from a wide range of sources. Many member states have shown the political will, demonstrated critical leadership and committed considerable resources to combating human trafficking.

Also, far more information, including basic data, comparative analyses and national assessments of human trafficking, has been compiled and made readily available by national authorities and international organizations than even a decade ago. The U.S. State Department, for example, issues an annual trafficking in persons (TIP) report that provides an updated global assessment of efforts to confront and eliminate human trafficking. The TIP report includes individual human trafficking narratives for some 189 countries and territories, with recommendations and evaluations of government prevention, protection and prosecution efforts.

In addition, the TIP report classifies countries into one of four human trafficking tiers according to their compliance with the minimum standards of the U.S. Trafficking Victims Protection Act. While the 2014 TIP report found 31 countries whose governments fully comply with the minimum standards, the governments of 23 countries do not fully comply and are not making significant efforts to do so. Also, another 89 countries do not comply with the minimum standards but are making significant efforts to come into compliance and 44 countries are on a watchlist concerning their compliance efforts.

Despite the noteworthy progress over the past decade, major challenges remain in implementing effective and comprehensive responses to human trafficking. Perhaps the foremost challenge in the implementation of antitrafficking policies and programs is the lack of sufficient financial resources. Without adequate funding, global and national efforts to prevent human trafficking, especially those in less-developed countries, will not be able to move beyond stating that trafficking in persons is a problem and reporting on it anecdotally.

Another widely recognized challenge is the continuing inadequacy of data, knowledge and research on human trafficking. Although the literature on trafficking has grown markedly, comparatively few studies rely on extensive, evidence-based research and the actual numbers or magnitude of trafficked persons continues to remain uncertain. Sound estimates about the extent and varied dimensions of human trafficking are essential in order to establish baselines, ascertain trends and assess the impact and effectiveness of policies and interventions. In addition, much of the existing research concentrates on the trafficking of women and children for sexual exploitation, neglecting other important forms of human trafficking, such as forced labor.

Improving the knowledge base on human trafficking will require further clarification of key trafficking concepts and a standardized and widely accepted methodology for better estimating the number of trafficking victims. Concepts such as "exploitation," "vulnerability" and "abuse of power" are often difficult to interpret and apply in possible instances of human trafficking, especially for government authorities working in the criminal justice system.

Also, agencies dealing with human trafficking should be encouraged to collect data systematically and consistent with international definitions, principles and practices. Smuggling and trafficking, in particular, need to be clearly distinguished and not confused in order to achieve certain political outcomes, such as regularization of illegal immigration status. Improvement is also is needed in the effective responses of the criminal justice system to human trafficking, which in the past has limited the usefulness of the reports emerging from law enforcement agencies.

An additional major challenge is the lack of monitoring and evaluation of efforts to combat human trafficking. Comparatively little independent evaluations of counter trafficking policies and programs have been carried out to assess their actual impact and effectiveness. Moreover, many of the agencies that are combating trafficking do not systematically collect and analyze data permitting evaluation of the effectiveness of programs in preventing and reducing trafficking, protecting victims, and punishing traffickers. Without such research and the corresponding data it is extremely difficult to identify best practices and assess which countries have been most successful in their efforts to combat trafficking.

The limited capacity of some countries is a further important challenge in addressing human trafficking. As the extent and dimensions of human trafficking vary by country, with the poorest being most vulnerable to exploitation, many governments, especially those of the least-developed nations, face financial and organizational limitations in combating human trafficking. Increasing the capacities of governments in the world's poorer regions would be a significant contribution as it would assist these countries in developing their relevant institutions and strengthening their technical skills, thereby permitting them to more effectively implement their antitrafficking policies and programs. Increased collaboration and cooperation at the regional and international levels, especially exchanges of good practices, would also be helpful in improving the capacities of countries to deal with human trafficking.

More than 150 people walk across Pariser Platz square during the 'Walk for freedom' demonstration in Berlin, Germany, October 18, 2014. The participants join a Europe-wide protest against human trafficking. (IMAGE BY © PAUL ZINKEN/DPA/CORBIS)

U.S. policy options

The U.S. government views human trafficking as both an international and a domestic crime that includes violations of standards relating to public health, labor, human rights and criminal law. As noted earlier, the U.S. antitrafficking policies center on programs of prevention, protection and prosecution (the three "Ps"). Important policies relating to prevention include public awareness campaigns, with education and employment opportunities for those at risk of trafficking, especially girls and women.

The provision of shelters, training service and assistance to victims of trafficking is a key part of U.S. protection programs. Depending on the specific need requirements, U.S. policy may include temporary housing, cultural orientation, transportation, job training and counseling. Legal aid and assistance are also available to victims in order to facilitate the prosecution of traffickers. To this end, U.S. policies may include training of law enforcement officials and judiciaries to enforce anti-trafficking laws.

In addition to technical and financial support, the U.S. policy options include the threat of withholding certain forms of assistance to influence and persuade governments to take needed and responsible action regarding human trafficking. Beside the possibility of withholding foreign assistance, the U.S. may apply sanctions and restrictions on countries as well as issuing explicit critiques of governments' policies and responses to trafficking in persons.

As is the case with many international efforts, U.S. policies and programs to combat human trafficking are often difficult to evaluate. It is difficult to accurately assess the extent of the problem, especially in diverse environments, insofar as the numbers of the various types of trafficking victims remain elusive. Consequently, the U.S. administration and the Congress, which are responsible for providing the funds, encounter serious challenges in evaluating whether the numbers of traffickers prosecuted and victims rescued reflect successful policies and strategies. Moreover, given the limited resources and growing needs for assistance both domestically and internationally, tough questions arise regarding the proper attention, emphasis and allocation of resources to be given to the major types of human trafficking. However, despite these challenges, the U.S. continues to be active and supportive in addressing the global problem of human trafficking. ∎

discussion questions

1. Various international organizations and governments have defined human trafficking. How would you define human trafficking? What specific activities or services should be included and excluded within human trafficking?

2. The term "exploitation" is a central aspect of human trafficking. How does one deal with exploitation in actual practice, especially as it relates to the wages and financial compensation for work as well as child labor?

3. Human trafficking and human smuggling are said to be different phenomena. What are the important differences between human trafficking and human smuggling? How does human smuggling and illegal migration contribute to exploitation, abuse and human misery?

4. Some believe that legal prostitution is exploitative and subordinates and victimizes women. Should authorities do away with legal prostitution? Should prostitution be criminalized and fall within the purview of human trafficking?

5. Governments and organizations around the world have agreed to confront directly human trafficking. How would you quantify or measure the extent and impact of human trafficking?

6. What are likely to be the most effective policies and programs to reduce human trafficking? Also, what are likely to be the most effective penalties for those who commit human trafficking?

7. Most victims of human trafficking have limited financial resources. Given their difficult financial and personal circumstances, who should cover the costs of providing aid, assistance and care to the victims of human trafficking?

suggested readings

Council of Europe and United Nations. **Trafficking in organs, tissues and cells and trafficking in human beings for the purpose of the removal of organs.** Strasbourg, France: Council of Europe, 2009. Available free online: <http://www.coe.int/t/dghl/monitoring/trafficking/docs/news/organtrafficking_study.pdf>. Joint report by the COE and UN on organ trafficking worldwide, the international standards in place and what can be done to combat it.

Axel Dreher, Seo-Young Cho and Eric Neumayer. "Measuring anti-trafficking policies: How do they spread across countries?" **VOX, Research-Based Policy Analysis**. Mar 10, 2011. Available free online: <http://www.voxeu.org/article/measuring-anti-trafficking-policies>. Looks at a new methodology for assessing the efficacy of anti-trafficking policies.

International Labour Organization. **Profits and Poverty: The Economics of Forced Labour.** Geneva: International Labour Organization, 2014. Available free online: <http://www.ilo.org/wcmsp5/groups/public/---ed_norm/---declaration/documents/publication/wcms_243027.pdf>. This article details the lucrative practice of exploiting labor markets.

Masci, David. "Human Trafficking and Slavery: Are the World's Nations Doing Enough to Stamp it Out?" **CQ Researcher**. Mar 26, 2014. Available free online: <http://www.sagepub.com/upm-data/31938_1.pdf>. Drawing from personal stories and extensive research, the author explains why human trafficking and modern slavery is a crime that continues to grow in the 21st century.

Shelley, Louise. **Human Trafficking: A Global Perspective.** New York: Cambridge University Press, 2010. 356 pp. This book examines the business and nature behind the global crime of human trafficking. The author draws from her research the conclusion that this global crime will continue to grow in the 21st century without new policy changes to intervene.

U.S. State Department. **Trafficking in Persons Report 2014**. Washington, DC: U.S. Department of State, 2014. Available free online: <http://www.state.gov/j/tip/rls/tiprpt/>. This report is the U.S. government's principal tool used to engage and assess foreign countries' efforts to fight human trafficking.

Benjamin Perrin, Philip Reichel and John Winterdyk (eds.). **Human Trafficking: Exploring the International Nature, Concerns and Complexities**. Boca Raton, Florida: CRC Press, 2011. 318 pp. From detection to support of victims and prosecution, this report combines the contributions of multiple leading experts on the growing crime of human trafficking.

TO LEARN MORE ABOUT THIS TOPIC AND TO ACCESS WEB LINKS TO RESOURCES GO TO www.greatdecisions.org

Brazil in Metamorphosis

by Juan de Onis

An aerial view of the construction site of a hydroelectric dam along the Teles Pires river, a tributary of the Amazon, near the city of Alta Floresta, Para state, June 19, 2013. (IMAGE BY © NACHO DOCE/REUTERS/CORBIS)

A new tropical civilization with global ambitions is being born in Brazil. For the first time, a technologically advanced, energy-driven society has been established in the tropics on a continental scale. Mastering the knowledge and skills of how to exploit its abundant natural resources, Brazil is producing a growing wealth of petroleum and mineral products for world markets and has converted its agriculture into a prodigious source of food for a hungry world. This economic expansion has elevated Brazil to a new role on the world stage.

At the heart of this transformation are the Brazilian people. Once called "the children of the sun" by a 19th-century French traveler, their identity is an amalgamation of different races and creeds. Now, Brazil is shedding its old shell that it developed as a rural patriarchal society of slave-owning landlords and has become an emerging market of global importance, an industrial society of mass consumers. With a population of over 200 million and an annual gross domestic output of $2.2 trillion, Brazil is now the world's seventh-largest economy, surpassing Italy and Britain. The keystone country of South America, Brazil is also the "B" in the acronym BRICS (Brazil, Russia, India, China and South Africa), a label for large emerging markets, countries that represent over 40% of the world's population and 21% of global production.

Yet, Brazil's metamorphosis is still a work in progress. Thanks to a deep divide over the country's "ideal" future and national purpose, Brazil repeatedly falls short of its full potential. The divide is inherently ideological, pitting notions of social justice against a need for rapid economic development. One school of thought, entrenched in political parties and academia, favors statist populism, with stifling bureaucratic control over economic decisions. Another, favored by those in the private sector, is committed to free-market capitalism with limited government oversight.

This conflict, with its roots in the post-World War I era, has persisted through a century of modernization, starting with the centralization of the economy under the dictatorship of Gétulio Vargas (1930–45). State control of the economy continued through a succession of authoritarian military regimes and, more recently, democratically elected constitutional governments, which achieved important advances in poverty

JUAN DE ONIS *is an American journalist who spent 23 years reporting in Latin America, the Middle East, the UN and Washington, DC, for* The New York Times. *He lives in Brazil where he wrote* The Green Cathedral *(Oxford University Press 1900), which researched ecological issues in the Amazonian rainforest. He continues to write frequently on Brazil through a blog and periodic publications.*

Brazil´s geography

Brazil is a subcontinent, an archipelago of diverse biomes, or ecosystems, contained within 4,575 miles of land frontiers bordering on six Spanish American countries and the three Guyanas. Its maritime frontier extends 4,660 miles from Oiapoque, a river town on the northern-most border with French Guiana, to Chui, a town bordering on Uruguay to the south. Brazil´s land mass of 3.3 million square miles is the size of the continental U.S. Adding the off-shore continental shelf, where Brazil claims exclusive economic rights, the total area under Brazilian sovereignty reaches over 3.9 million square miles. Brazil is an ecological mosaic of nine distinct biomes that go from the world´s largest wetland, called the Pantanal, where the Paraguay River begins in southern Mato Grosso, to the semi-arid Northeast region, where severe droughts are frequent. There are coastal biomes where rainfall is abundant but where native flora has been severely reduced, endangering endemic wildlife, like monkeys and hummingbirds. In central Brazil there is the cerrado, a savannah-like bush land with rich biodiversity that has been altered extensively by conversion to agriculture and cattle ranching. And, in the deep western reaches of Brazil, there is the Amazonian biome, covering 60% of Brazil's territory, where the world´s largest tropical forest is largely intact, but undergoing intrusions from highways, hydroelectric dams and other public works that attract new settlers.

The spatial diversity of Brazil is held together by its rivers. With the exception of the western Amazon rivers that have their headwaters in the Andes, nearly all the river systems in Brazil originate in the central highlands. There are no high mountain ranges in Brazil, like the Andes or the Himalayas, but there is a topographical crease running east-west that is a continental divider of waters. The division begins in the highlands of Minas Gerais, the "mother of waters," where three great systems originate: the San Francisco river that runs to the Northeast, providing that parched region with water and electricity; the tributaries of the Parana river that runs southward to join the Paraguay river, where both enter Argentina and form the River Plate estuary to the south Atlantic and the headwaters of the Araguaia river, which runs north until it joins the Tocantins, eventually reaching the Amazon delta near Belem. Historically, these rivers have been corridors for penetration of the interior and routes for primitive transportation. In recent times, they have been dammed and become major sources of electric power for Brazil's national grid. Now, they are also being used for irrigation systems and as inland waterways for fleets of barges carrying grains, minerals and other products of the interior. The same is happening on southern Amazon tributaries, like the Madeira, the Tapajos, and the Xingu, big rivers that join the Amazon near internal port cities, like Santarem and Manaus. These rivers unite Brazil, integrating isolated regions into the national economy, but highways, power dams and airports bring settlers to the interior who upset the traditional life of indigenous "forest people."

With support from environmental and human rights activists, Brazil has created an enormous system of reserves for Indian tribes and communities that extract products from the forests, as well as conservation areas. National parks, Indian reserves and conservation areas cover more than 370 million acres, or nearly 40% of Brazil's Amazonian biome. If adequately protected from illegal intrusion, these conservation areas would constitute an immense reserve for preservation of biodiversity, but many have been invaded by loggers and wildcat miners and burned out by cattle ranchers. Private land holders, who claim 25% of the Amazon biome, are required by law to maintain ecological reserves of up to 80% of their property, but this is hard to enforce on a wild frontier. Amazon land use needs to be better managed through a political commitment by federal and state governments to effective law enforcement, backed up by financing of ecologically sustainable uses of the primeval rainforest and its biodiversity, including payment for maintaining forests that capture carbon and sustain rain cycles. ●

---

reduction through large-scale income redistribution. The ambiguity borne of these tensions has a paralyzing effect on policy decisions that are vital for domestic and foreign investors. Henrique Meirelles, a former president of Brazil's Central Bank, summed up the nature of the problem in a statement in 2014:

Unfortunately, there persists in sectors of Brazilian thinking the belief, already discarded in countries with greater economic success, that a government with social preoccupations needs to be anti-business and anti-market, with a restrictive vision of the private sector—an inheritance from the Marxist tradition that sees profit as an improper appropriation of the wealth of laborers. The collapse of the Soviet bloc showed beyond doubt the failure of that system and the limitations of the producer State. This stimulated the search for economic efficiency and the capacity of the private sector to generate wealth and profits. These provide the resources, through taxation, to maintain social programs, education, and public health. And they finance the investments that generate employment, the great distributor of income. Despite the historic evidence, we still have great difficulty in accepting this reality in Latin America.

Under recent Brazilian governments dominated by the leftist Worker Party (PT), private investment has slowed and the economy has stagnated as inflation wiped out income gains and taxes soared. The decline deepened after 2010 under President Dilma Rousseff, the handpicked successor of President Luiz Inácio Lula da Silva, the historic leader of the PT. Lula da Silva, a pragmatic union leader, retained the orthodox development policies and fiscal disciplines

Brazilian States Grouped by Region

- AMAZONIA
- CENTER-WEST
- NORTHEAST
- SOUTHEAST
- SOUTH

Watershed and Wetland Areas

- AMAZON BASIN
- PANTANAL

LUCIDITY INFORMATION DESIGN, LLC

inherited from his predecessor, Fernando Henrique Cardoso of the centrist Social Democratic (PSDB) Party. Rousseff, however, undertook a number of aggressive economic policy interventions meant to reduce interest rates and electricity prices. In the end, the government squandered public resources needed for infrastructure investments by introducing politically popular, but unfinanced, consumer subsidies for petroleum products and energy services. These interventions backfired —deficits grew and by 2014, economic growth had shrunk to zero. Frustrated with government fail-

ures and evidence of widespread government corruption, many dissatisfied electors turned into opponents of President Rousseff´s bid for a second term.

Election

Yet, despite the many warning signs that Brazil´s economy is moving toward a crisis of growth stagnation with price inflation, Brazil´s 142 million registered voters chose continuity that preserves social payments, and gave President Rousseff a second four-year term in a presidential election in October 2014 that was a model of democratic

choice. After an ugly campaign marked by personal insults between the candidates and few tangible policy proposals, Rousseff edged out Aécio Neves, candidate of the opposition PSDB. Rousseff received a total of 51.65% of the valid votes providing a winning margin of 3 million votes over Neves.

This was the closest presidential race since democratic elections were restored in Brazil in 1989 after 21 years of military rule. Rousseff´s victory came because of a deep political divide in which Brazil´s poor and less-educated northeastern "red" states voted for the populist

PT candidate by a landslide 70%–30% proportion that wiped out the majority vote for Neves in the industrialized "blue" states of Brazil's southern region, centered in São Paulo. In the south and the agriculture frontier of central Brazil, the anti-PT sentiment favored Neves by a wide margin and ousted PT candidates for governor and federal senators in São Paulo, Parana, and Rio Grande do Sul. The tilt in favor of Rousseff came in Minas Gerais, the central state that is the second-largest electoral district after São Paulo, and the home state of Neves. This was a stunning defeat for Neves and the PSDB which will have to build for the future on a strong opposition role in the senate, where Neves, already a senator, will be joined by Jose Serra, a former presidential candidate, who was elected senator from São Paulo.

Brazil is badly split politically and President Rousseff in her new term will have a difficult time introducing economic reforms and applying the deficit reductions that she avoided during her first term. The populist political combinations that the PT and its allies made to win this election, including corrupt payments to other parties for a PT-led coalition majority in congress, are now going to aim for a new presidential election in 2018 when the likely PT candidate, former president Luiz Inácio Lula da Silva, is already negotiating with other parties, like the Democratic Movement Party (PMDB). There are 28 political parties in the Brazilian congress and many of these, starting with the PMDB, provide their votes to the highest bidder.

With a PT president holding the federal checkbook—the largest single source of public funds in Brazil—everything is negotiable with a congress dominated by interest groups and political opportunists. The money comes from shakedowns of contractors bidding for lucrative public projects in state-run companies like Petrobras. This leads to widespread political corruption involving officials who enjoy guarantees of immunity that have only recently begun to be challenged by public prosecutors in Brazil's evolving democracy. With national attention focused on an enormous corruption scandal in Petrobras, Roussef reset her populist economic policies for her second term, and named Joaquim Levy, a respected financial executive with orthodox credentials, as her new minister of economy.

Brazilians dream of becoming a more inclusive society that will set a democratic example to the world. In recent years, Brazil has pushed ahead with social programs that reduce inequality and moderate political unrest. Poverty—measured by the number of people living with incomes of less than $2 per day—has fallen markedly, from 21% of the population in 2003 to 9% in 2012. Personal income of the poorest 10% of the population grew 7% a year during that decade, while that of the wealthiest 10%, grew 1.7%. This helped decrease income inequality to reach a 50-year low in 2012.

But averages in Brazil can be deceptive. The disparity between the lifestyle and opportunities afforded to the wealthy minority and the poor majority remains enormous. The wealthiest 10% of the population earns as much annually as the 50% who make up the working class. Closing the gap requires strong economic growth and Brazil's social ideals are not always accompanied by practical ways and means to reach these goals. And when such opportunity does come about, Brazil finds it is poorly prepared to make the most of its good fortune. ■

Brazil in the world

Ecologically, Brazil is a global giant. The world's fifth largest country by area (see map), Brazil is experiencing a natural resource revolution in the use of water and land. Indeed, as possessor of the world's largest tropical forests, teeming with biological diversity, Brazil is making pioneering efforts to use its valuable ecosystems in renewable ways. Ecologists hope Brazil will become a "green" leader in environmental conservation, preserving the biodiversity of its tropical biomes (ecological communities) and contributing to stabilizing global climate change. With nearly 40% of the world's population living within the globe's tropical belt, Brazil's successes can set an example for many others as well.

South America's biggest country is a peacemaker. Brazil's military expenditures are modest. Despite an abundance of uranium, it has no nuclear arms program and is committed to nonproliferation. Culturally and historically, Brazil is part of the West, yet it has begun to pursue expanded trade with new markets in Asia, such as China and India, and close cooperation with Africa, where Brazil has strong cultural ties and economic interests. (This is sometimes referred to as a South-South alignment.) Still, only economic integration with its South American neighbors is awarded the status of a "special" relationship. Its "soft" diplomacy focuses on poverty remediation, conflict resolution, religious tolerance, and ethnic assimilation.

The arrival of Brazil on the global stage as a player to be reckoned with is the result of a long, often frustratingly slow process. Why has Brazil only now, at the start of the 21st century, entered a new era that brings its hopes of being an influential world power closer to reality? Is there a new dynamic that will overcome the bottlenecks in education, technical innovation and shoddy governance that have held back Brazil's development? As Brazil gains international stature, what role will it play in the world? What can Brazil contribute to global cooperation?

In an attempt to show off its advances to the world, Brazil chose to put itself on display in a series of international events. The first was the United Nations Conference on the Global Environment in 2012, dubbed Rio+20 because it came 20 years after a 1992 meeting (also in Rio) that made climate change into a global issue. In 2014 Brazil hosted the Soccer World Cup. In summer 2016 Rio de Janeiro will stage the Olympic Games. Finally 2022 will mark the 200th anniversary of Brazil's independence from Portugal. Brazil wants to show the world that its hour has come. ■

Brazil today

Between the tropics of Cancer and Capricorn that girdle the globe, more solar energy is shed year round than anywhere else on earth. The tropical zone, where the sun is always high in the sky, contains 39% of the world's land. Brazil's territory is the largest within this intertropical belt. The rivers that flow through Brazil provide the world's largest source of unfrozen freshwater. In the tropics, intense year-round photosynthesis produces dense forests that enclose highly diversified life systems.

In fact, no other ecological zone on earth has the same potential for increased food production as the tropics. It is no exaggeration to say that as global population grows toward 9 billion people in 2050, the output of Brazil's farms and ranches will increasingly be vital for world food security. Agriculture, cattle ranching, and timber extraction flourish, as do plantation forests for cellulose. The country is a leader in production of animal proteins—beef, poultry and pork—as well as soybeans, sugarcane, and the breakfast favorites, orange juice and coffee. There is great potential for expanded corn and dairy production. But what sets Brazil apart is that only half of its land suitable for agriculture, cattle ranching, and forest plantations is in use and most of its dense tropical forests remain intact. Brazil's food production could double with further deforestation. Brazil's farming know-how can show the way for other underdeveloped tropical lands, particularly in Africa.

Brazil is a land of discoveries, with multiple new frontiers. Until 50 years ago, the central plateau of Brazil, a well-watered, rolling bush land called *cerrado*, was considered virtually worthless because of soil nutrient deficiencies. When researchers discovered how to correct the soil, spreading limestone to reduce toxic acidity, and introduced new cultivars, like soybeans, nourished by chemical fertilizers, and *brachiaria*, a hardy African grass for pastures, an agricultural boom began in an area

Cows graze on deforested Amazon rainforest, next to another tract recently cleared and burned, near the city of Novo Progresso, Para state, September 23, 2013. The Amazon rainforest is being eaten away at by deforestation, much of which takes place as areas are burnt by large fires to clear land for agriculture. (IMAGE BY © NACHO DOCE/REUTERS/CORBIS)

covering 1.2 million square miles. The *cerrado* produced a land rush of farmers from southern Brazil who brought with them know-how, modern mechanized farming technologies and, above all, their families to settle in what had been considered a wasteland. These new settlements are a major source of the food that city dwellers consume as a result of a demographic revolution that has transformed Brazil´s population distribution from 65% rural in 1950 to 85% urban today.

Another recent breakthrough has been the discovery of major offshore oil fields along the South Atlantic coast, which stand to make Brazil not only self-sufficient in oil and gas but potentially a large exporter of crude oil and products. Drilling deep into the continental shelf, oil companies led by Petrobras, Brazil's state-owned energy firm, have found 16 billion barrels of proven oil and gas reserves. Industry analysts estimate Brazil's offshore fields could hold up to 55 billion barrels. The demand for drilling platforms, pipelines, ports, electronic technologies and naval construction for the oil sector has produced an industrial boom involving big foreign investments and imports of

equipment. Growing access to natural gas has revolutionized the energy sector and stimulated production of raw materials for the plastic and fertilizer industries. The energy market is becoming increasingly diverse, as suppliers convert sugarcane into ethanol to fuel cars and provide the raw materials for "green" plastics.

Although only a small part of Brazil's interior has been surveyed geologically, mining discoveries have produced another window of opportunity. Brazil has become the world's leading producer and exporter of iron ore. This development is symbolized by the great Carajas mining district, discovered when a geological exploration team made a forced landing in a helicopter at the jungle site of the future mine in the Amazonian state of Para. After building a 500-plus mile railroad to an Atlantic port in the state of Maranhao, Vale S.A., Brazil's mining giant, developed a fleet of ships that carry 150 million tons a year of high-quality iron ore to China, Japan, South Korea and Europe. Major deposits of bauxite are in production for aluminum refineries, and large amounts of manganese, copper, tin and gold are being mined. High-grade uranium deposits provide fuel for Brazil's nuclear power plants. Precious rare earths, providing high conductivity metals for electronic devices, have begun to emerge. The search is on.

Brazil's riches are not just a natural resource windfall—the country is also home to a vibrant consumer market that generates a wide spectrum of demand for food, energy and industrial products. Brazil is the fourth-largest auto vehicle market in the world. Demand for household durables, like refrigerators and television sets, grows 10% a year, spurred by easy credit and new housing. Brazilian construction contractors are among the biggest in the world, building highways, and dams in Brazil and throughout the world. A telecommunications revolution has connected about 142 million users to cell phone systems and drastically boosted Internet penetration rates. This network provides instant connectivity for banks, lotteries, schools, government institutions and bloggers. The expanding size of this national market and Brazil's proven capacity to produce commodity exports is what compels foreign investors to bet heavily on Brazil's rise. After the global recession of 2007–08 redirected capital toward emerging markets, Brazil received

substantial foreign direct investment and loans. By 2013 the total of foreign direct investment had passed $64 billion as Brazil's economy became increasingly globalized.

Brazil's great opportunities have given rise to great expectations, but the country has been slow to benefit. Brazil's glowing prospects are offset by the weaknesses it must overcome for the transition to succeed. It is facing the challenge of developing strategies to manage several new frontiers, all at the same time. There is the advancing agricultural frontier of the center-west that requires a new transportation system of railroads, highways and river canals along the approaches to the deep Amazon biome, an ecologically sensitive area that runs the risk of suffering environmental change of global importance if not well managed. There is the 4,660 mile maritime frontier where the development of off-shore oil and gas discoveries has placed an entire marine domain under ecological stress.

There is the urban frontier where metropolitan mega-centers, led by greater São Paulo's 20 million people and Rio de Janeiro's 11 million, head a list of 15 cities of over 1 million, with another 250 of over 100,000 people. Since 1960, Brazil's cities and towns

have received a massive influx of migrants fleeing from poverty in the rural interior in search of jobs in industry, construction and urban services.

Each frontier poses different problems requiring huge investments in infrastructure, housing, urban waterworks, public services, and communications that interlock one region with another in a vast national market. In the end, all the frontiers have in common the need to manage a territory in which human beings have to harmonize their economic and social activities with the natural surroundings.

Brazil's economic emergence was greeted initially as an accomplishment comparable to the successful launch of a spaceship. An eye-catching cover of *The Economist* in November 2009 gleamed with the statue of Christ the Redeemer, a Rio de Janeiro landmark, rocketing into the sky like a space vehicle over a title saying "Brazil Takes Off." Three years later this hasty triumphalism gave way to cold realism. Growth slowed as structural problems emerged in transportation and in the workforce. As the economy lost momentum, foreign investors pulled out of profitless steel mills and shipyards. The stock market fell sharply when Petrobras, the state oil company entrusted with development of the offshore oil discoveries, cut back predictions of oil and gas production and reported losses on its operations because of political manipulation of domestic fuel prices. A new cover showed the symbolic statue crashing into the sea.

Brazilian development is going to be a long, cumulative learning process, poorly organized, wasteful and full of contradictions until it overcomes a legacy of short-run economic improvisation. The main challenge is to develop infrastructure adequate to seize the opportunities created by abundant natural resources and Brazil's expansion into global markets. Choke points include woefully inadequate highways, railroads, inland waterways and ports for the transportation system unable to meet the needs of an expanding economy. Brazilian industry relies heavily on foreign technology and lags behind oth-

An aerial view taken in April 2006 of Paraisopolis, a slum located in the Morumbi neighborhood of São Paulo, South America's biggest city and one of the three biggest metropolises in the world. (IMAGE BY © PAULO WHITAKER/REUTERS/CORBIS)

er industrial countries, including China and India, in homegrown innovation.

Development is further weighed down by severe income equality, and limited opportunities for upward social mobility have created political tensions. Education and health are below the standards expected for a country that has an annual per capita income of roughly $12,000. Human capital is tested by a demand for managers, engineers and technical workers. Environmental damage to Amazonian forests and high crime rates in urban centers are both downsides of expanded land use and rapid urbanization. Poverty has dropped overall, but it remains a serious problem in large cities and rural areas. And even with its world-class agriculture, Brazil's food security agency said in 2010 that 11 million people were going hungry because they did not make enough money to feed their families.

Eliminating extreme poverty (per capita income of less than $2 a day) has been a priority for recent democratic governments, which have been more responsive to social demands than the authoritarian military governments of the recent past. Nevertheless, even the democratically elected leaders have been unable to stop political opportunists from plundering public money for private gain with virtual impunity, thanks to a weak judicial system. Improvement in governance is desperately needed, but reforms to clean up politics and increase accountability have been resisted by interest groups and the political class.

Crossing the threshold from a society plagued by a heritage of poverty and inequality into a dynamic forward-looking achiever of modern development poses new problems. The most important is social inclusion. The wealth created by economic growth has benefited some social classes and regions more than others. The political challenge is to provide more opportunities for those lagging behind in the creation of income. It is widely recognized that this requires improving education for 50 million students, many of whom are ill-prepared for employment and citizenship. Among 17- to

A demonstrator wears a costume that represents the Amazon rainforest during a march at the People's Summit at Rio+20 for Social and Environmental Justice in Rio de Janeiro June 20, 2012. (IMAGE BY © STRINGER/BRAZIL/REUTERS/CORBIS)

24-year-olds, only half complete high school, and, of those who advance to the university level, only 15% graduate. Until this waste of human resources improves, government programs that transfer cash to the poorest families provide a safety net that helps keep poorer children in school and off the streets. This "poverty entitlement" is politically popular, but handing out public alms to 16 million needy families can only lead to economic and social inclusion if education promotes labor skills, enterprise and innovation.

Another central problem for Brazil is a split over how it should manage its ecological endowment, regarded by many scientists as vital for control of global climate change and preservation of biodiversity. The main split is between proponents of the "feed the world" model—those for boosting Brazilian agriculture by intensifying use of land and water for food crops, cattle ranching and bioenergy—and the "nature preservation" model, defended by a very active ecological community that fights for legal limits on deforestation and conservation of biodiversity. This conflict taps into a desire for economic development to be compatible with sustainability, even if this means placing restrictions on individual economic gain. Some eco-strategists go further,

arguing that Brazil should be a world leader in reducing carbon emissions and protecting its biomes.

Whether Brazil becomes a "green" champion or a "villain" of environmental destruction depends on improving governance and fostering a new civic mentality that values law enforcement and an ecologically sustainable economy. Some policies of this nature have already been implemented. In 2012 a new forestry code regulating land use and water conservation, along with preservation of forest resources on private land, became law and Brazil reduced annual loss of tropical forest from a peak of 10,695 square miles (an area equal to Massachusetts) in 2004 to about 2,239 square miles in 2013.

As of now, less than 20% of Brazil's Amazon rain forests has been torn down; however, maintaining the remaining rain forest will require continuing efforts in law enforcement and mobilization of local communities to preserve their natural habitat. With major investments in hydroelectric stations, interstate highways and river transport now opening up the deep interior, preserving the ecological services of Amazonia´s forests, including the abundant rainfall for agricultural production in central Brazil, will be a difficult task.   ∎

Civil society

Modernization has not been limited to improvements in the economic sphere. Civil society has also come to life on issues involving social equity and political rights. Since the end of an authoritarian military regime in 1985 and the restoration of democracy, there has been an unprecedented expansion of nongovernmental organizations (NGOs) and nonprofit social initiatives, many supported by large enterprises. Most focus on education, environmental protection, political ethics and urban development. These civic organizations mobilize public opinion, monitoring government policies and performance, and in creating new technologies that offer innovative solutions to social problems.

A vibrant free press has brought to light corruption by law-breaking politicians and their business cronies. Brazil's justice system belatedly confronted the rampant corruption. In 2013 a majority of the Supreme Court convicted the top leadership of the PT for mounting a system of payoffs to bribe members of congress to vote with the PT government. The chief PT politicians were sentenced to jail time and lost their right to be elected. This was an unprecedented blow against impunity in Brazilian politics, but it did not recover millions of dollars in public money that were diverted to finance the bribery scheme properly called by the chief prosecutor "the worst scandal" in Brazilian political history.

The courts also began to enforce laws disqualifying candidates for elective office who were convicted of crimes confirmed by a court of appeal. A vice president of the chamber of deputies was expelled for corruption and two prominent former governors, Paulo Maluf of Sao Paulo and Jose Roberto Arruda of the Federal District of Brasilia, were legally barred from running in 2014. ∎

The future

The future has often seemed elusive, uncertain, even enigmatic in Brazil. In colonial times, European thinkers, like Montesquieu, saw Brazil as condemned to backwardness because of its tropical climate. The French savant said the tropics made people "inconstant," less capable of sustained or decisive action, excessively "amorous," and prone to practice slavery, which the author of *The Spirit of the Laws* roundly condemned. Theologians like Caspar Barlaeus, who also mapped a short-lived Dutch occupation of Brazil's northeast region, claimed that below the equator there was "no sense of sin."

Brazil's slave-owning elite were swept by the wave of racist pessimism after the country achieved independence in 1822. The ruling classes of Portuguese origin despaired of building a successful nation based on a mixed population drawing heavily on black slaves and Indians. Their official policy promoted European immigration to "whiten" the mix without going as far as formal apartheid. In practice, what prevailed was the "browning" of Brazil through extensive miscegenation. When a large influx of European immigrants came in the 19th century following a boom in coffee production that required more workers, pessimists said Brazil would never achieve modernity as a single-crop coffee exporter without developing a national industry for a domestic market. Even when industrialization advanced, doubts remained because Brazil showed little creativity in technology.

Stefan Zweig, a widely read author in Europe before World War II, sought asylum in Brazil from the Nazi persecution of Jews. He wrote an admiring book about his haven entitled *Brazil, the Land of the Future*. Ever since, when the future of Brazil is discussed, someone will inevitably say: "Yes, Brazil is the land of the future and always will be." Such skeptics argue that Brazil, free of wars and earthquakes and endowed with bountiful natural resources, is just a happy-go-lucky land that has never lived up to its opportunities. Indeed, there have been astonishing delays in the development of Brazil's potential in mining, fishery and tourism. Brazil's economic totem is not the swift Asian tiger. For Brazil, a candidate for totem could be the anaconda (*sucuri*), the gigantic python of Brazilian rivers that encoils and crushes its prey with brute strength. But Brazil needs a symbol that represents innovative intelligence in the use of its resources and stirs the creative imagination of its people. Preferred is the macaw (*arara*), a gorgeously plumed parrot with blue-green-red-and-yellow feathers that soars over the Amazon forests, perches on the tallest tree and can see, at a piercing glance, anything that moves below the canopy. That is what Brazil needs: clear vision. ∎

Flocks of Graza Mora, Pantanal Conservation Area, unesco World Heritage Site, Brazil, South America, in Jan. 2012.(IMAGE BY © MICHAEL RUNKEL/ROBERT HARDING WORLD IMAGERY/ CORBIS)

Political style

Since democratic government was restored in 1985 after two decades of military rule, two political parties have dominated Brazil's national politics: the centrist PSDB and the populist-left PT. In 1994 the political system was facing a major crisis. With a presidential election approaching, inflation was threatening to run out of control, a recurrent problem in Brazil, which had defaulted on its public debt in 1987. A group of creative economists, acting under the leadership of Fernando Henrique Cardoso, a politically experienced sociologist who was minister of finance in the government of then President Itamar Franco, successfully created a stabilization plan called Plano Real that tamed inflation and restored public confidence. Thanks to a well-managed transition to a new currency, called *real*, price increases were contained and the purchasing power of wage earners rose. The stabilization was so politically popular that Cardoso, as candidate of the PSDB, was elected president for two consecutive terms.

The Plano Real has proved to be the cornerstone of Brazil's political stability and economic boom. During the Cardoso government, the PT, led by Lula da Silva, a union organizer, denounced the Plano Real as a capitalist trick and voted repeatedly in congress against implementing legislation. Some tax and social security reforms that formed part of the stabilization plan were blocked, but the goal of providing a strong currency was achieved. Foreign investors began to see Brazil as a safe bet for long-term productive investments. They were unsure, however, about the political future if a "populist" government came to power. When Lula da Silva was elected president in 2002 he dropped his earlier resistance and embraced the stabilization principles of the Plano Real. He moved even further toward stability by accumulating over $300 billion in exchange reserves as insurance against foreign trade deficits. The now much admired "New Brazil" arose on this foundation.

Brazil's political synthesis maintains free-market incentives, property rights and public credit that stimulate private initiative and wealth creation. Efficient tax collection provides financing for social programs. Mass-market consumption is stimulated by income redistribution through wage policies that keep purchasing power ahead of inflation, by consumer credit that reaches the low-income majorities, by subsidized social security pensions for the needy, by public cash transfers to the poorest families, and by free public education and health coverage that is low in quality but universal. These policies promote social mobility and the growth of a middle class. The key word in the Brazilian consensus is "inclusion." The slogan for President Lula da Silva´s administration was "Brazil, a country for everyone." In other words, well-being should not be a privilege of the rich and uplifting the poor should be a primary goal of public policy.

Lula da Silva left office as the most popular president in Brazilian history and his successor, Dilma Rousseff, was elected on a platform that stressed "eradication of misery." The election, said Andre Singer, a PT political analyst, demonstrated that the public wants "distribution of income without political radicalism." But Eduardo Giannetti da Fonseca, a historian, has said that Brazil will always be "the country of the future" unless it begins to invest more in its future, transferring resources from current consumption to the formation of human capital through quality education. "There are no shortcuts to the future, we have to make the effort to save and invest now to improve our tomorrow," says Giannetti, who became a close adviser to Marina da Silva, an ecological militant born in an Amazon rubber-tapper community, who ran third in the presidential race in 2014.

But there are skeptics who question Brazil's economic future if commodity prices deteriorate and foreign credit dries up. They recall the collapse of the economic "miracle" promoted by the military regime in the 1970s when Brazil's gross national product (GNP) grew at 10% a year. The bust came when foreign oil prices soared and Brazil continued borrowing abroad to pay its oil bills until it could no longer meet growing foreign-debt payments. Now, Brazil enjoys much more favorable oil prospects. National production of oil

Brazil's president, Luiz Inacio Lula da Silva (L), poses for a photo with Brazilian President-elect Dilma Rousseff, celebrating her election victory at the Alvorada Palace, in Brasilia, capital of Brazil, Nov. 1, 2010. (IMAGE BY © AGENCIA ESTADO/XINHUA PRESS/CORBIS)

A Petrobras oil platform in Guabanara bay in Rio de Janeiro, Sept. 24, 2010. Brazilian state oil company Petrobras raised $70 billion in the world's biggest share offering, giving the company the financial muscle it needs to tap vast offshore oil reserves. (IMAGE BY © BRUNO DOMINGOS/REUTERS/CORBIS)

and gas is expected to double, reaching 4 million barrels a day in 2020. The offshore oil discoveries protect Brazil from spikes in international energy prices. With foreign investments pouring in and swelling exchange reserves, servicing Brazil's foreign debt should not be a problem. But as a big spender on government projects and public payrolls, overall public debt has grown at a faster rate than GNP, so Brazil has to tighten some loose screws in its public finances. With prudent management of its economy, Brazil is not condemned to endless boom-and-bust cycles, but there is the danger that reckless policies could undermine sustainable development.

Another concern raised by some analysts is that Brazil's oil discoveries and rising commodity exports will produce what economists call the "Dutch disease." This is what happens when a country becomes overly dependent on revenue from a single export, like oil, while crowding out other economic activities, such as domestic manufacturing. That scenario does not fit Brazil's

economy. The oil industry promotes investments in a wide range of industrial and service activities. Domestic energy demands absorb a major share of oil and gas production.

Like any commodity exporter, Brazil has to expect ups and downs in global prices, but with its mix of agricultural, mining, energy and industrial exports, Brazil is far from dependent on one commodity. Natural resource exports are not a "curse" if the revenues are invested productively in diversified development. Being competitive internationally depends on innovation, efficient management and labor productivity and infrastructure to reduce costs, all of which are part of Brazil's learning curve.

The real danger is not "Dutch disease" but what could be called "Brazilian disease." This is a tendency toward halfway measures that try to accommodate conflicting interests and postpone decisive action, with imprecise responses that lead to confusion. Sometimes this confusion is sought deliberately by wily manipulators, who

practice the deceits contained in the noxious Brazilian saying, "You may win, but you will not collect." Sometimes it reflects hope for magical solutions where what is necessary is hard thinking.

Nowhere is this more important than in economic policymaking. In constitutional terms, Brazil functions in the framework of a market economy with legal protection for private property rights and the sanctity of contracts. At the same time, there are strong political currents that favor state intervention in the economy and limitations on the use of private property, invoking doctrines that are supposedly not served by profit-seeking entrepreneurs. Still, political interests often prevail over economic criteria. Political groups capture control of state enterprises, such as Petrobras, and use the "strategic" energy company to control fuel prices and the allotment of huge public contracts that promote chosen sectors, regardless of efficiency. Public institutions, such as pension funds and state-owned banks, are used to finance friendly candidates in elections to control the state and its economic policies. This strategy involves appointment of tens of thousands of party loyalists to high-paying public-sector jobs, awarding contracts to bidders who frequently engage in corrupt practices, and extending social subsidies to low-income beneficiaries who are also voters.

The PT first came to power using this method, both on the metropolitan and national level. Maintaining this economically inefficient system requires heavy taxation to generate public revenues that can be used for political purposes. As a result, there was fierce resistance in the PT to privatization of sectors of the state-run economy, be it energy, education, toll roads, or airports that might deprive the political class of the benefits of this state-directed "political economy." These parasitic practices are embedded in Brazilian political customs and require constant vigilance by public ministries and regulators to contain the damage. Fiscal responsibility is essential for Brazil to achieve its goals. ∎

Brazil and the U.S.

In the age of the BRICS, Brazil is exploring a new range of foreign relations. A century of close Pan-American cooperation with the U.S. in peace and war has given way to an "independent" Brazilian foreign policy that has chosen to align Brazil with opponents of the U.S. This shift is partly due to Brazil´s powerful commercial expansion toward BRICS partners like China and Russia but it is also driven by ideological advocates of leftist nationalism in the foreign policy councils of the governing PT. In 2014, China displaced the U.S. as Brazil´s largest trading partner and a "strategic agreement" was reached during a visit to Brazil by Chinese President Xi Jinping to increase Chinese investments in Brazilian railroads, electricity generation, oil exploration and other infrastructure projects essential for Brazil´s economic development. This was extolled by former president Lula da Silva, the main PT strategist, as evidence that the BRICS hold the key to the world's economic future if they form an alliance that can supersede the Western economic bloc led by the U.S. In a "multipolar" world, said Lula da Silva, the BRICS would bring pressure on the rich countries to accept a "more just economic and political order" With this division of the world into the equivalent of class conflict, Lula da Silva cast the U.S. as "refractory" to "social justice" in international relations and the BRICS as champions of the poor.

In practice, what this has produced in Brazil´s recent foreign policy is a failed attempt to mediate in Iran´s nuclear dispute with the U.S., rejection of any international intervention in Syria´s civil war, one-sided support for the Palestinian side in the Gaza conflict, and support for violent repression of political protestors by Venezuela´s authoritarian regime. Beyond the Latin American region, Brazil has minimal influence in settlement of conflicts, but in the region Brazil has chosen to ally itself with Venezuela and Argentina, two authoritarian populist regimes that are the most evident economic failures in the region and chronic violators of human and political rights. But both are important markets for Brazil´s uncompetitive protected industries, like automobiles, and Venezuela is a major importer of Brazilian food products. In Brazil´s alignment with Venezuela, support for Cuba is also part of the deal. Venezuela is Cuba´s source of cheap oil and Brazil is contributing by its policy to the stability of the shaky government of President Nicolas Maduro. Brazil is also building a $1 billion port at Mariel on Cuba's north shore, facing the U.S., that is vital for Cuban exports if the Castro regime ever normalizes its trade relations. But none of Brazil´s moves in Latin America are coordinated with the U.S., as had been the case since Pan-Americanism was launched as a Western Hemisphere policy in 19th century. Brazil fought alongside the allies during World War II against the Nazi aggression, and joined U.S. forces in blocking an attempt by leftist guerrillas to take power in the Dominican Republic in 1965. No such joint action is imaginable today with Brazil reaching out to new anti-American partners.

There is no lack of opportunities for Brazil-U.S. cooperation if mutual mistrust is overcome and pragmatic diplomacy replaces ideological posturing. The most important areas are global food security through worldwide development of tropical agriculture; clean energy alternatives reducing carbon emissions; space exploration and telecommunications; and health research. Only a change in Brazil's government, bringing leaders with more creative thinking on the benefits of good political relations with the U.S., can change the current sterile situation.

After her reelection, President Rousseff received a congratulatory phone call from President Barack Obama, who renewed an invitation for an official visit to the U.S. This opened possibilities for a rapprochement in Brazil-U.S. relations that have been impaired since Edward Snowden´s revelations in 2013 of the secrets of the National Security Administration showed that Rousseff´s electronic communications were monitored by the U.S. government. This led Rousseff to cancel a scheduled visit to the U.S. •

A truck is loaded with sugar cane At Usina da Mata Ethanol, Sugar and Energy. Valparaiso, Brazil, Sept. 18, 2014. (IMAGE BY © PAULO FRIDMAN/CORBIS)

discussion questions

1. Brazil has advocated for a more equal playing field in the global community, challenging U.S. influence over international organizations. Would a seat on the UN Security Council bring Brazil more in line with U.S. interests because of their larger voice and greater responsibility on the global stage? Or is it more likely that Brazil would use this opportunity to assert its independence and its own interests on the world stage?

2. Brazil's investment in infrastructure for the 2014 World Cup caused protests from an unhappy middle class. With Brazil set to host the 2016 Summer Olympics and protestors demands left largely unmet, will demonstrations and unrest return ahead of the games? Can Brazil address the demands of its people?

3. Brazil is a vital member of the South American trade block Mercosur. Does Brazil's status as a BRICS member mean it will chase more lucrative trade agreements in the international community? id development? How will Brazil's stronger economy affect its relationship with other countries in the Mercosur trade bloc?

4. Brazil assumed more global responsibility when it held negotiations with Iran over its nuclear program. How effective has Brazil been in these negotiations? Are Brazil's negotiations with Iran counterproductive to what the U.S. would like to see as the outcome? If so, how?

5. A lot of discussion about the U.S.-Brazil relationship focuses on trade and cooperation. What other interests does the U.S. and Brazil share? What are their differences? How can they cooperate in the future?

---

suggested readings

Bethel, Leslie. **The Cambridge History of Latin America.** Cambridge: Cambridge University Press. 2008. 632 pp. This book offers a large-scale survey of Latin American from the past 70 years and examines profound political, economic and social changes Brazil experienced as it transitioned to the democracy.

Fishlow, Albert. **Starting Over: Brazil since 1985.** Washington, DC: Brookings Institution Press. 2011. 236 pp. This book covers Brazil's political and social change from authoritarian regime to democracy. Learn about the profound domestic transformation the country went through to reach the status it is at today.

Hunter, Wendy. **The Transformation of the Workers' Party in Brazil, 1989-2009.** Cambridge: Cambridge University Press. 2010. 252 pp. Relating to history, this book details Brazil's political evolution from the Workers' Party in 1989 to President Luiz Inacio "Lula" da Silva in 2009.

Reid, Michael. **Brazil: The Troubled Rise of a Global Power.**

New Haven: Yale University Press. 2014. 352 pp. This book claims that, among the other developing nations, Brazil is most overlooked. Picking up from the end of military rule, a detailed account of Brazil's rise to regional dominance and international prominence is presented.

Skidmore, Thomas. **Brazil: Five Centuries of Change**, 2nd Edition. Oxford: Oxford University Press. 2009. 304 pp. A lively political and economic narrative is provided to explain the last 500 years of Brazil's development. It offers in-depth coverage of the military coup in the 1960s, the return of democracy and concludes with the Luiz Inacio "Lula" da Silva presidency.

Thomas, Vinod. **From Inside Brazil: Development in a Land of Contrasts.** Redwood City: Stanford Univeristy Press. 2006. 224 pp. In a discussion of how Brazil's socioeconomic and political reforms will be pursued, the book examines presents a strong agenda for action and a plan for Brazil to achieve economic growth and improved welfare for its citizens.

✔ **DON'T FORGET TO VOTE!**
WWW.FPA.ORG/BALLOT

KEY TO ABBREVIATIONS AND ACRONYMS
FOR EACH ARTICLE NOW AVAILABLE ONLINE!

TO LEARN MORE ABOUT THIS TOPIC AND TO ACCESS WEB LINKS TO RESOURCES GO TO www.greatdecisions.org

Global Discussion Questions

No decision in foreign policy is made in a vacuum, and the repercussions of any single decision have far-reaching effects across the range of strategic interests on the U.S. policy agenda. This GREAT DECISIONS feature is intended to facilitate the discussion of this year's topics in a global context, to discuss the linkages between the topics and to encourage consideration of the broader impact of decisionmaking.

———————————————

1. Consider "Sectarianism in the Middle East" in the context of "U.S. policy toward Africa." How much influence has Islamic extremism in the Middle East had on growing extremist movements in Africa? Are there strong connections from African extremist groups to those in the Middle East? What can the U.S. learn from its experience fighting extremism in the Middle East that it should or should not apply to fighting extremism in Africa?

2. Consider "Sectarianism in the Middle East" in the context of "U.S. policy toward Africa." How much influence has Islamic extremism in the Middle East had on growing extremist movements in Africa? Are there strong connections from African extremist groups to those in the Middle East? What can the U.S. learn from its experience fighting extremism in the Middle East that it should or should not apply to fighting extremism in Africa?

3. Consider "Privacy in the digital age" in the context of "Brazil's metamorphosis." As the Snowden documents continued to be revealed, Brazil's relationship with the U.S. was badly damaged. With many countries in the region under Brazil's influence, did this damage the U.S. reputation with them as well? How will this affect Brazil's view on similar interests to the U.S.?

4. Consider "Russia and the near abroad" in the context of "Syria's refugee crisis." Russia's support for Bashar al-Assad's government in Syria is well-known. Not only does Russia speak up for Syria to the international community, but they provide material support as well. Does this give Russia a special responsibility to provide aid to refugees displaced by fighting? And should they play a larger role in resolving the conflict?

5. Consider "Human trafficking in the 21st century" in the context of "Syria's refugee crisis." Refugees in a crisis zone are at a high risk of being forced or coerced into human trafficking. Are governments and organizations involved with Syrian refugees providing enough security to stop this from happening? How can they ensure that local employers do not take advantage of the situation?

6. Consider "Privacy in the digital age" in the context of "Russia and the near abroad." There is evidence that Russia has engaged in state-sponsored cyberwarfare and cyberespionage. Will Russia receive the same backlash as the U.S. if revelations expose an international cyber espionage campaign as well? Will Russia adhere to international laws meant to control cyber espionage?

7. .Consider "Syria's refugee crisis" in the context of "Sectarianism in the Middle East." Countries like Lebanon have a distinct sectarian balance. As Syrian refugees pour across borders, could this threaten the stability of neighboring countries by adding large numbers of a different sect to a population? Is Syria's refugee crisis likely to disrupt Lebanon's fragile peace? If so, what can the U.S. and allies do to present sectarian conflicts from re-emerging?

8. Consider "Russia and the near abroad" in the context of "Privacy in the digital age." What can recent crackdowns on independent media and stricter regulations on speech tell us about Russia's approach to expression online? How has Russian media handled dissenting opinions both at home and abroad on hot button issues, such as the crisis in Ukraine?

For glossaries, additional readings and more, visit

www.GreatDecisions.org

1/DEFENSE TECHNOLOGY

How interested would you say you are in issues related to defense technology?

Very interested	48%
Somewhat interested	46%
Not too interested	6%
Not at all interested	n/a

How closely have you been following news about the U.S. government's use of unmanned aerial vehicles, commonly known as drones?

Very closely	29.3%
Somewhat closely	58.3%
Not too closely	11.8%
Not at all closely	0.6%

Assume the U.S. government is going to use drones to launch airstrikes in a foreign country. Do you agree or disagree that the U.S. government should obtain permission from the foreign country's government before launching the airstrikes?

Strongly agree	25.7%
Somewhat agree	46.5%
Somewhat disagree	20.1%
Strongly disagree	7.6%

Do you think the U.S. government should increase, maintain or decrease the amount of money it spends on programs to develop new defense technologies?

Increase the amount	40.1%
Maintain the current amount	38.8%
Decrease the amount	21.1%

Overall, do you think each of the following has made the United States safer from terrorism, less safe from terrorism, or hasn't made a difference?

	SAFER	LESS SAFE	NOT MADE A DIFFERENCE
The war in Afghanistan	30.8%	36.6%	32.6%
The NSA's phone and Internet surveillance programs	62.8%	14%	32.2%
The use of military drones to target extremists in countries such as Pakistan, Yemen and Somalia	66.7%	22.8%	10.5%

Do you think the U.S. government should or should not use drones to…?

	SHOULD	SHOULD NOT	NO OPINION
Launch airstrikes in other countries against foreigners who are suspected terrorists	54.1%	38%	7.9%
Launch airstrikes in other countries against U.S. citizens living abroad who are suspected terrorists	34.4%	55.5%	10.2%
Launch airstrikes in the U.S. against foreigners living in the U.S. who are suspected terrorists	10.2%	84.4%	5.4%
Launch airstrikes in the U.S. against U.S. citizens who are suspected terrorists	7.1%	87.2%	5.7%

2/ISRAEL AND THE U.S.

Should the U.S. government increase, keep the same, or decrease the following types of foreign aid it sends to Israel?

	INCREASE	KEEP THE SAME	DECREASE
Economic aid	5.2%	46.4%	48.4%
Military aid	6.8%	41%	52.2%

How interested would you say you are in issues related to "Israel and the U.S."?

Very interested	68.9%
Somewhat interested	28.4%
Not too interested	1.6%
Not at all interested	0.1%

In terms of resolving the dispute between Israel and the Palestinians, do you think the United States should be more involved than it is now, as involved as it currently is, or less involved than it is now?

More involved	17.8%
As involved as it currently is	59.8%
Less involved	22.4%

In the dispute between Israel and the Palestinians, do you think the United States should support Israel, support the Palestinians, or take a neutral position?

Support Israel	22.6%
Support the Palestinians	7.2%
Take a neutral position	70.3%

In the dispute between Israel and the Palestinians, which side do you sympathize with more, Israel or the Palestinians?

Israel	19.2%
Palestinians	27.7%
Both	44.4%
Neither	8.8%

People debate whether Israelis should be permitted to construct villages, called settlements, for Israelis in the Palestinian territories. Do you think Israelis should be permitted to build settlements in the Palestinian Territories, or do you think they should not?

Israelis should be permitted to build settlements in the Palestinian territories	12.1%
Israelis should not be permitted to build settlements in the Palestinian territories	87.9%

Do you think Israel and an independent Palestinian state could coexist peacefully with each other, or not?

Yes	78.7%
No	21.3%

What kind of effect has U.S. support for Israel had on U.S. relations with other countries in the Middle East?

Very positive effect	0.7%
Somewhat positive effect	54.2%
Neither positive nor negative effect	33.4%
Somewhat negative effect	5.1%
Very negative effect	6.6%

Following the political movements that started in 2010 known as the Arab Spring, new governments are being established in nations such as Libya, Egypt, and Tunisia. In your view, will these changes be mostly good for Israel, mostly bad for Israel, or will they have no impact?

Mostly good	23.4%
Mostly bad	48.4%
No impact	28.2%

Suppose Israel were to conduct airstrikes against Iranian nuclear facilities, Iran were to retaliate against Israel, and the two were to go to war. Do you think the U.S. should or should not bring its military forces into the war on the side of Israel and against Iran?

It should bring its military forces into the war on the side of Israel and against Iran.	34.3%
It should not bring its military forces into the war on the side of Israel and against Iran.	65.7%

3/TURKEY'S CHALLENGES

How interested would you say you are in issues related to "Turkey's Challenges"?

Very interested	42.4%
Somewhat interested	52.3%
Not too interested	5%
Not at all interested	0.4%

Please tell us whether you have a very favorable, somewhat favorable, somewhat unfavorable, or very unfavorable opinion of Turkey?

Very favorable	12.8%
Somewhat favorable	66.1%
Somewhat unfavorable	19.7%
Very unfavorable	1.3%

Generally speaking, do you think that Turkey's membership in the European Union would be...?

A good thing	66.8%
A bad thing	9.6%
Neither good nor bad	23.6%

How likely or not do you think it is that Turkey will join the European Union?

Very likely	3.7%
Somewhat likely	40.6%
Not too likely	48.2%
Not likely at all	7.5%

Some people say that the United States and Turkey have enough common values to be able to cooperate on international problems. Others say that the U.S. and Turkey have such different values that cooperating on international problems is impossible. Which is closer to your view?

Enough common values to cooperate on international problems	92.7%
Such different values that cooperating on international problems is impossible	7.3%

On international matters, with which one do you think Turkey would act in closest cooperation?

The countries of the EU	14.3%
The United States	5.2%
The countries of the Middle East	20.1%
Turkey would act alone	26.6%
All of the above	31.8%
None of the above	1.9%

On the issue of Turkey's membership to the European Union, to what extent do you agree or disagree with the following statements?

	AGREE STRONGLY	AGREE SOMEWHAT	DISAGREE SOMEWHAT	DISAGREE STRONGLY
Turkey's membership in the EU would help promote peace and stability in the Middle East.	17.4%	61.8%	17.8%	3%
Turkey's membership in the EU would be good in economic terms for Turkey.	41.2%	52.9%	5.1%	0.9%
Turkey's membership in the EU would be good in economic terms for the EU.	4%	9.6%	31.3%	55.1%
As a predominantly Muslim country, Turkey does not belong in the EU.	1.6%	8.4%	31.3%	55.1%
Turkey is too populous to be integrated into the EU.	2.8%	25%	46.5%	25.7%
Turkey's economy is too weak to be integrated into the EU.	18.1%	51.2%	27.8%	2.9%

How concerned are you that if Turkey's membership in the EU is delayed, the following things will happen?

	VERY CONCERNED	SOMEWHAT CONCERNED	A LITTLE CONCERNED	NOT AT ALL CONCERNED
Turkey will drift away from the EU.	16.1%	47.4%	25.1%	11.5%
Turkey will move toward the Middle East.	20.2%	42.3%	24.8%,	12.8%

Copies of the National Opinion Ballot Report are available upon request. The NOBR is also available at www.fpa.org as a PDF.

4/ISLAMIC AWAKENING

How interested would you say you are in issues related to the "Islamic Awakening" topic?

Very interested	64.9%
Somewhat interested	32.3%
Not too interested	2.6%
Not at all interested	0.3%

When it comes to recent changes in political leadership in Middle Eastern countries such as Egypt and Libya, do you think the United States should be more involved than it is now, as involved as it currently is, or less involved than it is now?

More involved than it is now	11.1%
As involved as it currently is	57.7%
Less involved than it is now	31.3%

In terms of the political situation in the Middle East, which is more important?

Democratic governments, even if there is less stability in the region	27.1%
Stable governments, even if there is less democracy in the region	72.9%

Suppose there is a Muslim-majority country that is not democratic and if it were democratic, the people would probably elect an Islamic fundamentalist leader. Do you think the U.S. should encourage democracy, discourage democracy, or take no position on the issue either way in that country?

Encourage democracy	37.6%
Discourage democracy	3.2%
Take no position either way	59.2%

Following the political movements that started in 2010 known as the Arab Spring, new governments are being established in nations such as Libya, Egypt and Tunisia. In your view, will these changes be mostly good for the United States, mostly bad for the United States, or will they have no impact?

Mostly good	36.4%
Mostly bad	38.5%
No impact	25.2%

Please select which of the following statements is closer to your own view:

Because Muslim religious, social and political traditions are incompatible with Western ways, violent conflict is inevitable.	17.8%
Because most Muslims are like people everywhere, we can find common ground and violent conflict between the civilizations is not inevitable.	82.2%

5/ENERGY INDEPENDENCE

How interested would you say you are in issues related to the "Energy Independence" topic?

Very interested	72.5%
Somewhat interested	25.9%
Not too interested	1.4%
Not at all interested	0.3%

Thinking about long-range foreign policy goals, how much priority do you think the U.S. government should give to reducing U.S. dependence on imported energy sources?

Top priority	62%
Some priority	36.3%
No priority at all	1.8%

How much do you favor or oppose expanding offshore drilling for oil and natural gas off the U.S. coast?

Strongly favor	23%
Somewhat favor	34.3%
Somewhat oppose	25.9%
Strongly oppose	n/a

How much of a threat to the vital interests of the United States in the next 10 years is U.S. dependence on foreign oil?

Critical threat	26.1%
Important but not critical threat	66.5%
Not important or critical threat	7.5%

Thinking about how to address America's dependence on foreign energy sources, please indicate whether you favor or oppose each of the following:

	FAVOR	OPPOSE
Creating tax incentives to encourage the development and use of alternative energy sources such as solar or wind power.	83.4%	16.6%
Requiring automakers to increase fuel efficiency, even if this means the price of cars would go up.	87.3%	12.7%
Building new nuclear power plants to reduce reliance on oil and coal.	59.3%	40.7%
Raising taxes on fuels such as coal and oil to encourage individuals and businesses to use less.	64%	36%

6/FOOD AND CLIMATE

How interested would you say you are in issues related to the "Food and Climate" topic?

Very interested	61.7%
Somewhat interested	34.3%
Not too interested	3.4%
Not at all interested	0.6%

Thinking about U.S. foreign policy goals, how important of a goal is combating world hunger?

Very important	56.1%
Somewhat important	35.1%
Not too important	1.9%
Not important at all	6.9%

Do you feel the amount the U.S. government spends on efforts to reduce hunger in poor countries is too much, too little, or about right?

Too much	15%
Too little	44.5%
About the right amount	40.5%

Please select which of the following two statements comes closer to your point of view.

The U.S. should only send aid to parts of the world where the U.S. has security interests.	12.3%
When hunger is a major problem in some part of the world, the U.S. should send aid whether or not the U.S. has a security interest in that region.	87.7%

When it comes to addressing the problem of hunger, there is a debate about whether the U.S. should just provide food or if it also should help poor countries develop their economies. Please select which of the following two statements you agree with more:

It is important to help poor countries develop their economies so that they can become more self-sufficient.	93.5%
Helping poor countries develop their economies is too complicated and it is impossible to tell if it is doing much good.	6.5%

Current U.S. food aid policy requires some of the food aid sent abroad to be grown or raised in the United States and shipped to countries in need. A current proposal before the U.S. government would relax these requirements and allow the U.S. government to give more flexible food aid, including purchasing food from local farmers or giving poor people in other countries money to purchase food themselves locally. Do you think the U.S. should maintain its current food aid policy or relax the current requirements to make food aid more flexible?

The U.S. government should maintain its current food aid policy.	24.4%
The U.S. government should relax the current requirements to make food aid more flexible.	75.7%

If you had to choose which countries should get U.S. aid, which of these would you select as most important?

Countries with the poorest economies	64.6%
Countries needed by the U.S. as trade partners	7.9%
Countries important to U.S. security	27.5%

Is it your overall impression, that over the last few decades the number of people in the world who do not have enough to eat has increased, decreased, or stayed about the same?

Increased	55.9%
Decreased	24.2%
Stayed the same	19.9%

There is a controversy over what the countries of the world, including the U.S., should do about the problem of climate change. Here are three statements. Please select which statement comes closest to your own point of view:

Until we are sure that climate change is really a problem we should not take any steps that would have economic costs.	6.6%
The problem of climate change should be addressed, but its effects will be gradual so we can deal with the problem gradually by taking steps that are low in cost.	28.2%
Climate change is a serious and pressing problem, and we should try taking steps now even if this involves significant costs.	65.1%

To deal with the problem of climate change, do you think the U.S. government is doing too much, not enough, or about the right amount?

Too much	9.7%
Not enough	73.4%
About the right amount	16.9%

There has been some discussion about the circumstances that might justify using U.S. troops in other parts of the world. Would you favor or oppose the use of U.S. troops to ensure the oil supply?

Favor	17.8%
Oppose	42.1%

Some people say that the world is facing some new problems that require new international institutions or agencies to deal with them. Do you think there should be new international institutions to monitor the worldwide energy market and predict potential shortages?

Should be	57.9%
Should not be	42.1%

How important is investing in renewable energy to the United States remaining competitive with other countries in the global economy?

Very important	68.5%
Somewhat important	23.6%
Not too important	6%
Not important at all	1.9%

How much do you agree or disagree that the United States should fund renewable energy projects over "traditional" energy projects, even if the payoff is not as immediately high?

Strongly agree	52.3%
Somewhat agree	30.4%
Somewhat disagree	9.8%
Strongly disagree	7.5%

7/CHINA'S FOREIGN POLICY

For each of the following possible future trends, please tell us if you would see it as mainly positive or mainly negative.

	MAINLY POSITIVE	MAINLY NEGATIVE
China becomes significantly more powerful economically	77.6%	22.4%
China becomes significantly more powerful militarily	6.8%	93.2%

How concerned are you about the following issues in U.S.-China relations:

	VERY CONCERNED	SOMEWHAT CONCERNED-	NOT TOO CONCERNED	NOT AT ALL CONCERNED
China's unwillingness to limit greenhouse emissions.	56.2%	33.1%	8.3%	2.4%
China's government limiting its people's access to the Internet.	45.3%	42.9%	10.5%	1.3%
China's keeping its currency cheap to make its exports more competitive.	41.4%	46.4%	10.5%	1.7%
China's repression of prodemocracy dissidents.	53.3%	38.6%	7.1%	1%
China's treatment of Tibet.	46.8%	38.1%	13%	2.1%
U.S. weapons sales to Taiwan despite China's objections.	12.2%	41.7%	37.1%	9%

How interested would you say you are in issues related to the "China's Foreign Policy" topic?

Very interested	60.4%
Somewhat interested	35.9%
Not too interested	3.6%
Not at all interested	0.2%

How much of a threat is China's emergence as a world power to the well-being of the United States?

Major threat	25%
Minor threat	54%
Not a threat	21%

All things considered, which of these descriptions comes closest to your view of China today? Do you think China is...?

An adversary of the United States	11.3%
A serious problem, but not an adversary	65.7%
Not much of a problem	23%

In general, do you think Chinese trade policy toward the U.S. is fair or unfair?

Fair	31.3%
Unfair	68.7%

Now thinking about U.S. foreign policy in Asia, do you think the U.S. should put a higher priority on building strong relations with traditional allies like South Korea and Japan even if this might diminish its relations with China, or put a higher priority on building new partnerships with China, even if this might diminish U.S. relations with its traditional allies?

Higher priority on building strong relations with traditional allies	47.7%
Higher priority on building new partnerships with China	52.3%

If China's economy were to grow to be as large or larger than the U.S. economy, do you think that would be mostly positive, mostly negative, or equally positive and negative?

Mostly positive	12.1%
Mostly negative	19.4%
Equally positive and negative	68.5%

In dealing with a rising China, do you think the U.S. should:

Undertake friendly cooperation and engagement with China	96.7%
Actively work to limit the growth of China's power	3.3%

When it comes to economic development do you think the way that the Chinese government manages its economy and its political system is more of an advantage or more of a disadvantage for China?

More of an advantage	47.1%
More of a disadvantage	52.9%

How worried are you, if at all, that China could become a military threat to the U.S. in the future? Please say whether you are very worried, somewhat worried, not too worried, or not worried at all?

Very worried	7.8%
Somewhat worried	42.6%
Not too worried	42.3%
Not worried at all	7.2%

8/TRADE

How interested would you say you are in issues related to U.S. trade policy?

Very interested	41.5%
Somewhat interested	51.1%
Not too interested	6.8%
Not at all interested	0.7%

People debate whether the U.S. government should increase restrictions on imports, keep restrictions on imports at current levels, or decrease restrictions on imports. What do you think the U.S. government should do?

Increase restrictions on imports	13.6%
Keep restrictions on imports at current levels	52.1%
Decrease restrictions on imports	34.3%

Do you think that reducing the U.S. trade deficit with foreign countries should be a very important foreign policy goal of the U.S. government, a somewhat important foreign policy goal, or not an important goal at all?

Very important foreign policy goal	26.8%
Somewhat important foreign policy goal	58%
Not an important foreign policy goal	15.3%

Do you think the Trans-Pacific Partnership, the free trade agreement the U.S. is negotiating with 11 countries in Asia and Latin America, would be a good thing or a bad thing for the United States?

Good thing	85.3%
Bad thing	14.7%

Do you think the Transatlantic Trade and Investment Partnership, the free trade agreement the U.S. is negotiating with the European Union, would be a good thing or a bad thing for the U.S.?

Good thing	92%
Bad thing	8%

Do you think the growing trade and business ties between the U.S. and other countries are a very good thing, somewhat good, somewhat bad, or a very bad thing for the United States?

Very good	65.1%
Somewhat good	33%
Somewhat bad	1.7%
Very bad	0.2%

Do you favor or oppose engaging in trade with the following countries

	MAINLY POSITIVE	MAINLY NEGATIVE
Cuba	86.1%	13.9%
Venezuela	75.9%	24.1%
Iran	49.3%	50.7%
North Korea	23.6%	76.4%
China	96.4%	3.6%

Overall, do you think the North American Free Trade Agreement, or NAFTA, is very good, somewhat good, somewhat bad, or very bad for:

	VERY GOOD	SOMEWHAT GOOD	SOMEWHAT BAD	VERY BAD
The U.S. economy	29%	55.5%	12.1%	3.5%
Consumers like you	31%	57.6%	9%	2.4%
The Mexican economy	52.1%	37.5%	8%	2.4%
Job security for American workers	7.8%	35.4%	44.7%	12.1%

Become a Member

For nearly a century, members of the Association have played key roles in government, think tanks, academia and the private sector.

As an active participant in the FPA's Great Decisions program, we encourage you to join the community today's foreign policy thought leaders.

Member—$250

Benefits:
- Free admission to all Associate events (includes member's family)
- Discounted admission for all other guests to Associate events
- Complimentary **GREAT DECISIONS** briefing book
- Complimentary issue of FPA's annual *National Opinion Ballot Report*

Visit us online at

www.fpa.org/membership

Make a Donation

Your support helps the FOREIGN POLICY ASSOCIATION's programs dedicated to global affairs education.

Make a fully tax-deductible contribution to FPA's Annual Fund 2014.

To contribute to the Annual Fund 2014, visit us online at **www.fpa.org** or call the Membership Department at **(800) 628-5754 ext. 232**.

The generosity of donors who contribute $500 or more is acknowledged in FPA's *Annual Report.*

All financial contributions are tax-deductible to the fullest extent of the law under section 501 (c)(3) of the IRS code.

FPA also offers membership at the SPONSOR MEMBER and PATRON MEMBER levels. To learn more, visit us online at www.fpa.org/membership or call (800) 628-5754 ext. 232.

Return this form by mail to: Foreign Policy Association, 470 Park Avenue South, New York, N.Y. 10016. *Or fax to:* (212) 481-9275.

ORDER ONLINE: WWW.GREATDECISIONS.ORG

OR CALL (800) 477-5836

FOR MEMBERSHIP: WWW.FPA.ORG/MEMBERSHIP

❏ MR.   ❏ MRS.   ❏ MS.   ❏ DR.   ❏ PROF.

NAME _____

ADDRESS _____

_____ APT/FLOOR _____

CITY _____ STATE _____ ZIP _____

TEL _____

E-MAIL _____

❏ AMEX   ❏ VISA   ❏ MC   ❏ DISCOVER

❏ CHECK (ENCLOSED)

CHECKS SHOULD BE PAYABLE TO FOREIGN POLICY ASSOCIATION.

CARD NO.

SIGNATURE OF CARDHOLDER

EXP. DATE (MM/YY)

PRODUCT	QTY	PRICE	COST
GREAT DECISIONS 2015 Briefing Book (FPA31639)		$22	
SPECIAL OFFER TEN PACK SPECIAL GREAT DECISIONS 2015 (FPA31646) *Includes 10% discount		$198	
GREAT DECISIONS TELEVISION SERIES GD ON DVD 2015 (FPA31640)		$40	
GREAT DECISIONS 2015 TEACHER'S PACKET (1 Briefing Book, 1 Teacher's Guide and 1 DVD (FPA31642) E-MAIL: (REQUIRED)		$65	
GREAT DECISIONS CLASSROOM-PACKET (1 Teacher's Packet & 30 Briefing Books (FPA31643) E-MAIL: (REQUIRED)		$506	
MEMBERSHIP		$250	
ANNUAL FUND 2015 (ANY AMOUNT)			
		SUBTOTAL	$
		plus S & H*	$
		TOTAL	$

For details and shipping charges, call FPA's Sales Department at (800) 477-5836.
Orders mailed to FPA without the shipping charge will be held.